AMERICA Is the Prison

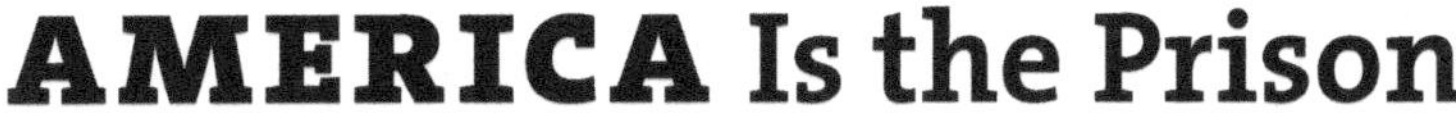

AMERICA Is the Prison

ARTS AND POLITICS IN PRISON IN THE 1970S

LEE BERNSTEIN

The University of North Carolina Press   Chapel Hill

Designed by Kimberly Bryant and set in Merlo, TheSerif, and TheSans types by Tseng Information Systems, Inc. The paper in this book meets the guidelines for permanence and durability of the Committee on Production Guidelines for Book Longevity of the Council on Library Resources. The University of North Carolina Press has been a member of the Green Press Initiative since 2003.

Library of Congress Cataloging-in-Publication Data
Bernstein, Lee, 1967–
America is the prison : arts and politics in prison in the 1970s / Lee Bernstein.
p. cm.
Includes bibliographical references and index.
ISBN 978-0-8078-3387-2 (cloth : alk. paper) — ISBN 978-0-8078-7117-1 (pbk. : alk. paper)
1. Prisoners as artists—United States. 2. Arts, American—20th century. 3. Arts—Political aspects—United States—History—20th century. 4. Arts and society—United States—History—20th century. I. Title.
NX164.P7B47 2010
709.73′09047—dc22 2009049999

cloth 14 13 12 11 10 5 4 3 2 1
paper 14 13 12 11 10 5 4 3 2 1

for L. G. C., M. W. B., *and* S. L. B.

and in memory of L. C. B. *and* W. E. C.

CONTENTS

ILLUSTRATIONS

ACKNOWLEDGMENTS

This book shows, among other things, that without the participants, volunteers, and employees of prison arts and education programs, the cultural life of prisons would be far bleaker. Many people and organizations doing this work today generously opened their programs, institutions, and ideas to me during the period I worked on this book, including incarcerated people and correctional staff at the Manhattan Detention Complex ("The Tombs"), San Quentin Correctional Facility, Eastern Correctional Facility in Napanoch, New York, and Shawangunk Correctional Facility in Wallkill, New York. Several people kindly hosted my visits, including Tom McCarthy of the New York Correction History Society; Aïda de Arteaga, director of Arts-in-Corrections at San Quentin; Laurie Brooks of the William James Association in Santa Cruz, California; and Max Kenner of the Bard Prison Initiative at New York's Eastern Correctional Facility. I also want to acknowledge the impact of the PEN American Center's Prison Writing Committee on my developing sense of the history and politics of prison cultural work; I especially wish to thank Bell Gale Chevigny, Jackson Taylor, Claudia Menza, and Sarah White. All went far beyond what I could have reasonably expected in including me in their efforts and sharing their experience and thoughts with me. My work with Susan Blase, head librarian at New York's Shawangunk Correctional Facility; Karanja Keita Carroll of the State University of New York at New Paltz; and John Vanderlippe of the New School for Social Research to connect college professors with prisoners is a source of great satisfaction and inspiration.

For research assistance on Jack Henry Abbott, many thanks go to Charlotta Äsell. Her own research on programming at Bedford Hills Correctional Facility provided a wonderful model of engaged scholarship. The Susan Turner Research Fund at Vassar College funded Charlotta's efforts. Brian Lehrer provided helpful research assistance on

Cell Block Theatre. The dean's office of the College of Liberal Arts and Sciences at SUNY New Paltz funded Brian's assistance. San Jose State University provided summer funding during the period when this book was first conceptualized. Erik Anderson, of the Naropa University Archive Project, tracked down and provided a recording of a Miguel Piñero poetry reading from the 1970s. Ellen Belcher of Special Collections at the Lloyd Sealy Library at the City University of New York's John Jay College of Criminal Justice provided access to key materials on Theatre for the Forgotten. Documentary filmmaker Peter Rosen spoke to me at length about his experience making the film *Sesame Street Goes to Prison*. He generously handed over his file and donated the use of a photograph for the book. Arnold Shapiro provided reflections on the controversy over *Scared Straight!* and donated the use of images from his film. For additional help with images, thanks to Joe Silvestri of Fox 5 New York, Sandy Quinn of the Nixon Library and Birthplace Foundation, the Museum of the Moving Image, and LeRoy Clarke, whose response to Attica serves as the cover image for this book. SUNY New Paltz provided a range of resources to enable completion of this book. I am grateful to Jim Schiffer, Gerald Benjamin, and Gwen Havranek of the College of Liberal Arts and Sciences and Kristin Charles-Scaringi of the Office of Public Affairs. I am fortunate to have colleagues who are enthusiastic and talented scholars, teachers, and critics. Susan Ingalls Lewis and Andy Evans provided feedback on several chapters. Joel Lefkowitz and Reynolds Scott-Childress introduced me to recordings of the various versions of "George Jackson." David Krikun provided access to his collection of political writings from the 1960s and 1970s.

Academic audiences at the American Studies Association, the California American Studies Association, SUNY Albany, and SUNY New Paltz helped me shape my general ideas into sharper arguments. I received additional feedback on portions of this book from Lisa Gail Collins, Margo Crawford, Lisa McGirr, Colin Palmer, Christopher Wilson, and Curtis Marez. H. Bruce Franklin and an anonymous reviewer for the University of North Carolina Press went well beyond peer review, suggesting fruitful avenues for further research and analysis.

Sian Hunter, Beth Lassiter, and Alex Martin of the University of North Carolina Press offered ongoing support for this book.

Conversations and debates with my friends and family kept this project moving forward through its long incubation. I am grateful for the support, encouragement, and patience of Mizue Aizeki, Matt Bernstein, Gabe Bernstein, Nate Bernstein, Nancy Bernstein, Nan Alamilla Boyd, Joyce Collins, Lydia Murdoch, Joe Nevins, Timea Szell, and Judith Weisenfeld. Luisa Paster and Harriet Bernstein demonstrated that a political position based on the simple premise of fairness achieves dramatic results. They are also wonderful grandparents to my boys. This book, more than my previous one, reflects a series of profound transformations in my own life. The passing of Bill Collins and Len Bernstein and the arrival of Memphis Bernstein Collins and Sasha Bernstein Collins all, in their own ways, shaped this period of my life.

For all she has meant to my being able to write, and to me, I thank Lisa Gail Collins. Her influence on this book will be obvious to people familiar with her scholarship on African American visual culture, but her stamp is also present in the ways I have grown by witnessing her courage to confront injustice with concrete efforts to leave the place better than she found it.

AMERICA Is the Prison

INTRODUCTION

> Prisons are really an extension of our communities. We have people who are forced at gunpoint to live behind concrete and steel. Others of us, in what we ordinarily think of as the community, live at gunpoint again in almost the same conditions. The penitentiaries, as they call them, and the communities are plagued with the same thing: dope, disease, police brutality, murder, and rats running over the places that you dwell in. We recognize that most of the militant-dissatisfied youth are off in the penitentiaries. Eighty percent of the prison population is black, brown, and yellow people. You look around and say, "what happened to my man. I haven't seen him for along time," then you get busted, go to jail, and there he is. Prisons are an extension of the repression. In these penitentiaries are the Malcolms, Cleavers, Huey P. Newtons, Bobby Seales and all other political prisoners. Now the inmates are moving forth to harness their own destinies. They're not relying on lying, demagogic politicians to redress their grievances. Of course, the courts didn't redress their grievances in the first place, so there's no sense in relying on them either. There's very little difference between the penitentiaries in California and those in New York, New Orleans, Alabama, or Chicago. It's the same system—America is the prison. All of America is a prison where the people are being held captive by the real arch criminals.—ZAYD SHAKUR, 1970

Writing just after his acquittal as part of the New York Panther Twenty-one, Zayd Shakur reflected a consciousness that prisoners were broadly representative of racism and inequality in the country. Drawing on insights developed by Malcolm X, Shakur, deputy minister of information for the New York branch of the Black Panther Party, declared that "all of America is a prison where the people are being held captive by the real arch criminals."[1] This insight underscored the high proportion of African Americans in prison, relative to other ethnic groups, and the ongoing racism and inequality pervading U.S. society. This view held great currency during the late 1960s and early 1970s. After her capture in 1970, Angela Davis wrote that "our enemies find themselves confronted with a growing awareness among the people that the concentrated effort to maim and murder revolutionaries is just another form of the daily genocide of police brutality, and impoverished living conditions of ghettos and barrios."[2] In his wildly popular *Soul on Ice*, Eldridge Cleaver similarly argued that "it is only a matter of time until the question of the prisoner's debt to society versus society's debt to the prisoner is injected forcefully into national and state politics, into the civil and human rights struggle, and into the consciousness of the body politic. It is an explosive issue which goes to the very root of America's system of justice, the structure of criminal law, the prevailing beliefs and attitudes toward a convicted felon."[3] This straightforward metaphor that America is itself a prison for African Americans helped the 1970s generation of inmates see themselves as potential leaders in movements for social change. As they grew to understand the political and historical dimensions of their confinement, some, like George Jackson, believed that incarcerated people would serve as the vanguard of a revolution. They hoped they would inspire large-scale revolt and unprecedented attention to the writings, thought, and creativity of incarcerated people.

As in Shakur's comment, debates over prisons and the criminal justice system became a way to more broadly contest the meaning of American history and society. The connection between the penitentiary and the plantation highlighted the sense of injustice. If America was a prison, it became one in the aftermath of slavery. Standing beneath of statue of Sojourner Truth in Detroit's Kennedy Square in December 1970, Fania Jordan urged her audience to understand activists who struggled to abolish prisons as akin to those who had fought to abolish slavery the century before: "We stand before the monument of Sojourner Truth, a Black woman liberation fighter," Jordan told the crowd. "She was on the slaveowners' most wanted list, just like Angela Davis, another freedom fighter, was on the FBI's most wanted list."[4] Jordan was Davis's sister and cochair of the National United Committee to Free Angela Davis. In speaking about and below the statue of the famed feminist and abolitionist, Jordan sought to make clear that people deemed enemies of the state should more accurately be understood as working to bring about a just society. In a California court appearance the following month, Davis stated that she believed the charges of kidnapping, murder, and conspiracy grew from a "political frameup which far from pointing to my culpability implicates the State of California as an agent of political repression."[5] The slavery of the past and the racism and class inequality of Jordan and Davis's own time did more than economically exploit its victims; those in power achieved widespread acquiescence in part by arguing that opponents of the social order were terrorists and criminals.

Davis's arrest and the press coverage of her trial largely centered on her communist politics and close ties to George and Jonathan Jackson. Jonathan had been killed in an attempt to free three San Quentin prisoners. His brother, George Jackson, was the most prominent prisoner in the country when San Quentin guards killed him in August 1971. The press coverage paradoxically decried the political nature of the defense. Even before Davis had been extradited from New York to California, the *New York Times* criticized her supporters for artificially "politicizing her case" in order to "deflect attention from the specific charges against her."[6] Davis, it turned out, would be declared innocent of all charges in June 1972. Many more activists of the period would not be so lucky.[7] The physical evidence against her amounted to the fact that the guns Jonathan Jackson used were registered in her name. In addition, Davis was a member of the Soledad Brothers Defense Committee and the Che-Lumumba Club, the African-American communist club in Los Angeles that went on to play a key role in her defense. Davis had been on the faculty of the philosophy department at UCLA, but the California Board of Regents did not renew her contract when earlier attempts to fire her on ideological grounds violated basic provisions of academic freedom. Most of the prosecution's case hinged on eyewitnesses who saw Davis with Jonathan Jackson in the days leading up to the escape attempt and on romantic letters between Davis and George Jackson. One key letter that Davis wrote to George Jackson stated, "to take our first step toward freedom we, too, must pick up the sword. Only a fighting woman can guide her son in the warrior direction. Only when our lives, or total lives, become inseparable from struggle can we, Black women, do what we have to do for our sons and daughters."[8] When the prosecution read this letter to the jury in the San Jose courtroom, it surely hoped that Davis's words—and her fingerprint on a book titled *The Politics of Violence*—would convince jurors that she had decided to pick up the sword and hand it to Jonathan Jackson.

The trial of Angela Davis came to signal a broader conflict in the meaning of the criminal justice system in general and prisons in particular during the 1970s. The era of prison reform was in full swing: prisoners had access to a wide range of prison programs and agitated for prisoner unions and political organizations. At the same time, prisons had become the center of a key ideological fissure shaping American life. Davis and many others saw prisons in political terms, as evidence of the continuing racism and economic inequality at the heart of U.S. society. Others saw them as failures precisely because they were too focused on alleviating social and cultural deficiencies that led to crime, instead of concentrating on punishment. This conflict played out in the political and cultural arenas of the decade, with, for example, George Jackson's *Soledad Brother* released by the nation's largest publisher of paperbacks. While President Richard Nixon went out of his way to compliment the FBI for its successful apprehension of Davis, Aretha Franklin—whose recording of Otis Redding's "Respect" topped the Billboard R & B charts in 1967—offered to post bond for Davis and headlined a concert with Sammy Davis Jr. to raise funds for the defense.[9]

The ways that Angela Davis's arrest, representation, and trial played out in the political and cultural realms was not unique. Rather, it was emblematic of the close linkage between cultural expression and political engagement throughout the decade. Some saw prisons and the criminal justice system as demonstrating larger patterns of injustice and racism in U.S. history. Others countered these views by articulating "law-and-order" policies that would lead to aggressive policing and long prison terms. People seeking to shed light on the injustices of the criminal justice system would, like Angela Davis, become subject to close scrutiny. This book argues that these individual incidents were embedded in and informed by a cultural and political transformation taking shape inside of America's prisons at the precise moment when the state and federal policymakers began to "get tough on crime." This was a political and ideological conflict, but it was also a culture war. We can think of "culture" as a system of beliefs that helps lend meaning to our experiences in the world and as the expressive practices that come to define a literary, artistic, or musical tradition. The cultural meaning of prisons was up for grabs during the period, with sharply contested ideas about their function. At the same time, cultural expression—music, literature, theater, mass media, art exhibitions—responded to and influenced the unfolding conflicts of the period. In that decade preceding the "culture wars" of the 1980s and 1990s, prisons became a flashpoint for a country in transition. Those who sought to move toward a just society expressed their view of the criminal justice system and American society and the forces of repression tried to figure out how to respond. In a revolutionary culture, prisoners would come to look more like Sojourner Truth, fighting for freedom against a racist institution in a repressive state.

Prisoners played crucial roles in this cultural and political conflict. Even while they responded to and helped shape the political conflicts of the period, prisoners also inherited prison cultural traditions that had long provided opportunities for solace, protest, humor, and solidarity. Prison cultural expression had a history that simultaneously reacted to and departed from the repressive characteristics of all prison life, regardless of which ideology dominated at any given moment. The road gangs and prison camps during the decades preceding the period covered in this book gave rise to a trove of stories and songs that alternated between, among other topics, bearing witness to Jesus and extolling heroes who escaped from the state farms or road gangs. Prison camp work songs like those collected at the Ramsey and Retrieve State Prison Farms in Texas by Pete and Toshi Seeger in 1956 demonstrate a collective response to conditions like those described in "Long John": "Long time ago, you could find a dead man right on your row. Well the dog man killed him. Well the dog man killed him 'cause the boy couldn't go."[10] The song's protagonist asks the dead man to wake up and "carry my row."[11] In a prison so bereft of hope that even the dead cannot rest, Long John escapes by putting a reversed second heel on each shoe so that he could not be accurately tracked. This call-and-response song bears the cadence of working a row of cotton even while imagining an improbable escape. The song's only hope is that "one day, one day, I'll be on my way."[12] For now, at least, escape lies purely in the song.

But if cultural expression provided an imaginative and sustaining release from the conditions of prison, it did so in a way that acknowledged and occasionally challenged the racial and social contexts of incarceration. Alan Lomax, who collected songs in the prisons of the Mississippi Delta in the 1930s and 1940s, linked the musical expression of southern prison farms to the ability to give even the most arduous tasks a sustaining sociability, linking inmates to each other and to an African ancestry and legacy of slavery: "In the burning hell of the penitentiaries the old comforting, healing, communal spirit of African singing cooled the souls of the toiling, sweating prisoners and made them, as long as the singing lasted, consolingly and powerfully one."[13] If the transfer wagon replaced the slave ship of old, the theme of being torn from loved ones to labor in an unjust system remained. H. Bruce Franklin most fully developed this historical and cultural link, showing us that "the evolution from plantation to penitentiary is perhaps best expressed in the work songs of African-American convicts. For the cultural corollary of this evolution was the metamorphosis of slave songs into prison work songs and blues, which then became the tap root of later blues, jazz, and rock, as well as a prime source of modern prison literature."[14] In this way, cultural expression provided the audible and visible acknowledgement of incarceration's political and social context.

By the 1970s culture continued to provide opportunities to express hope for spiritual or carceral salvation. Cultural traditions and expression provided one avenue for personal transformation and imaginative escape. Like the Jim Crow era studied by Lomax, the writing workshops, theater companies, painting workshops, classrooms, and inmate-generated reading groups in radical political thought provided avenues for sociability and self-improvement. Comparisons like Fania Jordan's of Sojourner Truth and Angela Davis would become common. For example, in 1971, Ronnie Reed, an inmate at the New York City Department of Corrections' Rikers Island, signed his facetious "Open Letter" from a released inmate, "your ex-slave." But Reed also signaled that something was different in the closing lines: "Well, sir, I just thought I'd let you know, I'll never forget your generosity and now I gotta go. Cause like yesterday I took a job that was offered to me working with a guy named Huey for the B.P.P."[15] These references to Huey P. Newton and the Black Panther Party were set to music by the band Soul Rock from the Rock, incarcerated musicians who played in the jazz-influenced style of Gil Scott-Heron. Reed's words reached a wider audience through the compilation album *From the Cold Jaws of Prison* (1971). There are no doubt more continuities between the history of slavery and the Jim Crow era and the culture of American prisons in the 1970s. Something new was also happening, however: the prison culture of the 1970s demonstrated widespread hopes for collective liberation brought about by a revolutionary movement with incarcerated people among its vanguard. It was not simply that culture could sustain inmates and connect them to one another; during the 1970s cultural expression became the vehicle for incarcerated people to participate in political and social movements seeking to transform and improve society as a whole.

Ironically, this faith in the transformative power of cultural expression also informed many of the reformist justifications for prison programming. Steeped in humanistic rationale rather than revolutionary politics, some prisons provided opportunities for inmates to both learn from and create literature, poetry, and visual art. Historical and political analysis took on a decidedly rehabilitative accent when an associate warden or cultural subcontractor placed it on a budget line. Correctional institutions during the 1970s operated in a climate of sharp disagreement over whether their practices should aim primarily to reform inmates or simply keep them in custody. "Reform" refers to efforts to make criminal justice institutions provide safe, educational, and professional environments to rehabilitate people convicted of crimes. The establishment of prisons in the early republic was itself the product of a reform movement, with subsequent efforts resulting in major changes in architecture, ideology, and programming. "Custody" refers to the belief that the criminal justice system's primary goal is simply to hold and punish convicts for the period of their sentence. Generally speaking, few efforts at education, training, or therapy take place in a custodial environment. Instead, custodial institutions seek to punish offenders for previous crimes, render them incapable of committing additional crimes during their period of incarceration, and deter others from committing crimes by raising the prospect of long sentences in unpleasant institutions.

Seeing the history of prisons in these terms, however, is an oversimplification: virtually all institutions demonstrate aspects of both ideologies, and the reform-or-custody view does not fully account for how criminal justice perpetuates class and racial domination. In fact, both paradigms leave unquestioned the role of criminal justice in maintaining patterns of exploitation and control of disenfranchised people. Neither the reform nor the custodial ideology directly seeks to empower convicts or the communities from which they come. Despite these shortcomings, the give and take between these paradigms has had a powerful influence on the culture of American prisons.

The prisons of the 1970s contained elements of previous reform movements, stretching back to the early years of the republic. In a crude way, the early American penitentiaries at Philadelphia and Auburn, New York, sought to reform convicts. Early prison advocates believed that people who committed illegal acts could reflect on the immorality of their criminal lives and learn patterns of thought and behavior that would lead to a law-abiding path. Through isolation, silence, and work, inmates would be shielded from negative influences, gain access to Christian teachings, and engage in the regular labor routines of an industrializing nation. In agricultural regions dominated by slavery, this reform movement took root only in Virginia under Thomas Jefferson's enthusiastic—if hypocritical—embrace of the Enlightenment. Reformers also argued that centralization, professionalization, and specialization would transform the then piecemeal, regionally differentiated, and often brutal prisons into effective institutions of transformation.

Between the Revolutionary War and the mid-nineteenth century, prison reform movements were driven by Enlightenment ideas about free will and moral responsibility. While ideas about social influences were not unheard of among the early proponents of the penitentiary, the institutions were primarily created out of a belief that solitary confinement, religious reflection, and silent labor would bring about a spiritual and moral transformation resulting in penitence. In New York, the earliest prisons provided Bibles to all literate inmates but also insisted that they be "kept constantly employed at hard labor during the daytime."[16] The first prison libraries and vocational education programs were established in the 1840s.[17] This decade also saw the hiring of instructors in the humanities at three New York prisons: Sing Sing, Auburn, and Clinton. Select inmates gained limited access to "the useful branches of an English education."[18] While important, the shortcomings were readily visible to the Prison Association of New York, a reform organization. In an 1870 report, it observed that "the system of instruction is so conducted as to amount to a farce."[19]

The 1870 critique by the Prison Association of New York marked a period of innovation in penology that Larry E. Sullivan calls the "emergence of the professional penologist": "To this new generation, knowledge was the key to social order, and social science the key to knowledge."[20] Enoch Wines of the prison association expressed the view of many reformers when he argued in 1870 that through scientific study one could "predict with wonderful precision, [the number of] crimes in a given year, and their general character."[21] This turn toward the social sciences in penology had several practical effects during the period. First, the state assumed greater authority over prisons, previously under local control in many places. Second, penologists sought to remove predetermined sentences imposed by law and trial. Instead, convicts would be rewarded with release from prison only after successful completion of a labor and socialization program.

Postbellum reformers felt that the old penitentiaries had lost sight of the goal of reforming the offender. Many believed that reform had been scuttled for financial reasons: the institutions stressed labor as a means to generate revenue to offset the cost of building and running prisons. The leasing of convicts to private contractors best exemplified this trend. States earned profits by leasing convicts to work on farms, road crews, heavy construction, mining, and other hard labor. In part to root out widespread graft in this system, several southern states turned former plantations into prison farms.[22] The reality of prison labor—whether on a prison plantation or in a factory—contradicted the belief that profitable work was indicative of rehabilitation.[23] Prison farms, for example, worked convicts literally to death, as memorialized in the song "Long John." Prison factories required long hours with little or no pay. This was slave labor, not reform. Virtually all prisons, including reformatories created following the Civil War, employed some form of convict labor. This was true even at the Elmira Reformatory, the New York institution that most completely invoked the principles of the 1870s reform movement in the design of its programs and facilities. Recognizing it for what it was, labor unions sharply criticized prison labor as modern slave labor, leading some states to begin passing anti–prison labor laws in the 1880s. States responded by reclassifying labor programs as "industrial training schools" but made few substantive changes to the regimen.[24]

When reformers discovered that scores of institutions were little more than warehouses for destitute and ignored members of society, they insisted that boards of charities pay closer attention to what was happening in prisons. Reformers increasingly argued that prisons, far from protecting society from immoral—or in the case of women, "fallen"—people, actually created criminality. This social determinist school of thought led to a greater consideration of such factors as home life, immoral literature, sexual exploitation, and economic desperation as fundamental influences on crimes and vice.[25] Reformers implemented classification systems that determined whether a convict was permanently degenerate, and thus should be forever segregated from society, or redeemable, and thus could be rehabilitated in reformatories.

In the early twentieth century, rehabilitation programs centered on basic literacy and vocational training.[26] The "Progressive era" agenda called for the classification of prisoners by type of crime, intelligence, and psychological state. It also urged the implementation of a comprehensive program of education and labor. Although far from universally applied, these reforms led some institutions to curtail beatings and gradually abandon customs like walking in lockstep and living in total silence that had been in place since the first American penitentiaries.[27] Even with these changes, however, the vocations inmates trained in—manufacturing license plates and road signs—were of little use to them when the prisoners were released. Estelle Freedman, in her groundbreaking study of women's prison reform, argued that Progressive reformers helped unseat biological arguments for criminal etiology.[28] Perhaps even more significant, they brought to wide public attention the plight of incarcerated women and children, leading to a pattern of building sex- and age-segregated institutions in the late nineteenth and early twentieth centuries.[29] But in the end, the few pieces of the Progressive vision that were implemented had a limited impact on prisons. The historian David J. Rothman describes a fundamental gap between "Progressive ambitions and day-to-day realities" that doomed the reformist agenda.[30] Freedman has only a slightly more optimistic assessment: "The first institutions failed to live up to their founders' ideals."[31]

Despite this shortcoming, Progressive reformers created new institutions and new programs in old institutions that would serve as models for postwar prisoner education programs and ultimately serve as crucial sites for the nurturing of the 1970s' artists and ideologues. The Progressive era saw a convergence of innovations in ideas and agencies similar to that of the prison reform movement of the 1870s. According to the legal scholar Edgardo Rotman, the social scientific model of the late 1800s gave way to a medical and therapeutic model in the early 1900s. The prisons were still run by professionals, but now these leaders were psychiatrists using "the methods and language of medicine to 'cure' offenders of their criminality."[32] The medical model of Progressive penology saw its fullest realization at the New York State Reformatory for Women at Bedford Hills. At Bedford Hills, most convicts participated in a treatment program. If it failed or if an inmate was defined as "defective-delinquent," she would be segregated for life. The head of Bedford Hills, Katherine Bemont Davis, was closely aligned with the eugenics movement and believed in social hygiene, but for those judged reformable, Bedford Hills embodied the psychological reform model of the Progressive era.[33] Other Progressive reformers worked in poor communities to improve the conditions of home life, poverty, and immorality that they believed led to criminal activity. To understand the Progressive reformers, one must look closely at the classification system that sent some people to reformatories and gave others, deemed degenerate, few opportunities for advancement.

During the New Deal began what practitioners of the time called "the new penology." New penologists viewed education as the lynchpin in a program of treatment that they hoped would bring about fundamental change in behavior. One advocate of the new penology generalized that "the socially maladjusted inmate must play a new and socially acceptable part after his release from prison. It includes efforts to combat emotional insecurity by combating cultural conflicts. It makes use of sound educational techniques for the purpose of giving prisoners the equipment they need in order that they may meet successfully the demands of contemporary socio-economic conditions."[34] In attending to emotional, cultural, and socioeconomic factors, the new penologists set out a broad context for criminal behavior. Their efforts focused on changing individual behavior rather than social conditions. In doing so, the new penologists envisioned penal institutions as schools with every employee having a pedagogical or therapeutic role to play in transforming criminal behavior. One advocate urged a complete reinvention of the penitentiary:

> A large part of the treatment which is fundamental in the procedure of the new penology, as recent experience indicates, comes within our conception of the meaning of the term "education." But it is education defined broadly. In the penal institution, "education" is the process or the means of achieving the reformation, correction, or rehabilitation of inmates in correctional institutions. It comprehends all of the experiences which such an institution can bring into the lives of inmates. It goes beyond the programs of academic and vocational instruction commonly found at the present time and includes the activities of every department or division of the institution with which inmates have contact. It makes prisons and reformatories basically educational institutions.[35]

People who believed that education could reform criminals in ways that religious reflection or hard labor could not came, not surprisingly, from the ranks of professional educators.[36]

The new penology helped influence the architecture and programming at the Norfolk Prison Colony (now the Massachusetts Correctional Institution at Norfolk). Inspired by the theory of social learning, Howard Belding Gill and Maurice N. Winslow, the first two commissioners at Norfolk, instituted programs that sought to create model societies behind prison walls. If, as the social learning model posits, behavior is a product of what we learn in our communities, then it makes sense to artificially create communities behind prison walls that emulate the qualities penologists would like to see in convicts. Doing away with cell blocks in favor of a system of cooperative houses, Norfolk combined a system of therapeutic treatment, inmate education, and a system of joint officer-inmate governance.[37] The most famous participant in the Norfolk regime was the future Nation of Islam minister and crusader for social justice Malcolm X. If his conversion to Islam at Norfolk marked a turning point in his life, his remarkable knowledge of world history, religions, and politics can be attributed at least in part to his access to the prison library. He understood prisons primarily as the embodiment of African American oppression, but Malcolm X also described his time in Norfolk during the 1950s as transformative. Subsequent biographers downplayed the institutional role in Malcolm Little's transformation, preferring to see him as a product of self-invention. Malcolm X himself made clear, however, that the move from Charlestown's pre-Revolutionary walls to the program at Norfolk enabled him to dedicate himself to personal and social change.

If the new penology emphasized treatment, education, and self-governance, other forces would undermine these goals. Politicians and correctional bureaucrats advocated the creation of larger and larger institutions that privileged an economy of scale over reform. In particular, in the 1920s and 1930s massive new cell blocks were built at older prisons like San Quentin and Sing Sing and at new institutions in Stateville, Illinois, and Jackson, Michigan. This limited the effectiveness of the new penology. The shear scale of these new institutions—Jackson housed more than six thousand inmates by 1952, and twenty-five hundred was common—allowed Progressive penology little more than a token role in lives dominated by a "treadmill and mechanical quality of existence."[38] In the early 1930s, one inmate described inmate governance at Stateville as "gangs of prisoners runnin' wild over the yard."[39]

Amid these contradictions and shortcomings, an observer during the 1970s could see elements of all these previous reform movements: in some places and to varying degrees, prisoners governed themselves and received education; psychologists, psychiatrists, and social workers held therapy sessions; convicts were classified by types of crime and security threat; racial segregation and forced labor remained; and beatings and solitary confinement continued. In fact, progressive penologists continued to hold prominent posts during the postwar period, but they either naively believed that their institutions exemplified lofty principles or found themselves unable to create model reformatories in the face of political opposition, economies of scale, and inmate skepticism. Even reform-minded prisons had become primarily custodial, with correctional officers ill equipped to execute the reformist programs of the administration. Between 1951 and 1953, unprecedented prison rebellions highlighted the distance between the ideal and the reality of criminal justice.[40] Self-mutilation was a frequent protest tactic; thirty-seven convicts at Angola in Louisiana slashed their heel tendons with razor blades in 1951. Larry Sullivan attributes this rise in violent protest to the bureaucratization of prisons over the previous decades: "In the postwar period, prisons in the North and West became bureaucratized and professionals took over many of the functions, such as handing out job and cell assignments, that convicts had previously held."[41] Postwar penal institutions sent dramatically mixed messages to inmates: therapists and other professionals continued to employ a therapeutic model of personal transformation in large, hierarchical institutions where correctional officers used primarily coercive—and to the inmates, arbitrary—power to maintain control through extensive regulations.

These competing trends can be seen in the development of postsecondary education in prisons, which coincided with these changes. During his early years in Stateville Correctional Center, Nathan Leopold, whose trial for murder received national press attention in 1924, sought intellectual engagement. He took courses in math and Hebrew through Iowa State University's "Home Study Department" as the only available option. As the new penology took root, Leopold was able to take courses through the University of Michigan and Columbia, and ultimately to conduct research with Clifford Shaw of the famous sociology department at the University of Chicago.[42] Leopold's work was published in leading academic journals, including the *Journal of Criminal Law and Criminology*.[43] In 1953 he helped the University of Southern Illinois establish the nation's first inmate college at Stateville.

Leopold's upper-class background, educational achievements, race, and gender shed light on another key element of the reform movements. While correctional authorities greatly expanded arts and educational offerings, access was not even across race and gender lines. Programs in women's prisons lagged far behind those in men's institutions. When Leopold was busy with his studies, for example, the political prisoner Kate Richards O'Hare found that the women's prison in Jefferson City, Missouri, had no library at all. After complaining, she gained access to the library on the men's side. Beyond that, there "were no provisions in our prison for educational or vocational training."[44] While O'Hare won the right to use the men's library, other inmates were not able to gain access to education. The Chicano poet Jimmy Santiago Baca wrote of his thwarted attempts to enter a GED program.[45] In the 1960s and 1970s this trend continued. Programming increased, but access remained limited. While prisons contain much higher proportions of the poor and people of color than the rest of the United States, prison classrooms historically do not. For example, while San Quentin was 54 percent white in 1968, its college program was 70 percent white. African Americans, 30 percent of the general prison population, made up 20.2 percent of students in the college program; Chicanos, 15 percent of San Quentin prisoners, comprised 9.2 percent of students. One explanation for this discrepancy is that eligibility for the program was determined by "mental status" and IQ, notoriously racist measurements.[46]

In this sharply paradoxical context many incarcerated people benefited from the increase in writing and artistic opportunities available in correctional facilities. Between 1965 and 1973 the number of college-level programs in U.S. prisons increased more than fifteenfold, to 182. By 1982 there were 350 programs in forty-five states, with roughly 10 percent of all inmates attending a prison college. In addition, the National Endowment for the Arts funded the publication of prisoners' works, while other organizations began major initiatives to create free-standing programs behind prison walls. State departments of corrections and arts commissions throughout the nation undertook unprecedented joint projects. The private nonprofit sector saw the founding of the PEN American Center's famous Prison Writing Program and literary competitions, the Black Emergency Cultural Coalition's Prison Arts Program, along with many individual and small-scale courses, workshops, and performances.

This era is framed by a series of well-known events: the election of Richard Nixon in 1968 on a "law-and-order" platform, the rhetoric and actions of George Jackson and the Attica riot of 1971, the popular appeal of Miguel Piñero's *Short Eyes* in its off-Broadway run, the influence of the Black Arts movement, the television documentary about New Jersey's "Scared Straight" program, and the saga of incarcerated intellectual Jack Henry Abbott. In between, the high-profile incarceration of everyone from G. Gordon Liddy to Patty Hearst to Angela Davis occupied the nation's consciousness during the decade. Prison writers were being compared to Jean-Paul Sartre, winning New York Drama Critics Circle awards, and landing major book deals. They were lampooned on *Saturday Night Live* and excoriated on the editorial pages of major newspapers. The 1970s saw wide interest in the public writings, images, and speeches of incarcerated or formerly incarcerated men and women. The efforts of the previous generation's rehabilitative regime took full shape just as its basic assumptions about reform and rehabilitation came under aggressive critique.

Prisoners expressed themselves in places where display of emotion and common humanity can present risks; nevertheless, prison workshops, classrooms, and studios became places for personal revelation, growth, and imaginative intimacy. Some of the names associated with prisons during this period are well known, but the culture of prisons had an immediate and little understood impact on American public life. The cultural world of prisons in the 1970s had a reciprocal relationship to artists outside prisons, including Norman Mailer, Larry Neal, and Faith Ringgold. In addition to the Black Arts movement, their voices and aesthetics would help shape the Nuyorican writers, "New Journalism," and political theater, among the most important aesthetic contributions of the decade. Perhaps most important, through their cultural work as much as their riots, incarcerated men and women insisted that they had a stake in the public debates of the day. They, along with the other social protestors of the era, led the Harvard political scientist Samuel Huntington to argue that a new "excess of democracy" needed to be scaled back.[47] Others saw the creativity and political transformation of incarcerated people as an exciting harbinger for large-scale social transformation.

CHAPTER ONE

WE SHALL HAVE ORDER

THE CULTURAL POLITICS OF LAW AND ORDER

During the 1968 presidential campaign, Richard Nixon made Lyndon Johnson's attorney general, Ramsey Clark, a target of his "law-and-order" campaign strategy. In accepting the GOP nomination at his party's national convention in Miami, Nixon exhorted that whomever he nominated for attorney general would "open a new front against the filth peddlers and the narcotics peddlers who are corrupting the lives of the children of this country."[1] Once in the White House, Richard Nixon made the law-and-order rhetoric of his campaign a cornerstone of his first term, naming his campaign manager, John Mitchell, to the post formerly held by Clark. Mitchell immediately distanced himself from his predecessor. "There's a difference," he told the *New York Times*, "between my philosophy and Ramsey Clark's. I think this is an institution for law enforcement, not social improvement."[2]

The political ideology underlying this difference between "law enforcement" and "social improvement" reflects perhaps the most important transformation of the U.S. criminal justice system in its long history. This transition led to the sharp rise in repressive policing, high rates of incarceration, and the end of postwar liberalism.[3] As a political and social flashpoint, "law and order" brought together conservative contempt for government programs and professional experts while drawing on growing public concern about urban uprisings, radical protest, and street crime. The Johnson administration—and later Hubert Humphrey's failed presidential campaign—could not develop a coherent and convincing liberal response to the growth in the fear of crime.[4] Law-and-order politics, along with the limits of Johnson's Great Society and the failures in Vietnam, helps explain the decline of liberalism as a potent political force on the national stage.[5]

If 1968 marked the apogee of law and order as a political strategy, it was also the source of, at first, the expansion of heavily armed law enforcement and, over time, an explosive increase in prison populations.[6] While the Nixon administration's "law-and-order" politics laid the groundwork for federal, state, and municipal governments to transform and expand police departments and correctional facilities, broader social and economic factors help explain the shift in criminal justice ideology and tactics.[7] The prison building boom of the 1980s and 1990s was closely linked to major political and economic changes of the late 1960s and early 1970s. As Ruth Wilson Gilmore points out, 1968 was the moment when "revolutionaries around the world made as much trouble as possible in as many places as possible."[8] The Watts riot of 1965 ushered in several years of "militant urban antiracist organizing."[9] In response, law-and-order politics sought to subdue what the government saw as domestic insurgencies. Economically, 1968 was the end of the three-decade "golden age" of U.S. capitalism that began with the buildup for World War II. Not all Americans enjoyed the benefits of that economic growth, and in the postwar period some made ambitious efforts to oppose inequality. As the economic crisis deepened during the 1970s, the country saw dramatic surpluses in land, labor, and population amid continuing unrest. Gilmore makes clear that prison building puts "certain state capacities into motion, makes use of a lot of idle land, gets capital invested via public debt, and takes more than 160,000 low-wage workers off the streets."[10] If law-and-order politics played a decisive role in the decline of postwar liberalism, it was also the result of a shifting political economy.

Law-and-order politics provide a useful way to understand the explosive growth in the U.S. prison population. By looking closely at the cultural and ideological underpinnings of the 1960s and 1970s shift in crime-control policy, we can see the place of crime control in the postwar decline of liberalism and rise of conservatism. These political and economic factors deeply influenced the cultural life of American prisons—and the place of prisons in American culture—during the 1970s. They did so, however, in ways that help explain the mainstream "tough on crime" consensus that would later develop around criminal justice. If 1968 was the beginning of the end of postwar liberalism, it was also when a consensus began to coalesce around abandoning rehabilitation for more purely punitive criminal justice. This shift would be gradual and indirect, but it had its roots in the 1960s and developed momentum during the 1970s.

The post-1968 shifts in the criminal justice system were firmly rooted in the Great Society's liberalism while simultaneously inspiring what would later be termed neoconservatism. The Nixon campaign and administration did not replace the Great Society's criminal justice apparatus. Rather, they employed a cultural strategy of assigning new meaning to key features of postwar liberalism such as "civil rights," "freedom," and "order." Rather than work solely through the criminal justice system or through legislative channels, neoconservatives produced television ads, political speeches, and public policy books for a popular audience. This cultural strategy enabled the rapid discrediting of sociohistorical approaches to social problems like crime, poverty, and unequal access to health care. In particular, concerns over racial inequality—as well as the shape and pace of reform—were the central narrative in the cultural production of crime and criminal justice during the late 1960s and 1970s. Linked bureaucratically, however, liberal and neoconservative criminal justice both tended to distance themselves from explicit naming of racial differences as a factor in their policymaking decisions. The new cultural constructions of criminality and race that took shape during the 1970s simultaneously linked criminality as an assault on the "civil rights" of "decent citizens" and discredited civil rights activists in and out of prison who asserted an ongoing pattern of discrimination in the criminal justice system.

If law-and-order rhetoric enabled the conservative ascendancy it was also an invisible link between Johnson's Great Society and Nixon's silent majority, facilitated in part by crucial domestic policy advisors to Johnson like Daniel Patrick Moynihan and James Q. Wilson, both of whom also advised Nixon. In addition, the growth of a primarily repressive criminal justice system can be traced to bureaucratic and cultural resignification. That is, the bureaucracies of the Great Society and its language of civil rights and social improvement were not replaced by a new, more repressive government infrastructure. Rather, the institutions of the Great Society became conduits for repression and incarceration. At least as far as criminal justice was concerned, policymakers saw no need to replace or repeal the bureaucratic structures of postwar liberalism when shifting from "social improvement" to "law enforcement."

Scholars have hastily reached a consensus on the meaning of this shift, seeing it largely in terms of the future war on drugs, the rapid rise in prison populations and the boom in prison construction. Nevertheless, the structural and political studies of the transition allow us to gain only a preliminary understanding of the cultural politics of the transition. A shift in the cultural significance of criminality and criminal justice accelerated during the late 1960s and 1970s amid polarized debate over the significance of repressive state power. Was the state a representative body with the power to carry out public demands for security and order? Or did the government use criminal justice to control the "dangerous classes" and maintain racial inequality? In order to shape the answers to these questions, the Nixon campaign and the administration's policymakers entered the cultural realm, substituting postwar liberalism's narrative of "social improvement" with one of law enforcement. Over time, this shift would become a neoconservative reframing of crime control. However, the cultural politics of crime control in the late 1960s and early 1970s reveals a more complicated story of continuity and reversal. Although Ramsey Clark and the Great Society may have been convenient rhetorical foils for John Mitchell and Richard Nixon, Clark's liberalism also was a useful bureaucratic and ideological structure for the repressive policing and incarceration that would come to dominate criminal justice.

Like all U.S. political campaigns of the postwar period, the Nixon campaign ran advertisements that advanced its ideological agenda. While the campaign did not specify what policies and practices Nixon's administration would implement, the ads did demonstrate what Michael Denning calls "aesthetic ideology." This refers to the ways that political expression engages forms and conventions that "establish ways of seeing and judging, canons of value."[11] For example, different genre conventions contain class inflections, political assumptions, and audience expectations. These ads did more than make a case for electing Nixon, they reflected and pushed for shifting "canons of value" toward more repressive state responses to disorder after 1968. Christopher P. Wilson explored this terrain of cultural narrative and political work in his analysis of police procedurals and organized crime narratives. Rather than dismiss the formulaic elements of popular crime and policing narratives as deceptive and unscholarly, Wilson asks us to consider the ways law enforcement and criminal justice intersect with—and depend on—"journalistic norms and literary conventions."[12] Much like the "aesthetic ideologies" mapped out in Denning's *The Cultural Front*, these norms and conventions provide a way of seeing criminality and criminal justice that imply political affiliations, modes of policing, and, as Wilson notes, the political economy of crime and the role of the state.[13]

Just as cultural forms offer insight into particular social and ideological locations, the political field draws on aesthetic ideologies in its campaign ads and policy initiatives in order to reformulate political blocs and direct state resources toward favored initiatives. Furthermore, as the 1970s wore on, policymakers made it increasingly difficult for prisoners to engage in cultural politics or offer "ways of seeing and judging" criminality that might call into question the state's repressive solutions. These substitutions, distortions, and attempted erasures call for a different kind of analysis. Rather than what Denning calls "the politics of the cultural field itself," the shift in emphasis from "social improvement" to "law enforcement" necessitates an understanding of the cultural production of the political field itself.

Questions of racial inequality permeated the political field of the late 1960s. In particular, African American observers in and out of prisons increasingly saw the criminal justice system as a key enforcer of racial inequality. The police and prisons symbolized broader patterns of injustice throughout the era. The years preceding the 1968 election saw increasing attention to the racial context for crime, policing, and prisons. Most notably, the Nation of Islam developed analyses of prostitution and drug use in black communities that emphasized their origins in internalized racism and white domination. Furthermore, the Nation of Islam explicitly confronted police violence in African American communities while organizing and converting African American inmates. The specific appeal of its critique went well beyond members of its mosques. In *The Fire Next Time* (1963), James Baldwin explains that an interaction with police officers at age thirteen helped him realize "how little one could do to change one's situation." While crossing Fifth Avenue, far from his Harlem home, Baldwin was asked by a police officer, "Why don't you niggers stay uptown where you belong?"[14] Baldwin saw the unchecked ability of police officers to frisk and harass African Americans as a constant reminder of white power and a key means to limit the geographic and social mobility of African Americans. Echoing this sentiment in his 1973 Grammy award–winning single "Living for the City," Stevie Wonder told the story of a hardworking African American unable to find a job in Mississippi. After he migrates to New York City, the naive man is tricked into transporting drugs, arrested by viscously racist police officers, and sentenced to ten years in prison.[15] By the early 1970s, it was not just activists and intellectuals like the Black Panthers, George Jackson, Robert Chrisman, or Angela Davis who would articulate the view that the criminal justice system was a primary means and manifestation of state power and racial oppression.[16]

In this political climate, white support grew for repressive criminal justice amid the seemingly contradictory increasing acceptance of the principal of racial equality. This contradiction would ultimately be resolved in the cultural realm as conservative advertisements, books, and articles drew on the language of civil rights, equal citizenship, and defense of liberty as primary justifications for repressive policing and increased incarceration. By drawing on seemingly universal ideals of citizenship, personal responsibility, and community control, conservatives explicitly invoked and avoided a language of race while engaging in a pattern of racial control. As the sociologist Katherine Beckett reveals, polls during the late 1960s showed that Americans generally supported the principle of racial equality but also worried that the policies of the Johnson administration "pushed integration too fast."[17] For example, while many whites claimed to oppose segregated schools, they also opposed court-ordered efforts to integrate them. Moreover, Beckett found a correlation between white opposition to busing and support for punitive policing. Regardless of their party affiliation, respondents who opposed specific remedies to segregation and racial inequality tended to support conservative, punitive forms of law and order.[18]

Richard Nixon's 1968 presidential campaign crafted television advertisements that specifically confirmed and emphasized this correlation. Short political ads emerged as a crucial element only during the 1964 presidential campaign. Drawing on dramatic news footage, jarring or suspenseful music, and quick montage, Nixon's 1968 ads revolutionized the young genre.[19] While the ads of Hubert Humphrey and George Wallace, his opponents in the race, featured stiff and defensive candidates standing behind a lectern or awkwardly conversing with voters, Nixon's ads unleashed fears of social disintegration, with a first screen warning viewers, "This time vote like your whole world depended on it," then a second giving them the only hope of a return to normalcy: "NIXON." These advertisements marked more than a shift in political campaign strategy, they provided the core means to reframe political protest and street crime as fundamental issues in need of repressive "law-and-order" solutions.

In these ads, made by Eugene Jones—the filmmaker best known for *A Face of War* (1967), his wrenching cinéma vérité documentary about a Marine rifleman in Vietnam—law and order appeared in two forms: the first concerned student protests and urban rioting; the second focused on violent crime.[20] The ads conflated the two. In fact, while Nixon's campaign released separate ads for each form of lawlessness, they relied on several of the same images and phrases, creating an odd equivalence of political protest and violent crime. An ad called "The First Civil Right" featured news photos of student protests (including one of a banner with the word "socialism" prominently displayed) and burning buildings. In it, Nixon's voice avowed: "It is time for an honest look at the problem of order in the United States. Dissent is a necessary ingredient of change, but in a system of government that provides for peaceful change there is no cause that justifies resort to violence. Let us recognize that the first civil right of every American is to be free from domestic violence. So I pledge to you, we shall have order in the United States."[21] The revolutionary violence of groups like the Weather Underground and others would occur in the near future. Here, Nixon referred to the rioting that followed Martin Luther King's assassination and, more specifically, to the violent protests outside the 1968 Democratic Convention at which Hubert Humphrey received his party's nomination. During the convention, the images of the Chicago police attacking protesters in Grant Park symbolized the growing political divide within the Democratic Party. The fighting in the streets mirrored the primary battle between Humphrey and antiwar candidates like Eugene McCarthy and the recently assassinated Robert F. Kennedy. In addition, journalists covering the fighting in the streets emphasized that the police attacks were largely unprovoked.[22] By seeing the political rebellion and what amounted to a police riot in terms of "disorder," Nixon effectively absolved the Chicago police of any responsibility for the melee and reframed the event's meaning in time for the general election.

Nixon's voice-over linked antiwar activity to an undemocratic process and then interpreted the movements as a threat to the "first civil right of every American." In a society with free elections, Nixon argued, there was no place for protest. This understanding of "civil rights" would be unrecognizable to those advocating for racial equality. Because the ads appeared in the months after Martin Luther King's assassination and after consecutive summers of tension and violence between police officers and African Americans, this marked a significant reversal and diffusion of previous meanings of the term. In addition, it repudiated recent decisions by Earl Warren's Supreme Court that criminal defendants and convicted prisoners must have their civil rights protected from violations of due process, cruel and unusual punishment, and equal protection. No longer a strategy to promote the rights of African Americans or those accused of a crime, "civil rights" as employed by the Nixon campaign reversed the advances of the civil rights movement.

In other ads, Jones linked the two types of disorder—student unrest and street crime—by clearly defining their mutual opposite. The people threatened by the protesters and criminals were "decent citizens." One ad contained a typically vague employment of "decent citizens." In this ad, Nixon—in a convincing impersonation of Robert Stack's Eliot Ness in the early 1960s TV hit *The Untouchables*—reported that "in recent years, crime in this country has grown nine times as fast as the population. At the current rate, the crimes of violence in America will double by 1972. We cannot accept that kind of future for America. We owe it to the decent citizens of America to take the offensive against the criminal forces that threaten their peace and their security, and to rebuild respect for law across this country. I pledge to you, the wave of crime is not going to be the wave of the future in America." As Nixon recited his script, the screen displayed images of drug users, crime victims, a rainbow of "decent citizens," and, finally, of criminals cowering before police officers. Here, the Nixon campaign built on the theme of "order" by identifying a strategy of rebuilding "respect for law." Although Nixon did not specify in words how he would do this, images of uniformed officers arresting young thugs made clear his intentions. In his use of the idea of a "decent citizen," Nixon could draw on a homey phrase while invoking threatening images and foreboding statistics. The images and statistics supported Nixon's belief that the normal coercive controls that govern the behavior of most people were not in place in some parts of the United States. He pledged to restore them.

The third advertisement in this series provided the most dramatic invocation of the threat that crime posed to decent citizens. It featured an apparently wealthy, middle-aged woman in a fur coat walking down a dark city street. She clutched her purse close to her chest. As her heels clicked past shuttered storefronts the professional voice-over read alarming statistics: "Crimes of violence in the United States have almost doubled in recent years. Today a violent crime is committed every sixty seconds. A robbery every two-and-a-half minutes. A mugging every six minutes. A murder every forty-three minutes. And it will get worse unless we take the offensive. Freedom from fear is a basic right of every American. We must restore it." Like the other ads, this one ended with the same threatening appeal: "This time vote like your whole world depended on it: NIXON." This ad echoed one of Franklin D. Roosevelt's two famous uses of "fear" as a rallying cry. In his first inaugural address in 1933, Roosevelt assured a nation mired in the Great Depression that it could overcome its economic difficulties: "The only thing we have to fear is fear itself—nameless, unreasoning, unjustified terror which paralyzes needed efforts to convert retreat into advance."[23] Nixon did not invoke this use of fear. In fact, the ad provoked just the kind of fear Roosevelt warned against, leading viewers to conclude that it was just a matter of time before they would be robbed, mugged, or murdered.

Nixon directly echoed Roosevelt's second invocation of fear. In the buildup to the U.S. entry into World War II, "freedom from fear" became one of the "four freedoms" in Roosevelt's post–Pearl Harbor State of the Union Address of January 1942: "Our own objectives are clear; the objective of smashing the militarism imposed by war lords upon their enslaved peoples, the objective of liberating the subjugated Nations—the objective of establishing and securing freedom of speech, freedom of religion, freedom from want, and freedom from fear everywhere in the world."[24] Roosevelt framed "freedom from fear" as a "basic right," in part to sell the nation on his plan to enter World War II. Just as Roosevelt translated a European threat into the homey four freedoms (soon immortalized in a series of Norman Rockwell magazine images), Nixon personalized street crime and political disturbances in his foregrounding of domestic law-and-order policies. This would not be a struggle against poverty and economic depression, like Roosevelt's New Deal or, more to the point, Johnson's Great Society. Rather, if elected, Nixon would declare war to protect the basic rights of decent citizens.

These advertisements showed a country spinning out of control. The first ad implied that street protests threatened the democratic process itself. The second suggested a link between political violence and street violence. The third tapped into wartime propaganda to drive home Nixon's campaign slogan that "your whole world depended on it." Other parts of the campaign amplified these massages. During its early months, Nixon published an article in *Reader's Digest.* In it, he described the urban unrest as a product of "the decline in respect for public authority and the rule of law in America."[25] Nixon tapped into a resonant issue. In his study of the political effects of urban unrest, James W. Button wrote "81 percent of the public believed that 'law and order has broken down in this country,' and 54 percent responded that 'they personally feel more uneasy on the streets.'"[26] Nixon's ads reflected his attempt to translate this unease into votes. Voters understood that a vote for Nixon was a vote for a more repressive criminal justice system. Fully half of all voters questions by the Gallup Poll in 1968 felt that the police should "shoot on sight" anyone found looting during "race riots."[27] In a 1970 poll 75 percent of registered Republicans and 61 percent of registered Democrats agreed with the statement that the courts were too lenient with criminals.[28]

Despite all the disruption within the Democratic Party and the Nixon campaign's fear-mongering, Nixon defeated Humphrey by half a million votes out of more than 7 million ballots cast. Once in office, the Nixon administration translated these campaign slogans into policies and practices. The specific steps that it took to combat what it saw as disorder reveal that the late 1960s and early 1970s was a period both of progressive experimentation in the criminal justice system and the dawning of the repressive regime that continues in the early 21st century. The country was in a transition during which the Nixon administration tapped into Great Society institutions to funnel federal resources away from Clark's goal of social improvement and toward Mitchell's goal of law enforcement.[29] The most dramatic and lasting outcome of this strategy would be a sharp reduction in federal sponsorship of antipoverty and inmate rehabilitation anticrime efforts. In their place and in keeping with the wartime "freedom from fear" rhetoric of Nixon's campaign advertisements, law and order would be implemented using coercive and custodial criminal-justice techniques.

As with Nixon's election campaign, a shift in cultural politics accompanied the policy transition. The changes in the criminal justice system called for by leading right-wing figures like Richard Nixon, Ronald Reagan, and John Mitchell grew from their explicit dismissal of dominant ideas about the social and environmental origins of criminality. At the same time that conservatives sharply critiqued liberals, leftist criminologists advocated structural and materialist arguments about crime and the function of policing that allowed little room for reform efforts like the Great Society. Tony Platt, Paul Takagi, Richard Quinney, and the French theorist Louis Althusser influenced the development of a Marxian criminology that saw the state as a fundamentally exploitative institution.

Political scientists and urban policy advisers like Daniel Patrick

Moynihan, William Ker Muir, and James Q. Wilson helped shape what would become a neoconservative response to crime by appealing directly to the public in trade books aimed at a wide readership. While their works never achieved the wide public consumption of a campaign commercial, they provide insight into the cultural politics of law and order in crucial ways. If Nixon's campaign reframed the meaning of disorder and civil rights to coincide with his vision for government, these works helped usher in a perspective on criminality that emphasized cultural and behavioral deviance as its primary cause. This emphasis marked a significant shift away from both the environmental causes that dominated the liberal response to crime and the structural causes that dominated the radical critique of the criminal justice system and state power. However, they also disrupt easy polarities between "liberal" and "conservative" criminal justice policy. During the Johnson administration, James Q. Wilson—and, in a different context, Daniel Patrick Moynihan—advocated for his belief that poor communities lacked the organic checks on criminal behavior necessary in a civilized, democratic society. This view came to shape a more coercive, less rehabilitative criminal justice regime. Wilson tended to dismiss liberal policies—and demonize liberal policymakers—but he also looked to bureaucratic responses to what he described as pathological communities.

Rather than a polarity between "Left" and "Right," both the Great Society and the law-and-order responses to crime similarly opposed the radical critique of the criminal justice system, which generally saw the police and prisons as blunt instruments in an overall system of oppression in and domination of poor communities. This argument took shape under the influence of Marxist, anticolonialist, and antiracist political philosophy. Radical criminologists argued that the rise of coercive policing and incarceration methods were self-conscious reactions to increasingly unruly disempowered communities and their advocates. This view was most explicitly articulated in a now famous essay by Althusser that first appeared in English in 1971 as "Ideology and Ideological State Apparatuses."[30] Early in the essay, Althusser agrees with the following Marxist definition: "The State is a 'machine' of repression, which enables the ruling classes to ensure their domination over the working class, thus enabling the former to subject the latter to the process of surplus-value extortion."[31] Althusser theorized that this domination takes place via either repressive or ideological tactics in order to facilitate the continuous operation of capitalism. Theoretically, capitalist enterprises ensure that workers will show up each day by providing them wages sufficient for basic survival. These enterprises do little, Althusser argues, to ensure that workers agree that capitalism is itself a system beneficial to the laboring class. In addition, the enterprises have few assurances that future workers will have the skills and worldviews necessary to make them effective employees. Althusser agreed with the Marxist idea that "state apparatuses" provide the support necessary to ensure the continuation and expansion of the labor force. Public schools, military service, and training facilities provide the basic skills needed in various labor markets. Still other "ideological state apparatuses" (ISAs) reproduce "submission to the rules of the established order."[32] In other words, workers—and their managers—learn to accept the belief system that ensures "subjection to the ruling ideology."[33] This ideological education, according to Althusser, also takes place in schools and in military service, but it can also occur via ideological apparatuses not controlled by the state, like churches or the mass media.

At moments when the ideological education breaks down or alternative ideological forces threaten the control of the ruling class, "repressive state apparatuses" fill the void. Even when ISAs are functioning relatively effectively, a small police force and criminal justice system are used to repress crime that poses little threat to the current order. If an unexpected labor dispute or racial crisis develops, the military can respond. If the crisis expands, an extended period of repression could ensue. It appeared to those who subscribed to this belief that during the years leading up to Nixon's campaign and also during his term of office, just such a crisis developed. As Christian Parenti, a contemporary critic of the criminal justice system, points out, in those years,

> the Panthers—Black Marxists and fully armed—stormed the California state capitol. In Newark, Watts, and Chicago, Black people shot back at cops and National Guardsmen in Detroit, African

> American snipers were joined by transplanted urban "hillbillies." In New Mexico, armed Chicanos fired on a county court house, trying to kill the sheriff. Chants of "Black Power," and "Red Power" rose from all quarters. Gay men, routinely pilloried as "sissies," were knocking out cops during pitched battles following a police raid on the Stonewall bar in New York City. Meanwhile, women burnt bras and, more importantly, filed suits, protested against discrimination, and won the right to reproductive choice. Not even the US army could be trusted. . . . Gung-ho officers in the field started getting "fragged" with terrifying regularity, as drug addiction, madness, and open insubordination became the norm among GIs.[34]

Conservatives responded to what they saw as a crisis with an unprecedented expansion of the criminal justice system and an increasing reliance on custodial facilities with few rehabilitative programs. Prisons represented a consolidation of state power to the radical criminologists of the 1960s and 1970s. Paul Takagi, a criminologist at the University of California at Berkeley, argued in a 1975 article that Philadelphia's Walnut Street Jail (founded in 1790) was not the Quaker experiment in humane criminal justice that most historians described. Rather, it "came into existence when penal powers came to be monopolized by the State. The significance of a state prison . . . was not so much the architectural design and the classification of prisons, but the concept of a centralized state apparatus."[35]

If indeed the criminal justice system represented a repressive response to political upheaval, the rhetoric focused instead on order and community. In contrast to the radical critique of the criminal justice system, popular "social problem" books written by emerging neoconservative intellectuals demonstrated the problem of crime by telling stories about deteriorating black communities. Police violence and urban rioting would be chalked up to poor relations between police officers and African Americans. These narratives downplayed racial and economic inequality, emphasizing instead a loss of values. They also avoided criticizing government bureaucracy in the same ways they confronted other aspects of the Great Society. Rather than seeing criminal justice as a repressive regime that established and maintained control of actual and potential critics of a fundamentally exploitative economic system, the criminal justice system represented the interests of law-abiding citizens. Thus, existing institutions—in this case the criminal justice system—could be used to tell very different kinds of stories about state power, citizenship, and inequality.

Rather than seeing the police as representatives of a racist, oppressive state, conservative intellectuals emphasized the ways individual officers interacted with criminals. William Ker Muir reframed the politics of crime control in terms that emphasized individual interaction rather than state control and inequality of power. In some cases, he depoliticized explicitly political groups like the Black Panthers. But it is in Muir's ideological assumptions that we see the cultural politics of crime control most clearly. After several years as a consultant to the Berkeley and Oakland police departments, Muir interviewed twenty-eight Oakland police officers in the early 1970s, a period when armed political activists highlighted the effects of policing on African American communities. The resulting book, *Police: Streetcorner Politicians* would be nominated for the Pulitzer Prize, and Muir would later serve as a speechwriter for conservative politicians, including Vice President George H. W. Bush and California Governor Pete Wilson.

Muir did not fundamentally disagree that policing could be repressive. Rather than seeing these actions as part of a repressive system, however, Muir saw repression as one strategy among many employed by individual police officers in performing their duties. Rather than being a manifestation of a mounting racial crisis, coercive means were simply one tactic among many used by police. Muir identified three techniques: coercion, reciprocity, and inspiration. He defined coercion as "a means of controlling the conduct of others through threats to harm."[36] Muir understood policing through threats of physical harm as a right granted to public officials by a willing public. Muir did not see this as the most effective means of policing. Instead, he argued that reciprocity (overcoming resistance through exchange) and inspiration (encouraging people to act a certain way because they share the heartfelt conviction that it is the right thing) are more effective and attractive options.[37] In reciprocity, a classic barter system means that peace is best assured when all parties feel satisfied with the fairness of the exchange. The tactic of inspiration, Muir argued, is the most "civilized." In evaluating these tactics, Muir was particularly interested in the effect each form of policing would have on the officers themselves.

Many significant differences separate the political rhetoric and traditions Althusser and Muir drew on in theorizing the function of policing, but the core difference lies in how the two men saw the function of government. For Althusser, bourgeois governments were a "means of oppression" that represented the interests of the capitalist class and were antagonistic to the laboring class. To Muir, the state and its functionaries were public officials with legitimate authority freely granted by a public eager to protect its safety and freedom. As such, Muir's study of an Oakland Police Department then engaged in controlling political violence primarily described and analyzed the individual interactions and views of the officers. Following the social science convention of his book, Muir renamed Oakland as "Laconia" and the Black Panther Party as "Overseers." The Overseers were mentioned twice in the book. In the first instance, Muir described a "vigilante band of black youths" who "tried to modify the behavior of police within black areas—through surveillance, threats, and firearms."[38] In the second instance, they were completely depoliticized as a "black youth gang."[39] This dramatically downplayed the political context in which the Oakland Police Department operated.

Muir's focus on individual interactions marked what would become a trend in neoconservative criminal justice: a resistance to structural explanations for criminality or police violence amid the rhetorical transformation of political conflict into "controlling disorder" and protecting citizens. Muir, concerned primarily with the moral and intellectual lives of police officers, ultimately concluded that coercive policing placed an extraordinary burden on the officers. The contradictory aims of social work and coercive control left many of the officers Muir interviewed shaken and damaged. Muir was particularly disturbed by the trend toward creating highly coercive SWAT teams that did none of the reciprocal or inspirational work that Muir found more effective.[40]

Muir's preference for ideological over coercive tactics was echoed by the man who would become the most important theorist of criminal justice in the late twentieth century. Where Muir focused on the tactics of police officers in containing street crime, James Q. Wilson's early works on criminal justice attempted to understand the sources of criminal behavior before offering new tactics of policing. Like Muir's, Wilson's reputation as a New Right political theorist took shape in the cauldron of the late 1960s and early 1970s. In the 1990s Wilson, then a professor of government at Harvard University, would emerge as one of the architects of "broken windows" policing. The broken windows theory of crime, which described urban deterioration as fostering an environment conducive to criminal behavior, provided a basis for the adoption of "community oriented policing" programs and "quality of life" programs in municipalities around the United States.[41]

These approaches to criminality emerged as part of a broader critique of social and behavior disorder that focused closely on African American communities. Like Muir's resignification of interactions between the Oakland Police Department and the Black Panther Party, Wilson's narratives about African Americans acknowledged a racialized context for criminal justice but saw high rates of poverty and disproportionate representation in prison in the context of dysfunctional communities rather than an oppressive state. In 1963, Wilson made the argument that would be taken up in *The Negro Family: The Case for National Action*, popularly known as the "Moynihan Report" after its principal author, Daniel Patrick Moynihan.[42] Moynihan served as assistant secretary of labor in the Kennedy and Johnson administrations before joining Wilson at Harvard. While in Johnson's Department of Labor, Moynihan argued that the structure of African American families hindered upward mobility by encouraging welfare dependency. This contention would result in charges that Moynihan was a racial neoconservative. However, as Daryl Michael Scott argues, Moynihan was a "racial liberal" in the Johnson administration, arguing in favor of "equality of results" that drew on race-conscious policies like targeted hiring practices.[43] While the characterization of Moynihan's work as explicitly racist may have been unfair, his critics surely recognized that his calls to reform families came perilously close to blaming African Americans—and African American women in particular—for poverty.

Thus, while Moynihan may have seen himself as a liberal in that he emphasized the social causes of poverty and inequality, he was conservative in that he saw these social causes within African American communities.

For Moynihan, alleviating poverty required changing the culture of African American families and communities. For Wilson, controlling crime required similar long-term social and cultural transformations. In the meantime, if social disorganization and damage resulted in criminality, poor black communities needed intensive, community-level policing and clear consequences for deviation from majority norms. For example, *City Politics* (1963), which Wilson coauthored with Edward C. Banfield, argued that the primary reason for low African American political participation was "the social disorganization which is characteristic of lower-class Negroes and which is reflected in their high rates of crime, delinquency, desertion, divorce, and illegitimacy. This is in great part the result of the weakness of the family unit. The plantation system during the period of slavery made it difficult to form stable Negro families; the continuing lack of economic opportunities since then has made it difficult for Negro men to acquire the economic self-sufficiency to become the head and breadwinner of a family. Female-centered households are common among Negroes, and the 'wandering male' who is only a part-time worker and part-time husband has contributed to the high percentage of Negro families supported by either working mothers or welfare checks or both."[44] Using sources from the late 1930s and mid-1940s and thus ignoring the massive political mobilization of the postwar civil rights movements, the authors concluded that black people in the early 1960s faced economic hardship primarily because of "cultural and economic factors."[45] Wilson would go on to apply and expand the same logic to the problem of policing and crime. In 1968 (and in expanded form in 1975) Wilson argued that crime was primarily a problem of deteriorating community controls.[46] Wilson pointed out that despite falling unemployment and rising national wealth, crime rates and the use of government antipoverty programs like Aid to Families with Dependent Children went up throughout the 1960s. This "paradox of the sixties," Wilson argued, could be explained by looking at social disorganization evidenced by the emergence of rebellious young people, the use of illegal drugs, and the breakdown of traditional control mechanisms. Wilson argued, for example, that "the contacts of upper-middle-class suburban youths with ghetto blacks as a result of civil rights programs increased access to the drug culture."[47]

In order to combat this "breakdown," Wilson favored crime-control measures that emphasized moral values and the consistent use of predictable penalties. The homogeneity of small towns and suburbs provide a model of "local self-government" being used to "reinforce informal neighborhood sanctions."[48] In such a place, crime control could be primarily an ideological affair. Policing and prisons would be a temporary and repressive way to reestablish community controls, not the permanent fixture of a welfare state seeking rehabilitation.[49] In much of urban America, however, Wilson saw the departure of "persons with an interest in, and the competence for, maintaining a community."[50] This emphasis on loosening community control was a common feature of 1960s popular nonfiction on social problems, including works written by liberal observers. For example, Jane Jacobs argued in *The Death and Life of Great American Cities* (1961) that during the postwar period people became far less likely to intermingle on city streets. Jacobs believed that routine interactions—rather than the more physically coercive strategies of police departments—enabled communities to maintain and enforce informal controls on unwelcome behavior. In her assessment of the "slum clearance" housing projects championed by New York City's Robert Moses and other city planners, Jacobs wrote that

> the first thing to understand is that the public peace—the sidewalk and street peace—of cities is not kept primarily by the police, necessary as police are. It is kept primarily by an intricate, almost unconscious, network of voluntary controls and standards among the people themselves, and enforced by the people themselves. In some city areas—older public housing projects and streets with very high population turnover are often conspicuous examples—the keeping

> of public sidewalk law and order is left almost entirely to the police and special guards. Such places are jungles. No amount of police can enforce civilization where the normal, casual enforcement of it has broken down.[51]

Jacobs's desire to restore feelings of community is admittedly a far cry from Nixon's and Wilson's desire to restore "respect for law," but her writings did provide some of the rationale for different kinds of policing.[52] Wilson believed that African Americans had the greatest difficulty enforcing community controls that reflected "middle-class values": "The creation of a middle-class community requires that middle-class values dominate, and this applies with equal force—perhaps with special force—to blacks. If a family sends its children to schools in which many students reject school work, if they live in an area where illegitimacy is as common as marriage, if they regularly encounter on the streets persons for whom self-expression is more attractive than self-control, the family will either find itself conforming to a standard it does not value or isolating itself from its neighbors."[53] Where Jacobs saw the absence of formal community controls to be a result of the wrongheaded ideologies of past and present city planners; conservative crime-control scholars of the late 1960s and early 1970s saw—and urged policymakers to see—the problem as cultural and behavioral.

For Wilson, class became a descriptive feature of certain bad and good values, not a category of relative wealth and power. Most notably, Wilson felt that the loss of "middle-class values" could be seen in the entire social landscape. Whether discussing pornography and lurid paperbacks sold in drugstores, run-down buildings and yards full of crabgrass, offensive language used in public places, immodest fashion, "rowdy" teenagers, or panhandling, Wilson couched his disapproval as a loss of values. In this way, the New Right's "law and order" became a critique not of Marxists with guns, but of a tradition of progressive reform that saw the state as a potential force for alleviating social problems via noncoercive institutions and strategies. Wilson argued not simply for more police in urban areas but for a categorically different way of understanding police work. If authorities increased the number of "beat patrols," also known as "preventive patrols," police officers would be constantly visible in high-crime areas. Rather than merely respond to a criminal infraction, police officers would continuously drive or walk around a neighborhood when not responding to a call.[54] Crime control, both Wilson and Muir believed—should be primarily an ideological affair. Repressive policing and prisons should be a temporary way to reestablish community controls, not the permanent fixture of a welfare state seeking rehabilitation.

Wilson was responding to the increasing interest among U.S. urban police departments in accelerating the process of centralization, professionalization, and specialization that had been spreading, slowly but clearly, since the proliferation of uniformed urban police forces during the second half of the nineteenth century. Cities and police forces had been developing in relation to each other for at least the previous century: "The growth of uniformed urban police forces," the historian Eric Monkkonen argues, "should be seen simply as part of the growth of urban service bureaucracies."[55] Just as urban dwellers increasingly relied on municipal government to tend to other areas of public welfare like firefighting, garbage removal, and water service, they also expected their government to take responsibility for control of the "dangerous classes."[56] Thus, the late nineteenth century saw increased reliance on uniformed police officers, as well as increased use of scientific modes of detection and identification that relied on new technologies like mug shots, fingerprinting, and the Bertillon system of physical measurement.[57]

With these new professionals, the ideologies of social scientific study, professional management, and centralization would become key components of the next era of criminal justice, as it became a central feature of municipal, state, and federal governments. Reformers who believed that government bureaucracies, university researchers, and social welfare agencies could work together to increase professionalization further influenced policing and criminal justice during the Progressive and New Deal eras. Reform movements in municipal courts and prison systems followed the model of centralization and professionalization that characterized the formation and proliferation of urban police departments. Michael Willrich describes a "managerial revolution" in Progressive-era Chicago that facilitated the transformation of a largely private and disconnected system of police courts into a public, unified Municipal Court system overseeing the "conflicts and transgressions of the modern city."[58]

This managerial transformation saw the creation of new professional organizations and a federal crime-fighting bureaucracy that further removed policing strategies from the control and oversight of the communities being policed. These methods were championed by new organizations like the International Association of Chiefs of Police, founded in 1893 specifically to promote the sharing of information. The trend reached its apogee during the first twelve years of J. Edgar Hoover's long directorship of the Federal Bureau of Investigation. Between his appointment in 1924 and his declared end of the "war on crime" in 1936, Hoover created a federal law enforcement bureaucracy that, as Clare Bond Potter notes, "articulated good policing as a central characteristic of a modern state."[59] Hoover and his supporters saw good policing as professional, free from corruption, and employing scientific modes of detection. During the Depression, mass media valorized the exploits of Hoover's "G-men" as they went after John Dillinger, Ma Barker, and Alvin "Creepy" Karpis. But perhaps more significant than these moments of great cultural power were the institutional changes they helped bring about. By the early 1930s, the FBI issued the Uniform Crime Reports (UCR) and *Fugitives Wanted by Police* to connect municipal departments to one another and the federal crime-fighting bureaucracy.[60]

With the creation of a federal crime-fighting agency and the influence of Progressive-era reforms, the stage was set for further transformation of urban police departments. Police reform centered on rooting out corruption and encouraging professional efficiency, goals shared by the reformers and Hoover's FBI. Hoover's deft publicity campaigns argued primarily that a professional, well-trained police force would be the most effective means of crime control. In the Los Angeles and New York police departments, for example, progressives argued that elected officials should no longer control the police. Los Angeles reformers believed that corruption grew from political control. According to the historian Edward Escobar, the "chief or an official body within the department appointed by the chief had sole authority over all personnel issues, including promotions and questions of discipline."[61]

In addition, reformers implemented new recruitment and training programs and raised the pay of police officers to curtail corruption and raise the professional status of police officers. All these steps imitated innovations of policing on the federal level. In New York, the anticorruption Lexow Commission and the reform mayor Fiorello LaGuardia recommended and instituted similar changes. Most of these reforms would not take final form until the 1950s and 1960s, but they trace their origins to the 1930s. Despite institutional aversions to working closely with the federal agents, urban police administrators refashioned their administrations on the model of the G-men. This was particularly true among new units created during the reform period. While beat cops continued to wear uniforms and follow a militaristic chain of command, new investigative units and anticorruption officers donned suits and ties, much like other professionals. Furthermore, police administrators centralized the command structure and frequently reassigned officers in order to target high-crime areas.[62]

To progressives from the New Deal to the War on Poverty, it made sense that the state should take on the most pressing social problems of their age. Thus, while progressives did not necessarily seek to control "dangerous classes" or generally side with management in labor disputes, they did welcome the opportunity to create and fund agencies that would help define and fight wars on crime. This bureaucracy, it turned out, would ultimately implement law-and-order policies.

These cultural shifts would ultimately have dramatic implications for criminal justice funding and outcomes, but they also helped shape how the postwar liberal state could be put to repressive ends. Many scholars of the criminal justice system have accepted at face value the polarities that Nixon and Mitchell drew between the Johnson administration and their own approach to criminal justice policy. The cultural advocacy for transformation in the criminal justice system seemed to indicate that there would be a new approach to criminal justice under Nixon. In truth, there were significant changes in the criminal code and sentencing practices that would lead to the incarceration of an unprecedented number of people. The Nixon administration, however, inherited everything it needed to fight its war on crime from the Johnson administration it so sharply criticized. Despite the tendency to see Nixon's law-and-order politics as either the end of postwar liberalism or the beginning of a more conservative approach to crime control, the impact of Nixon's crime-control agenda lay in the cultural realm. That is, law-and-order politics shaped a cultural epistemology of crime control. Nixon, Wilson, and Muir engaged in what Christopher P. Wilson calls "cultural storytelling and political rhetoric."[63] The policy changes had already been made by Nixon's predecessor.

James Q. Wilson's political career during the 1960s is exemplary of the continuities between liberalism and conservative criminal justice institutions. Wilson's influence can be seen as early as 1966, when he served as an adviser to the Police and Science and Technology Task Forces of the President's Commission on Law Enforcement and the Administration of Justice. This commission, and the last years of the Johnson administration generally, provides an important backdrop to the anticrime efforts of the Nixon administration. Wilson would later argue that Johnson's attention to criminality was a specific reaction to the use of crime by Barry Goldwater during the 1964 presidential campaign. This might help explain why the Great Society's "social improvement" and the Nixon administration's "law enforcement" had so much in common. On the campaign trail, Goldwater continually charged that Johnson was not doing enough about crime. As Wilson later recalled to an interviewer, "In 1964, crime became a decisive issue in American politics, because Barry Goldwater made an argument about crime in the streets in his campaign against Lyndon Johnson. And Lyndon Johnson, being the kind of man he was, was not going to let any charge go unanswered. So after he won decisively in 1964, he immediately created a national commission on law enforcement and the administration of justice, determined to do whatever was in his power to reduce crime."[64] Wilson saw the commission as a political response to a conservative challenge.

Johnson's actions on criminal justice responded not just to Goldwater but to the public anxiety that brought people to the Republican campaign.[65] Concerns over crime posed a direct threat to a liberal coalition of big cities, urban African Americans, and college students. Since African Americans and the student Left were the objects of some of these fears, responding with a straightforward "tough on crime" approach posed significant political risks. Nevertheless, there is little in the commission's final report, *The Challenge of Crime in a Free Society*, that distinguishes it from the response typically labeled as conservative.[66] Like William Ker Muir and Wilson himself, the commission argued that poor "police-community relations" hindered crime control, especially in "minority-group communities."[67]

That high crime rates were seen as partly resulting from poor community relations offers insight into the marginalization of liberal criminal justice policies in subsequent years. This finding also appeared in the 1965 report of the McCone Commission,[68] formed in response to Los Angeles's Watts riot of August 11–13, 1965. The riot began after a California Highway Patrol officer hit Marquette Frye with a baton during a drunk driving arrest. During the rioting, thirty-four people lost their lives—virtually all at the hands of Los Angeles police officers and California National Guard soldiers, who swept through the city shooting at rock throwers and looters—and more than one thousand people were injured. During its investigation, the McCone Commission heard testimony regarding more than seventy cases of police brutality prior to the riot. Rather than see the riot as a response to police brutality that disproportionately impacted communities of color, the commission concluded that a climate of public distrust and poor public relations were the primary causes of the violence.[69] The commission discounted citizen complaints yet urged the Los Angeles Police Department to more effectively investigate grievances. Where the McCone Commission discounted the importance of police brutality as a legitimate problem, the president's commission, in *The Challenge of Crime in a Free Society*, did not mention it at all.[70] Seeing the problem as one of community relations rather than of state violence or social inequality, the report recommended focusing on retraining police officers as community relations specialists.

In contrast to its typically narrow consideration of the causes of violent urban protest, the president's commission would sharply diverge from previous and future opinion on the proper use of incarceration. On any given day in 1965, approximately 426,000 people resided in U.S. correctional facilities, over half of them awaiting trial.[71] The commission was surprised to find that few personnel showed concern for the rehabilitation or basic rights of inmates. In a recommendation that mirrored the optimism of many of the Johnson administration's Great Society programs, the commission urged federal, state, and local jurisdictions to conduct careful risk assessments and to divert as many offenders as possible into community-based corrections. They urged the creation of smaller, more flexible facilities where teachers, managers, and counselors would largely replace officers. Treatment, education, vocational training, and community building, the commission advised, should be the wave of the future.[72] Like Muir, the McCone and president's commissions both concluded that repressive criminal justice tactics were a symbol of failure, but where the McCone Commission urged an acceleration of public relations campaigns in poor and African American communities, the president's commission framed the problem in terms of an expansion of treatment. Both, however, failed to see rioting and crime as responses to police misconduct and brutality, not to mention systemic inequality and oppression.[73]

If liberal crime rhetoric mirrored that of conservatives, the bureaucracy of crime control was similarly consistent. The two major institutions now widely associated with Nixon's law-and-order campaign were already in place when he arrived in Washington. Johnson transformed the Federal Bureau of Narcotics into the Bureau of Narcotics and Dangerous Drugs (BNDD) and shifted it from the Treasury Department to the Justice Department.[74] In addition, Johnson created the Law Enforcement Assistance Administration (LEAA), claiming it to be one of the last major initiatives of the Great Society. However, as Malcolm M. Feeley and Austin D. Sarat noted, the Omnibus Crime Control Act of 1968—which mandated the creation of the LEAA—was less a well-defined response to rising concerns about criminality than the "product of a political atmosphere in which the Great Society coalition was in decline and in which no single political vision had arisen to replace it."[75] The BNDD and LEAA would lead to dramatically different outcomes than those hoped for by the president's commission or the broader War on Poverty, but because they lacked a coherent agenda they required few revisions in order to achieve those different ends.

It is telling that the Omnibus Crime Control Act of 1968 quickly became known as "the Safe Streets Act," a name given it by Housing and Urban Development Secretary Joseph Califano, a liberal member of the Johnson administration.[76] By emphasizing the "street" as a site of insecurity, Califano gave an urban cultural meaning to a set of policies and practices that would ultimately make the concerns of potential victims of crime central to a conservative coalition. While it contained some funding for antipoverty programs and arts and educational programs in prisons, its overall thrust was a far cry from a call for community-based corrections and neighborhood-level policing. The LEAA would primarily distribute weapons and provide training to local police departments. The Safe Streets Act also expanded the use of wiretaps and made confessions administered while in police custody admissible evidence in court.[77] In hindsight, one might be tempted to see this as the beginning of the conservative turn in criminal justice. It is true that Johnson signed the bill despite sharp opposition from congressional Democrats and his own misgivings.[78] Even these controversial steps, however, merely sharpened tools already put in place by Robert F. Kennedy's Justice Department to counter organized crime.[79]

A tough-on-crime approach had never been incompatible with postwar liberalism. Nixon tapped into a belief held by prominent social critics who believed that postwar urban policymakers had retreated from effective control of criminal activity and created a system of dependency and handouts. During the 1960s, the War on Poverty led to the creation of programs like Title I, Head Start, Job Corps, and Vista, as well as expanded benefits under Social Security. As Bruce Schulman points out, these programs were quickly denounced by conservatives like Ernest Van Den Haag, who called them "a wasteful hodgepodge [that] only trapped and humiliated the poor."[80] Because of these critiques we tend to forget that the Great Society included funding for intensive, coercive policing.

The criminal justice system was perhaps the Nixon administration's most visible use of the very social programs conservatives criticized to implement policies of neglect and repression. Jonathan Simon correctly points out that despite Nixon's and other conservatives' advocacy of "New Federalism," crime-control policy was as "imperially federal as any Great Society program, indeed more so."[81] While earlier administrations targeted political enemies as foreign radicals or communists, John Mitchell's Department of Justice viewed the Black Panther Party and other New Left organizations as criminal gangs rather than militant political organizations. Emboldened by the Safe Streets Act's allowance of electronic surveillance, Mitchell approved the wiretapping of the Black Panther Party and charged the Chicago Seven, including Black Panther founder Bobby Seale, with criminal conspiracy.[82] The LEAA always encouraged and funded tactical training and stockpiling of weapons by local police forces. The overall budget for the LEAA rose from $63 million in 1969 to almost $700 million by the end of Nixon's first term. The legislation directed the LEAA to make "riot-related" grants to states, resulting in large-scale purchases of tear gas, guns, communications and surveillance equipment, and other hardware. For example, James Button found that "65 percent of all state riot-related funds went for hardware in 1969, while only 35 percent of these monies were allocated for community relations efforts."[83]

While the LEAA provided the conduit for the expansion of repressive policing, the creation of the BNDD—which in 1973 became the Drug Enforcement Administration—facilitated the further erosion of the reform tradition in American prisons. Violent protest from previously peaceful movements, increasing rates of use of highly addictive narcotics, and greater fears of violent crime were all present during the late 1960s.[84] In linking these shifts, Nixon effectively argued that there was a breakdown in civil society, despite the fact that each factor alone affected a small number of people with sharply divergent experiences.[85]

Even though Nixon sought to blame liberal reforms, the antiwar movement, and the counterculture for disorder, he used administrative structures put in place throughout the twentieth century as hallmarks of progressive and liberal reform. During the reforms of the Progressive era (1900–1914), Congress passed the Smoking Opium

Exclusion Act of 1909 and the Harrison Narcotic Act of 1914.[86] Before World War II, people addicted to narcotics would be confined to the U.S. Narcotics Farm in Lexington, Kentucky. With passage of the Boggs Act in 1951, first offenders received a prison sentence of two to five years. If they offended again, they received a sentence of five to ten years. After that, the sentence increased to ten to twenty years.[87] As the decade wore on, heroin use had disproportionate effects on African American communities. According to the historian Jill Jonnes, half of all heroin addicts during the postwar years were African American.[88] Coinciding with this shift, Congress extended the sentences. With the Narcotics Control Act of 1956, Congress increased the sentence for first-time offenders to two to ten years. Second offenders would serve five to twenty years and third offenders ten to forty years.[89]

Nixon's drug control policies called for returning to an emphasis on drug treatment using methadone maintenance but also for using the funding apparatus of the Great Society's Law Enforcement Assistance Administration to emphasize the get-tough approach. These policies differed in scale, but not in ideology, from the mixture of criminalization and treatment that characterized the postwar era. In response to a successful Department of Corrections-based narcotic treatment program in Washington, D.C., Nixon created the first White House drug office. His administration, according to Robert L. DuPont, a psychiatrist specializing in treatment of addiction who served as Nixon's second "drug czar," "committed the federal government to unprecedented investments in addiction treatment."[90] The contradictions of crime control during the Nixon years is exemplified by Nixon's National Commission on Marijuana and Drug Abuse, which urged state and federal lawmakers to decriminalize marijuana.[91] Although Nixon did not support or implement its conclusions, many states did weaken their marijuana laws. In addition, under the auspices of the Special Action Office for Drug Abuse Prevention (SAODAP), the White House examined the use of heroin in urban areas and by U.S. soldiers in Vietnam. In addition, SAODAP coordinated federal drug policy and developed treatment programs throughout the nation. SAODAP's first director, Jerome Jaffe, was surprised to learn that, according to a 1971 study, 42 percent of Army enlisted men had tried heroin. Half of these—

approximately 20 percent of Army enlisted personnel—had become dependent on heroin.[92] As the image of the heroin addict shifted from urban African Americans to soldiers and veterans (of all races), the White House response also changed. By 1974, two-thirds of SAODAP's $784 million budget was devoted to what Jaffe called "demand reduction": treatment, education, and research.[93] SAODAP devoted only the remaining third to traditional "supply reduction" strategies of using law enforcement agencies to combat drug trafficking.[94]

Although the actions of Nixon's White House show that his law-and-order politics and practices had much in common with the postwar trends, activity on the state and local level reveals a more consistently repressive approach. State governments and parole boards were responding to alarming rates of violent crime and property crime during the 1960s. Official crime rates increased sharply during the 1960s. According to the FBI's Uniform Crime Reports, the number of violent and property crimes (as reported by state and local police departments) rose from 3,384,200 in 1960 to 6,720,200 in 1968. By 1970 the number reached 8,098,000.[95] Several states began to significantly increase the length of prison sentences for a variety of offenses. The federal government provided support for drug treatment, while state and local governments expanded a tougher approach. The historian Bruce Schulman argued that Nixon "pioneered what came to be called devolution—transferring authority from the federal government to state and local governments and from the public sector to the private sphere."[96] While SAODAP could provide money for treatment, federal dollars would also be funneled back to the states through the LEAA.

In New York, Governor Nelson Rockefeller championed and implemented the most draconian drug sentences in U.S. history. In May 1973 Rockefeller pushed through the state legislature a set of laws to deter citizens from using or selling drugs and to punish and isolate from society those who were not deterred. As the journalist Dan Baum argues, "It was thought that rehabilitative efforts had failed; that the epidemic of drug abuse could be quelled only by the threat of inflexible, and therefore certain, exceptionally severe punishment."[97] The new drug laws, which have since become known as the "Rockefeller Drug Laws," established mandatory prison sentences for the unlawful possession and sale of controlled substances. Generally, the statutes required judges to impose a sentence of fifteen years to life for anyone convicted of selling two ounces or possessing four ounces of narcotics such as cocaine or heroin.

The structure of federal crime control did not change in dramatic ways during the Nixon administration. Making this structure more repressive did not require replacing or repealing the criminal justice framework of the Great Society. What had been called "social improvement" under the Johnson administration was merely renamed "law enforcement" under the Nixon administration. As Michael Massing notes, the Nixon administration expanded funding for access to methadone maintenance at roughly the same time that it shifted the emphasis toward more intensive policing.[98] Mitchell and the Nixon administration more generally laid the groundwork for a future apparatus—to borrow the materialist metaphors of Althusser and Marx—of intensive, coercive policing and large-scale incarceration. Even before he took office, Nixon's campaign used crime control as a way to make sense out of the chaos that many Americans saw around them. This effort, however, included more than Nixon's cunning manipulation of a frustrated "silent majority." In fact, the transition was part of a larger transformation of the Great Society. In the realm of criminal justice, Mitchell and Rockefeller—like Muir and Wilson—lamented the failure of reform-oriented criminal justice and instead constructed new laws requiring stiff sentences. Under their leadership, law and order lost any connotation of corrections or rehabilitation in favor of an openly repressive state apparatus. Ultimately, however, some people who, like Moynihan and Wilson, came to politics during the Great Society would craft the Nixon-era policies. Two of the Great Society's most important bureaucratic legacies—the Bureau of Narcotics and Dangerous Drugs and the Law Enforcement Assistance Administration—provided conduits for the massive expansion of policing and prisons.

Criminal justice had gone through several major transformations in the nation's history, but the rapid and unprecedented expansion of coercive policing and correctional strategies was something altogether new. Until the 1970s, incarceration was a relatively minor, if severe, element of the nation's overall criminal justice system. This would change in the 1980s and 1990s, a period of massive growth in urban police departments and federal law enforcement. During these decades prisons also became the primary public answer to the question of how the United States would control lawbreakers.[99]

The shift from "social improvement" to "law enforcement" also can be seen in the cultural redefinition of "liberalism" itself. Once an expression of postwar optimism, liberalism by the beginning of the 1980s was seen as a primary cause of the social problems—including crime—that its proponents sought to alleviate. In a speech before the National Sheriff's Association in 1984, President Reagan remarked that a "hardened criminal class" had been created by "liberal social philosophy." Recalling his years as California governor in the late 1960s and early 1970s, Reagan ridiculed arguments that contextualized criminality as "schemes" that "saw man as primarily the creature of his material environment." Liberals had wrongly assumed that "individual wrongdoing was always caused by a lack of material goods, and underprivileged background, or poor socioeconomic conditions. And somehow, and I know you've heard it said—I heard it many times when I was Governor of California—it was society, not the individual, that was at fault when an act of violence or a crime was committed. Somehow, it wasn't the wrongdoer but all of us who were to blame." In this speech, Reagan announced the completion of John Mitchell's shift: "The increase in citizen involvement in fighting crime through such initiatives as the Neighborhood Watch programs, spearheaded by the Sheriff's Association; the tough, new State statutes directed at repeat offenders; the widespread public outcry against leniency in our court system; and the sweeping new steps we've taken at the Federal level show that the years of the pseudo-intellectual apologies for crime are now over."[100] Conservatives could finally claim for themselves the repressive manifestation of the Great Society.

CHAPTER TWO

THE AGE OF JACKSON

GEORGE JACKSON AND THE RADICAL CRITIQUE OF INCARCERATION

During the late 1960s and early 1970s, conservative politicians steered the national debate regarding criminal justice policy toward increasing repression. At the same time, the culture of American prisons became increasingly radical. Influenced by the New Left, the civil rights movement, and revolutions in Latin America, Asia, and Africa, a growing number of inmates interpreted the convergence of liberal and conservative criminal justice policies as the evolution of an increasingly reactionary, repressive, and neocolonial state. If Richard Nixon saw himself as the standard-bearer of a return to order that would protect the civil rights of "decent citizens," many prisoners would agree with the assessment by the radical Guyanese historian and politician Walter Rodney that Nixon was "America's chief prison warder."[1] If, as Arthur Schlesinger believed, the 1830s and 1840s could be deemed the "Age of [Andrew] Jackson," then the radicalization of American prisoners during the 1970s ushered in a second age of Jackson—George Jackson. George Jackson inspired his generation of incarcerated intellectuals and writers to insist on the importance of their perspectives in shaping public debates over a host of key issues. Though it would be hard to overestimate the influence of Malcolm X and Angela Davis on the cultural and intellectual output of incarcerated people during the 1970s, the brief, intense, and uncompromising revolutionary life of Jackson made him the icon for a range of critics of the prison system.

Between his first national exposure as a "Soledad Brother" in early 1970 and his violent death in August 1971, George Jackson achieved a level of celebrity rarely attained by an incarcerated person. Jackson both generated and was the product of the increasing political and cultural engagement of American prisoners. In the weeks and years that followed his death, prisoners around the country memorialized Jackson in a remarkable series of protests. Jackson was a key participant in debates over incarceration, colonialism, and racism. While he is often only remembered for the ideological extremes of his book of letters, *Soledad Brother*, as well as his rhetorical and possibly physical use of violent tactics, George Jackson has not been recognized for his participation in an organized system of covert education that presaged theories of internal colonialism, his popularization of arguments about the political qualities of incarceration, and his insistence that prisoners can contribute to movements for social change as symbols, intellectuals, and leaders. It is telling that the largest and most visible prison rebellion of the era occurred on the other side of the country only weeks after his death. While observers have noted the connection between Jackson and Attica, the tactics and demands of the "Attica Brothers" have been described as strange or unrealistic. Once placed in the proper context of the prison culture of the 1970s, their calls for unity, amnesty, and removal to a neutral—that is, postcolonial and Marxist—country seem far from outlandish. Indeed, the claims seem firmly rooted in the political culture and climate of American prisons of the 1970s.

For a period after Jackson's death, his image and ideas permeated the culture of the American Left. The San Francisco Mime Troupe staged multiple productions of Bertolt Brecht's *The Mother* between 1973 and 1975. Brecht's 1930 script calls for the set to be hung with placards quoting Marx and Lenin but the Troupe instead placed quotes by George Jackson and Richard Nixon, personifications of the extremes of 1970s political activism. These signs hung on an apparatus the company used in many of its productions, described by a theater producer as a "revolving cloth T.V. set" known as a "cranky."[2] The troupe, founded in 1959, had a well-earned reputation for opposing war, sexism, and capitalism. Even if the audience members were unaware of the substitution, they would have easily seen the ideological and political message the troupe sent. Brecht's notes called for a projection of Marx's "Theory turns into a material force once the masses have understood it!"; the Mime Troupe instead projected Nixon's "Communism is evil because it defies God and denies man." Brecht's stage directions called for projecting Lenin's "Prove that you can fight!"; the Mime Troupe substituted Louis Farrakhan's "All of us are in prison. Those locked up are merely in solitary confinement." Where Brecht's script called for a repetition of Lenin's line later in the play, the Mime Troupe invoked a letter George Jackson wrote to his mother: "You are free—to starve."[3]

Written during the Great Depression, *The Mother* dramatizes the political transformation of the mother of a communist. At the play's opening, she opposes revolution. At its end, she is a revolutionary. In the program notes of a production after Nixon's resignation, the Mime Troupe made clear its belief that Depression-era calls for revolution applied to the 1970s: "The San Francisco Mime Troupe decided to do *The Mother* because of the present crisis in America. Another Great Depression looms. A Rockefeller is chosen to share power with our first non-elected president; and together they call on the American people to make sacrifices. There is no possible reconciliation between labor and management. The people who do the work must have the power. Revolutionary changes are necessary in America, but they can only be made if we all work like 'good small moles.'"[4]

Performers and writers outside of prison clearly recognized the role Jackson could play in promoting revolutionary politics. By the time the San Francisco Mime Troupe used the quotes, Nixon was out of office and Jackson had been shot dead by San Quentin correctional officers. But by the middle of the decade it was already common to link the two men in order to send a useful symbolic message. Walter Rodney was perhaps the first to connect Nixon and Jackson. In a 1971 article, he wrote that "there is some considerable awareness that ever since the days of slavery the U.S.A. is nothing but a vast prison as far as African descendants are concerned. Within this prison, black life is cheap, so it should be no surprise that George Jackson was murdered by the San Quentin prison authorities who are responsible to America's chief prison warder, Richard Nixon."[5] Here, Rodney echoes Malcolm X's argument that America is a prison for African Americans who faced a constant if shifting struggle for freedom.

In the same year that Rodney referred to Nixon as the nation's chief jailer, Bob Dylan recorded his ballad "George Jackson":

> Sometimes I think this whole world
> Is one big prison yard.
> Some of us are prisoners
> The rest of us are guards.
> Lord, Lord,
> They cut George Jackson down.
> Lord, Lord,
> They laid him in the ground.[6]

Building on Rodney's image of the United States as a prison, Dylan muses that "this whole world" can be thought of as a division between keepers and convicts. Where Rodney names Nixon as the "chief jailer," Dylan leaves it to his listeners to identify the "they" who "cut George Jackson down." Jackson's iconic status would be repeated and amplified throughout the Left of the 1970s. Even before the San Francisco Mime Troupe replaced Lenin's quotes with Jackson's, C. L. R. James compared Jackson's *Soledad Brother* to the work of Lenin, writing shortly after Jackson's death that "the letters are in my opinion the most remarkable political documents that have appeared inside or outside the United States since the death of Lenin."[7]

In short, the imprisonment and killing of George Jackson was a potent symbol of American racism, colonialism, and other forms of oppression. To the Mime Troupe, Dylan, James, and Rodney, Jackson represented the prototypical African and African American experience in the United States. In the climate of the 1970s, the president was a warden and Jackson was attached to a long legacy of bondage. George Jackson was a particularly attractive figure to the movements of the New Left. Even before publication of *Soledad Brother*, Eric Cummins argues, "left-wing romanticism attached to the Soledad Brothers reached the dimensions of cult worship."[8] The Soledad Brothers Defense Committee counted among its supporters a broad range of political activists, celebrities, and writers, including Julian Bond, Pete Seeger, Allen Ginsburg, Tom Hayden, and Angela Davis. This attraction remains a crucial element in Jackson's cultural and historical importance, but his writings and actions are not solely a product of leftist "cult worship." To prisoners, Jackson was as much a teacher of radical political philosophy and a spokesperson for the crisis behind bars as a symbol of oppression. His education while incarcerated and his uncompromising politics would come to serve as a model for prisoners. As these prisoners became interested in political and social change, Jackson's insights into black consciousness, the sociology of racism, and radical political philosophy served as a central counterargument to Nixon's law-and-order politics. This counterargument had ideological and institutional antecedents that shed light on the place of prisons and prisoners in U.S. culture during the 1970s. Jackson's words and actions—like Nixon's—are best understood as part of both the long history of prison reform movements and the debates over U.S. culture and politics inside and outside 1970s prisons.

Jackson's intellectual and political development marked his personal transformation from petty criminal to revolutionary. Jackson was introduced to radical politics through a circle of inmates engaging in covert education. In fact, as Cummins argues, an "elaborate covert educational system" existed in California's prisons in the late 1960s and early 1970s.[9] This system ramified elsewhere in the country with, for example, the poet Raul Salinas founding Chicanos Organizados de Rebeldes de Aztlan, a study group at Leavenworth Penitentiary in Kansas. Salinas also published a journal, *El Aztlan de Leavenworth*, in 1970 and 1971.[10] Some prison study groups were connected to ongoing criminal enterprises. A Chicano prison gang, La Nuestra Familia, had an education department that sent instruction guidelines first to cell blocks in San Quentin and eventually to other institutions in the California Department of Corrections. To be sure, much of this education served an aggressive criminal organization seeking to profit from drug sales and prostitution.[11] But as more overtly political organizations emerged, their curriculum would include political education classes with reading lists spanning the work of Malcolm X, Eldridge Cleaver, Mao Zedong, Ho Chi Minh, Che Guevara, and Karl Marx. Censors placed some limits on what inmates could read, but Jackson's *Soledad Brother* was sold in some prison canteens.[12] Jackson was part of a network of incarcerated people who read, agitated, and publicized.

The historical context for the emergence of this educational and political network—the disintegration of reformist programs first created during the Progressive era—is crucial to understanding its meaning. The network also arose amid startling and unprecedented valorization of incarcerated people in American radical and youth cultures. This second factor led to a substantial market for works by and about incarcerated people like George Jackson. Literacy, vocational, and other educational programs had long been a central feature of inmate rehabilitation. Jackson's writing and its impact is representative of a shift in the meaning of these programs when American penology began abandoning its rehabilitative mission and prisoners began calling into question the premise that they—and not American society—needed to be fundamentally changed.

Jackson's first entry into California's adult prisons began in 1960 with a robbery. Jackson—then a nineteen-year-old who already had served seven months for burglary in an institution run by the California Youth Authority—allegedly drove the getaway car in a gas-station robbery. Despite agreeing to cooperate with prosecutors in exchange for a light sentence, Jackson received a sentence of from one year to life. California sentencing guidelines were still ruled by the practice of indeterminate sentences. He could expect to come before the parole board every year to have his case reviewed. A federal law—the Indeterminate Sentence Act of 1958—allowed corrections officials to parole inmates after they completed one third of their sentences. Eligibility for release typically centered on participation in group therapy or other social work sessions.[13] Conversely, participation in behavior deemed disruptive by corrections officials could result in what seem to be capriciously long sentences for minor crimes. Compliance with the expectations of correctional authorities would come to be a touchstone of this system and ultimately a factor leading to its dismantlement by many states in the 1980s.

In Jackson's case, the parole board annually denied him parole as he grew from a leader of a prison gang into a political revolutionary. According to the political philosopher Joy James, Jackson was first introduced to radical political thought by W. L. Nolen.[14] A group initially calling itself the "black guerrillas" included Nolen, James Carr, and

William Christmas. Jackson read widely in African American history and radical political economy, including the works of Marx, Lenin, Trotsky, and Mao. According to some accounts, after Jackson's death this reading group became the Black Guerrilla Family, an organization advocating prisoners' right to self-defense that eventually became one of the most notorious prison gangs in California.[15]

In 1969, Jackson and Nolen were transferred to Soledad Prison. Racial tensions ran high in Soledad. In the midst of a fight between African American and white prisoners, Nolen and two other African American inmates were shot to death by a guard. After the killings were ruled justifiable homicide, a white guard, John Mills, was killed on George Jackson's cell block. Jackson was indicted for the murder of the guard, along with John Clutchette and Fleeta Drumgo. These three men would become known nationally as the "Soledad Brothers."

The Soledad Brothers' articulation of radical politics, personal stories of injustice, and a willingness to use violence against a brutally racist prison regime made them compelling figures to the activist Left. Huey P. Newton, a founder of the Black Panther Party, took note of their plight. His lawyer, Fay Stender, soon became legal counsel to Jackson. She also helped found the Soledad Brothers Defense Committee.[16] Jackson's political ideology reached a wide audience with the publication of *Soledad Brother*, a collection of Jackson's letters to family, friends, and supporters. With the publication of this book, people in and out of the various social justice movements of the day gained access to the political education and prison environment that led Jackson toward his ideals and tactics. The letters routinely requested or recommended reading material. These requests detail a political philosophy that developed over time in relationship to the key revolutionary texts of the era: *Ramparts* magazine, Mao's "Little Red Book," *The Autobiography of Malcolm X*, *Malcolm Speaks*, and Robert Ardrey's *African Genesis* and *The Territorial Imperative*.

The letters also reveal the key role anticolonial liberation movements in Angola and the Congo played in Jackson's turn toward revolutionary politics. In a 1964 letter to his mother, Jackson wrote, "I clearly understand that my future rests with the black people of the world. I am trying in every way possible to adjust my thinking habits so that their ways of life won't seem as strange and alien to me as these people over here would have it. After I am finished with myself, an observer who could read my thoughts and watch my actions would never believe that I was raised in the United States."[17] As the decade wore on, Jackson continued reading, writing, and acting according to his growing sense that violent revolution would be the only avenue toward personal and collective liberation. His support for the anti-colonial struggles in Africa led Jackson to see the United States as itself a colonial power. He learned everything he could about the Indian wars in the United States, U.S. imperialism in the Philippines, and the Vietnam War. Convinced that this represented a consistent pattern of racist, colonial domination, Jackson used his education to inform his politics, writing, "The people of the U.S. are held in the throes of a form of colonialism. Control of their subsistence and nearly every aspect of the circumstances surrounding their existence has passed into the hands of a clearly distinct and alienated oligarchy."[18]

As his view deepened that the United States was a colonial power, Jackson increasingly understood African Americans as a colonized people. These philosophies led Jackson to look toward successful anticolonial revolutions in Asia, Africa, and Latin America for tactical guidance. Jackson's views in this area drew on the work of Ernesto "Che" Guevara, the Argentine-born revolutionary and architect of the Cuban revolution. To "Z.," a woman correspondent with whom he sought a romantic relationship, Jackson asked, "Can we 'do it in the road' until the people's army has satisfied our territory problem? That is important to me whether or not you are willing to 'do it in the road.' You dig, I'm more identifiable with Ernesto than with Fidel. When this is over I immediately go under."[19]

In the late 1960s the Chinese Revolution inspired anti-imperialist struggles throughout Asia, Africa, and Latin America. Mao's writings on revolutionary philosophy and tactics circulated widely among American radicals of the 1960s and 1970s. *Quotations from Chairman Mao Tse-tung*, popularly known as the "Little Red Book," was first issued in China during the Cultural Revolution of the late 1960s and early 1970s, when it inspired the Red Guard, made up of high school and college students intensely devoted to Mao and the Communist

Party. In the United States it became a kind of talisman for committed revolutionaries and student activists, particularly on the West Coast. An inmate in Soledad at the same time as Jackson recalled that there were several copies of "the Red Book" circulating among Soledad inmates in the late 1960s and early 1970s.[20] In the preface to the second edition, Lin Biao—Mao's second-in-command and a key leader of the Cultural Revolution before Lin's death in 1971—made clear that the "sound-bite" quality of the text was an intentional effort to "help the masses learn Mao Tse-Tung's thought more effectively."[21] Perhaps the most famous quote to come from this book was "Political power grows out of the barrel of a gun." Mao saw the use of armed force as among the most important elements of a revolutionary movement: "Revolutionary war is an antitoxin," Mao wrote, "which not only eliminates the enemy's poison but also purges us of our own filth."[22] War quite literally "clears the way" for a new form of government; as it does so, it simultaneously transforms the mind of the revolutionary. In giving oneself over to collective struggle, the revolutionary simultaneously claims and legitimizes his or her power.

As the "Little Red Book" migrated across the Pacific, Mao's writings also spoke directly to the United States as an imperialist power. In the 1960s, with revolutions in Vietnam and the Congo making strides toward eventual victory, the U.S. military and intelligence agencies intervened on behalf of leaders who promised continued U.S. influence. U.S. involvement in thwarting anti-imperialist struggles in Asia, Africa, and Latin America was a cornerstone of Cold War foreign policy. These policies and practices enabled Mao to link the United States to the exploitative imperialist regimes its money and military aided. In an essay that appeared in the United States in 1969, Mao accused the U.S. government of murdering the Congolese leader Patrice Lumumba and suppressing his liberation movement.[23] This directly spoke to concerns raised as early as 1961, when African American protestors broke up a session of the United Nations Security Council in protest of U.S. involvement in Lumumba's murder.[24] Mao argued that U.S. intervention in the Congo, Vietnam, Laos, Cambodia, Malaysia, Cuba, and "all Latin America" represented a form of neocolonialism. But Mao offered an alternative vision: "U.S. imperialism and the reactionaries of all countries are paper tigers. The struggle of the Chinese people proved this. The struggle of the Vietnamese people is now proving it. The struggle of the Congolese people will certainly prove it too. Strengthening national unity and persevering in protracted struggle, the Congolese people will certainly be victorious, and U.S. imperialism will certainly be defeated. People of the world, unite and defeat the U.S. aggressors and all their running dogs!"[25] In the end, Mao did more than provide an historical lesson in the victory of a people's struggle. His writings described a link between U.S. policies and imperialism at the same time that the Chinese government provided material support to revolutionary movements around the world. As George Jackson and other African American activists became interested in anticolonial struggles in Southeast Asia, Africa, and Latin America, Mao's thinking increasingly influenced their politics and tactics. For example, in a letter to Angela Davis later included in *Soledad Brother*, Jackson precisely echoes Mao's sentiment: "It's not possible for anyone to still think that Western mechanized warfare is absolute, not after the experiences of the Third World since World War II. The French had tanks in Algeria, the US had them in Cuba. Everything, I mean every trick and gadget in the manual of Western arms has been thrown at the VC [Viet Cong], and they have thrown them back, twisted and ruined; and they have written books and pamphlets telling us how we could do the same."[26]

The writings of Frantz Fanon served as a key supplement to Mao's vision of the eventual victory of anti-imperialist struggles. Although Fanon died in 1961, translations of his three most important books, *A Dying Colonialism*, *The Wretched of the Earth*, and *Black Skin, White Masks*, first reached the American reading public in mass-market paperbacks in the 1960s. Although they would be confiscated from Jackson's cell in January 1970, he continued to recommend them to new acquaintances.[27] These works did not merely mimic Mao's rhetoric; by focusing on the racist component of imperialism, Fanon provided a crucial element for U.S.-based leftists that had been missing from Mao's writings: the relationship between colonialism and racism. In a 1956 speech before the First Congress of Negro Writers and Artists, Fanon, a psychologist by training, urged his Paris audience to think about the cultural components of racism. In answer to his own question, "How does an oppressing people behave?" Fanon replied:

> We witness the destruction of cultural values, of ways of life. Language, dress, techniques, are devalorized. How can one account for this constant? Psychologists, who tend to explain everything by movements of the psyche, claim to discover this behavior on the level of contacts between individuals: the criticism of an original hat, of a way of speaking, of walking. Such attempts deliberately leave out of account the special character of the colonial situation. In reality the nations that undertake a colonial war have no concern for the confrontations of cultures. War is a gigantic business and every approach must be governed by the datum. The enslavement, in the strictest sense, of the native population is the prime necessity. For this its systems of reference have to be broken. Expropriation, spoliation, raids, objective murder, are matched by the sacking of cultural patterns, or at least condition such sacking. The social panorama is destructured; values are flaunted, crushed, emptied.[28]

The process of colonization, according to Fanon, relies on racism to devalue the cultural attributes of the colonized people. The cultural work of racism also mirrors the militarized destruction of opposition and the exploitation of any possible economic resources. It does so by "breaking" the "systems of reference"—the values, kinship systems, religious beliefs, languages, and the like—that give colonized people an oppositional framework.

In *The Wretched of the Earth* (1968), Fanon more directly identified the police and the military as the key upholders of colonialism; it is they who are empowered to break "the natives":

> In the colonial countries, the policemen and the soldier, by their immediate presence and their frequent and direct action maintain contact with the native and advise him by means of rifle butts and napalm not to budge. It is obvious here that the agents of government speak the language of pure force. The intermediary does not

> lighten the oppression, nor seek to hide the domination; he shows them up and puts them into practice with the clear conscience of an upholder of the peace; yet he is the bringer of violence into the home and into the mind of the native.[29]

The linking of racism, colonialism, and police power provided the essential backdrop for people like Jackson who experienced policing and incarceration firsthand. Fanon—like Mao—showed that resistance was not only possible; it was the only option for those who rejected a position of submission. According to Fanon, a revolution can occur when colonized people come to devalue the culture of their oppressor and embrace a new culture that valorizes decolonized ways of life. In *A Dying Colonialism* (1967), Fanon described the comprehensive quality of this reversal: "The same time that the colonized man braces himself to reject oppression, a radical transformation takes place within him which makes any attempt to maintain the colonial system impossible and shocking."[30]

Once George Jackson accepted this, the correctional officers who controlled much of his daily life began to take on a different significance. Fanon described this change in a different context: "The symbols of social order—the police, the bugle calls in the barracks, military parades and the waving flags—are at one and the same time inhibitory and stimulating: for they do not convey the message 'Don't dare to budge'; rather, they cry out 'Get ready to attack.'"[31] Jackson's writings convey the assurance that the colonialism impacting African Americans would be overturned by the power of the people's struggle. He saw clear proof of this in the revolutions in China, Cuba, and Vietnam. Furthermore, he was uninterested in using the avenues of electoral politics to achieve change: "People's war, class struggle, war of liberation means *armed* struggle. Men like Hoover, Reagan, Hunt, Agnew, Johnson, Helms, Westmoreland, Abrams, Campbell, Carswell, are dangerous men who believe that they are the rightful führers of the world's people. They must be dealt with now. Can men like these be converted? . . . Will they allow anyone to maneuver them out of their positions of power while they still live? Would Nixon accept a people's government, a people's economy?"[32] Jackson and a growing number of incarcerated revolutionaries felt strongly that the time for analysis and negotiation had passed. As C. L. R. James observed shortly after Jackson's death: "It is quite obvious that where [W. E. B.] Du Bois and myself were observing a situation, taking part, organizationally in our various ways, but guided by theoretical, that is to say intellectual development, the generation to which Jackson belonged has arrived at the profound conclusion that the only way of life possible to them is the complete intellectual, physical, moral commitment to the revolutionary struggle against capitalism."[33] Jackson's *Soledad Brother*, then, provides more than a window into a curriculum of covert prison education; it reveals the covert action of a growing group of people who saw themselves, in Jackson's words, as "the vanguard, catalyst, in any meaningful change."[34]

By the time Jackson was working on his final works, published posthumously as *Blood in My Eye*, the explicitly revolutionary aims of his violence clearly escalated. According to Luis Talamantez, a tier tender at the Adjustment Center in San Quentin and a future member of the "San Quentin Six," the inmates charged in the events preceding Jackson's death, even in that highest security unit books circulated by "Marx, Mao, Lenin, Fanon, Hegel, Trotsky, Ho Chi Minh, General Giap, Nkrumah, Fidel Castro, Che Guevara, and other revolutionary authors."[35] Jackson may have been uniquely situated to read such a broad range of revolutionary literature, Talamentez believes, because of legal support and oversight provided by the Soledad Brothers Defense Committee. Nevertheless, once on the tier, these works circulated extensively among inmates. Contraband books would be copied by hand and passed among the tiers. One former inmate realized after release from prison that he had read behind bars a hand-copied version of *The Communist Manifesto*—with no visible notation of the author or title.[36] Jackson and others grew to believe that they would instigate the revolution.

When, on August 7, 1970, Jackson's younger brother Jonathan entered the Marin County courthouse, armed Ruchell Magee, James McClain, and William Christmas, and took as hostages a judge, an assistant district attorney, and three jurors, it appeared to some to be a revolutionary act in keeping with Jackson's letters. Jonathan Jackson may have believed that San Quentin's infamous "no hostage" policy—in which prison authorities refused to negotiate for the release of hostages under any circumstances—would not be observed in the courtroom. He was mistaken. San Quentin guards opened fire on Jonathan, the inmates, and the hostages, killing Jonathan, McClain, Christmas, and the judge and wounding the assistant district attorney and Magee. As of 2009, Magee remained in a California prison.

Even prior to his national celebrity, George Jackson, then at Soledad, achieved the rank of field marshal in the Black Panther Party (BPP). Huey P. Newton assigned this rank to him while Newton was in the California Penal Colony facing murder charges.[37] Jackson's task was to recruit and educate new members for the party. Founded in Oakland in 1966, the BPP valued a critique of the criminal justice system much more than previous civil rights activists. The Panthers are often understood as representing a key break from the earlier nonviolent strategies of boycotts, sit-ins, and mass demonstrations exemplified by the Southern Christian Leadership Conference, the Student Nonviolent Coordinating Committee, and the Congress of Racial Equality. It is important to remember, however, that a critique of the criminal justice system was central to those organizations as well. For example, Martin Luther King Jr.'s "Letter from a Birmingham Jail" (1963) explains the moral justification for breaking unjust laws: "A law is unjust if it is inflicted on a minority that, as a result of being denied the right to vote, had no part in enacting or devising the law."[38] Disobeying the law also had a tactical appeal to King. By filling the jails with civil rights protestors, King hoped to raise the cost of segregation so high that it would lose its practical appeal to municipalities. With the founding of the Panthers, the critique of the criminal justice system expanded to include—in line with the thinking of Fanon—discussion of the system as a primary means used to oppress African American communities. Three of the points in the Panthers' "Ten Point Program" (1966) concerned the criminal justice system; they called for an end to police brutality, the release of all black men from jails and prisons, and a jury trial made up of black people for black defendants. This manifesto brought extraordinary police scrutiny, but it also attracted the attention of incarcerated people.

Incarcerated African Americans were close observers of the civil rights movement long before the Panthers, but they had few avenues to directly participate in the movement. This is not to say that they did nothing. For example, the Deuel Vocational Institution in California experienced two major racial conflicts per year during the early 1960s. Riots coincided with and were inspired by racial conflicts outside the prison, including the boxing victories of the aging welterweight Sugar Ray Robinson and anticolonial rioting in the Congo in 1959 and 1960.[39] It is important to point out, however, that the rioting in Deuel was between incarcerated groups of different racial identities rather than against prison administrators. As expressions of racial pride and antagonism, the riots responded to national and international conflicts but did not explicitly articulate local grievances or the structural critique of the late 1960s and 1970s. Incarcerated people increasingly embraced the philosophies of Marx, Mao, and Fanon, but they made clear that the criminal justice system and correctional officers would be a primary target for their activism.

Over time, the Panthers would be key allies of incarcerated activists and intellectuals. Eldridge Cleaver became active in the BPP and its minister of information shortly after his release from San Quentin. Furthermore, the BPP's scrutiny of the Oakland Police and its dramatic display of weapons at the State Capitol building in Sacramento in the spring of 1967 attracted attention. Increasingly, the Panthers themselves would be jailed in large numbers. In October 1967, Huey Newton, one of the two founders of the party and its most visible spokesperson, was charged with murdering a police officer. In March 1968 a second shootout with the police resulted in the death of the young Panther Bobby Hutton and the arrest of seven Panthers. Several others fled the country to avoid arrest.[40] Newton beat those charges in time to be present at the funeral for Jonathan Jackson and William Christmas, where his eulogy pushed King's analysis of the relationship between racial oppression and civil disobedience of unjust laws: "There are no laws that the oppressor makes that the oppressed are bound to respect."[41]

In addition to Cleaver and Newton, cofounder Bobby Seale was in federal prison stemming from charges in the Chicago Seven conspiracy trial of 1969–70. Fifteen members of the Detroit organizing committee of the Black Panthers were arrested after an altercation with the police. In 1969 the East Coast leadership of the Black Panther Party was arrested on conspiracy charges and not acquitted until May 1971. People incarcerated for other crimes also formed Panther chapters. In Louisiana's notorious Angola State Prison, Albert Woodfox and Herman Wallace founded a chapter in 1970 and would be confined to single-cell solitary confinement.[42] Other chapters were founded at San Quentin, Walla Walla State Penitentiary in Washington, and Attica.[43]

One year after the death of Jonathan Jackson, a corrections officer shot and killed George Jackson. The Department of Corrections explained the shooting as resulting from an escape attempt. Prison officials alleged that Stephen Bingham, Jackson's attorney, smuggled in a gun that Jackson hid in his hair. With gun in hand, Jackson forced the opening of thirty of the Adjustment Center's one hundred cells. Some of these inmates used razor blades to kill three guards and two white prisoners who worked in the Adjustment Center. Jackson fled from the center and ran toward a twenty-foot stone wall topped with barbed wire. A guard then fired on Jackson from a tower.[44] This official story stretched the limits of the imagination. Georgia Jackson, Jackson's mother, felt that her son was set up: "They killed him and set him out in the yard and photographed him and then said he tried to escape."[45] While Tom Wicker of the *New York Times* stopped short of this theory, he acknowledged in a column that "many persons would not believe the official explanation of George Jackson's death."[46] James Baldwin later wrote more specifically: "No Black person will ever believe that George Jackson died the way they tell us he did."[47]

More plausible explanations fit the killing into a continuous pattern of police violence and intimidation. In February 1968 the South Carolina Highway Patrol shot and killed three students from South Carolina State University in Orangeburg.[48] In December 1969 the Chicago Police Department shot into the headquarters of the Illinois Black Panther Party at 4:45 A.M., killing Fred Hampton and Mark Clark while they slept.[49] In May 1970, the Ohio National Guard opened fire on a peaceful protest at Kent State University, killing four students and wounding eleven. Two more students were killed at Jackson State in Mississippi ten days later. This violence shocked many Americans, including those behind bars. The particular impact of the killing of George Jackson, however, confirmed for many incarcerated people that time for collective action had come. There were memorial services, work stoppages, and silent protests at prisons around the country, but the most dramatic response to Jackson's death occurred at Attica State Prison in western New York.

The official McKay Commission report found that the Attica riot was not planned, but it also found ample evidence of a radicalized inmate population. As at prisons across the country, discussion groups led by the Nation of Islam, the Black Panthers, the Five Percenters, and the Young Lords debated the social and political issues of the day. The white radical Sam Melville was also active at Attica. These discussion groups filled the gap left by the lack of an official education program. Whereas fourteen hundred inmates performed some form of institutional maintenance, the education department enrolled fewer than three hundred inmates in basic skills, high school equivalency, and public speaking classes.[50] This led those inmates seeking more intellectually challenging or socially conscious content to turn to one another. Several formed an inmate-led sociology class in the summer of 1971.[51] According to the McKay Commission, these classes, discussion groups, and informal debates led to a series of organized protests that summer. Despite these strides, politically active inmates found it very difficult to unify people from different racial, religious, and ideological backgrounds. Although they had worked hard to establish a broad base of support and claimed to represent "all races and social segments" of the prison, it is telling that only five inmates constituted the Attica Liberation Faction in July. These five—Frank Lott, Herbert X. Blyden, Donald Noble, Carl Jones-El, and Peter Butler—were among the most experienced activists in Attica. Blyden had participated in a rebellion at the Tombs prison in New York City the previous year, helping to write the rebels' list of demands. Others had been involved in a sit-down strike at Auburn prison.[52] Blyden is credited with demanding that the prisoners be transported to a nonimperialist country as a condition of ending the takeover. While deemed impractical by one of the outside observers, this demand grew logically from the political education many inmates received while in prison.[53] Blyden and Jones served on the negotiating committee during the takeover.

Blyden was a member of Attica's Nation of Islam community, and Carl Jones-El and Donald Noble were members of the prison's Moorish Science community. The relationship between Islam and African Americans is historically linked to the pan-African movement of the late nineteenth and early twentieth centuries.[54] In the early twentieth century, several Islamic societies and temples took root in Detroit's African American community, preaching solidarity among people of color across the world. One adherent of the Detroit-based Fard Muhammad's Temple of Islam, Elijah Muhammad, went on to found the Nation of Islam. Elijah Muhammad developed a theology that emphasized economic development of black communities and liberation from the racist underpinnings of inequality and exploitation, leading him to take strong political stands and receive government attention. During World War II Muhammad was jailed for sedition after voicing his support for Japan. After Muhammad's release, he continued to focus on the spiritual and political development of incarcerated African Americans. Malcolm X would be among the many prisoners he corresponded with after their terms of incarceration. In 1964 Clarence 13X, a member of the Harlem Mosque of the Nation of Islam, parted ways with the Nation of Islam and founded the Five Percent Nation of Gods and Earths, or the Five Percent Nation. Five Percenters and members of the Nation of Islam continued to disagree on major theological questions, but both groups played key roles in the political life of Attica.[55]

In addition to the Panthers, the Five Percent Nation, and the Nation of Islam, the Young Lords maintained an active presence in Attica. The Young Lords held many views similar to those of the Black Panther Party, situating these ideas in the specific context of Puerto Rican politics.[56] The Young Lords were founded as a street gang in the 1950s but became a revolutionary political organization after Young Lord José "Cha Cha" Jiménez met Fred Hampton when both were in prison in 1968.[57] Hampton, the charismatic leader of the Chicago branch of the Black Panther Party, forged an alliance with the Young Lords and the Young Patriots, a group of white working-class radicals. Puerto

Rican activists in New York took note of the new political orientation of the Young Lords and formed a satellite chapter. The New York chapter modeled its Thirteen Point Program on the Panthers' Ten Point Program. The Young Lords called for the freeing of all Puerto Rican prisoners, an end to the U.S. military presence in Puerto Rico, and self-determination. Soon after their transition to a militant political organization, the Young Lords combined militant tactics with crucial services in poor communities, providing, for example, free breakfast and clothing in El Barrio—New York's East Harlem—and occupying a church when it refused to provide space.[58] Their calls for reproductive rights, however, were not part of the Panthers' program.[59]

The Attica Liberation Faction sent a list of demands—based largely on the Folsom Prisoners' Manifesto—to Commissioner of Corrections Russell Oswald and Governor Nelson Rockefeller, including calls for improved medical care, food, clothing, and working conditions. They wrote to Oswald that they were determined to "do this in a democratic manner."[60] Oswald acknowledged receipt of the demands, but he did not act on them other than to refuse Attica Superintendent Vincent Mancusi's request to transfer the five. Mancusi responded by increasing the frequency of cell searches, censoring all references to prison conditions from news sources, and announcing that there would be no prizes awarded to the winners of the upcoming Labor Day sporting competitions.[61] Although angered by these developments, the major organized groups at Attica—including the Five Percenters, Young Lords, the Nation of Islam, and the Black Panthers—remained divided in their priorities for change, tactical approaches, and basic beliefs.

After recalling how difficult it had been to convince people to work through their differences to establish a unified front in working toward much needed reforms, Donald Noble, a member of the Attica Liberation Faction and a signer of the July 2 list of demands, recalled that the situation changed dramatically and immediately when Attica prisoners learned that Jackson had been killed:

> What really solidified things was George Jackson's death. This had a reaction on the people, one that we were trying to accomplish all along, to bring the people together. We thought, "How can we pay

> tribute to George Jackson?" because a lot of us idolized him and things that he was doing and things that he was exposing about the system. So, we decided that we would have a silent fast that whole day in honor of him. We would wear black armbands. No one was to eat anything that whole day. We noted that if the people could come together for this, then they could come together for other things.[62]

Many inmates had only a peripheral knowledge of the political organizing of the Attica Liberation Faction prior to Jackson's death, but now they were willing to participate in a coordinated protest. Frank Smith did not even know who Jackson was prior to going to breakfast on the morning after Jackson's death. "I didn't know anything about George Jackson. So, when we got to the mess hall that morning, everything was quiet. No one was saying nothing, and you're talking about five, six, seven hundred people! Inmates! So, I said to my buddy, 'What's up, man?'"[63] After Smith's friend told him about Jackson, Smith decided not to eat as well. He would go on to be a member of the negotiating committee during the rebellion and was singled out for torture after the prison was retaken by the Department of Corrections.

This peaceful protest was a turning point: multiracial lines of inmates indicated their solidarity and mourning by wearing black armbands. After marching single-file into breakfast, they sat silently and refused to eat. One corrections officer described his impression of the protest: "I was scared shitless."[64] On August 30 three hundred inmates staged a second peaceful protest, this time signing up for sick call and occupying the hospital area to dramatize the substandard health facilities. In just one week, inmate leaders managed to turn the unity of the Jackson memorial into a protest with a clear goal. Where only the five members of the Attica Liberation Front were willing to state their demands the previous month, now there were hundreds of participants. The atmosphere was clearly tense at Attica, but the inmates remained organized and peaceful. Finally, on September 2, Commissioner Oswald recorded a message that was played over the prison public address system, warning inmates that it would take time to implement the requested changes. The inmates interpreted this as stonewalling, but it would not directly lead to the riot.

As with many riots, the violence at Attica was touched off by the perception that the police—or in this case correctional officers—used excessive force. On September 8 there was an altercation between correctional officers and two inmates. Later that day, correctional officers led two inmates whom they believed to be responsible to Housing Block Z (HBZ), the disciplinary housing unit where inmates were locked down for twenty-three hours per day.[65] Ray Lamorie, one of the two, had not been involved in the altercation. Observers saw officers strike Leroy Dewer, the other inmate, while taking him to HBZ. Inmates believed that HBZ was a site of routine, brutal beatings by correctional officers. Correctional officers encouraged these rumors in an "attempt," according to one officer, "to try and keep the inmates in line."[66] The following day, September 9, inmates subdued Lieutenant Robert Curtis in a tunnel that divided the prison yard into quarters. A group of fifteen to twenty-five inmates eventually overpowered four guards and locked them in cells. The uprising quickly spread to the other cell blocks, with more than twelve hundred inmates congregating in Cell Block D.

None of the members of the Attica Liberation Front participated in the initial rioting. However, they quickly took advantage of the opportunity the riot provided to move the inmate population toward more explicit demands for reform.[67] The inmates created a committee to negotiate with Commissioner Oswald and demanded that outside observers be present. The prisoners requested the presence of elected officials, members of the press, prisoners' rights organizations, leftist lawyers, Juan Ortiz and José Paris of the Young Lords, Louis Farrakhan of the Nation of Islam, and Bobby Seale of the Black Panthers. Although Farrakhan had written about the plight of prisoners in *Muhammad Speaks*, he did not go to Attica, reportedly on orders from Elijah Muhammad.[68]

On September 13, 1971, state troopers and correctional officers stormed the prison and engaged in a retaliatory frenzy that would shock the country. In the end, forty inmates and prison employees died during the revolt and the retaking of the prison. This was a reminder that life inside U.S. prisons was a stark manifestation of American repression. In the wake of Attica and other prison uprisings of the 1970s, some guards advocated white supremacy and Nazi ideology. Edward Bunker, a California prisoner during those years, recalled, "If [the white guards] had been secret bigots, they now turned into outright racists."[69] It is particularly notable that in 1971, no African Americans were employed as correctional officers in Attica at a time when roughly 54 percent of the inmate population was black. One African American was employed in the education department. There was one Puerto Rican correctional officer, while 9 percent of inmates were Puerto Rican. Although some of these officers may not have harbored racist feelings, it is notable that upon retaking the facility, one anonymous correctional officer scrawled on a wall "32 dead niggers."[70]

As with the killing of Jackson, prisoners around the country protested the brutality exhibited in the retaking of Attica. Women incarcerated at the Federal Reformatory for Women in Alderson, West Virginia, staged a work stoppage during a memorial service for the people killed at Attica. According to the *New York Times*, "Between 100 and 200 women occupied the prison's former garment factory for four days, refusing to report to their jobs. They presented prison officials with a list of forty-two demands, which ranged from speedier action by parole boards to more vocational training, disinfectants for cottages and lower prices on commissary items."[71]

Perhaps the fullest expression of the prisoner and correctional system response to Jackson and Attica occurred in Massachusetts. In 1972 a Harvard undergraduate named David Dance taught a class on African American history at Walpole Prison. Robert Heard, a member of the Black Panther Party, helped teach the class. Heard would later spend time in Norfolk Prison, where he earned two degrees from Boston University.[72] As with many such classes taking place around the country, the curriculum provided curricular fuel for the process of political and cultural transformation taking place in prisons. The reading list Dance and Heard chose centered on classic texts by Richard Wright, Langston Hughes, and Ralph Ellison. The administration at Walpole approved the reading list. Ralph Hamm, a student in the class who had already begun to embrace the Nation of Islam, described the course as turning his world upside down.[73] Hamm and the other eleven students embarked on a second curriculum that including readings not approved by the administration. As part of a new organization that they dubbed Black African Nations toward Unity (BANTU), the men read many of the key revolutionary texts of the era in a covert curriculum that included work by Frantz Fanon, Kwame Nkrumah, Amilcar Cabral, and others. They kept this material secret, along with revolutionary tracts by the Weather Underground and the Black Panthers.[74]

The willingness of Walpole's reform-minded administration to sponsor the black history course and create an inmate advisory council were nods to calls for greater representation by many African Americans during the period. BANTU had the larger goal of prisoner control of the institutions. Some members of the Nation of Islam had earlier asserted their control over a racially segregated cell block, just as white prisoners had earlier done in a different cell block. BANTU, however, inspired by anticolonial intellectuals, aspired to complete self-determination within the limits of the prison structure. In March 1973 reformers in the Massachusetts Department of Corrections resolved a dispute between the correctional officers and the department by giving inmates increased control over the facility under the banner of the local chapter of the National Prisoners Rights Association (NPRA), a prisoners' union. Founded in Rhode Island, the NPRA advocated on behalf of prisoners and sought greater visibility for them with the general public.[75] This control lasted until May, when state authorities retook control of the prison and placed some of the NPRA leadership in punitive segregation.[76]

While only temporary, the Walpole experience represented the culmination of the broader critique of prisons that emerged in the mid-1960s. George Jackson's transformation into a revolutionary resulted from the collective effort of a group of prisoners engaged in radical self-education. As these prisoners grew increasingly interested in Third World revolutionary thought, they understood their incarceration as the result of a concerted and consistent effort to humiliate and control African Americans in a deeply racist and imperialist country. Jackson soon became connected to the broader revolutionary movement, most notably to the Black Panther Party. As tensions mounted, evidence supporting the view that prisons reflected the colonial status of African Americans grew when correctional facilities responded to prisoner demands with violence. The views and murder of George Jackson sent a clear message to prisoners around the country: the time to act is now. The power to bring about change is within your grasp. Prison officials also watched these events closely, responding to prisoner demands in later weeks and years with, in the case of Attica, extraordinary brutality. In other cases, however, they showed an unprecedented willingness to engage in experimental forms of correctional reform. Inmates and correctional authorities had raised the stakes in the early 1970s, but it was still entirely unclear how it would all play out. They did cut George Jackson down, but the Age of Jackson would develop in surprising ways.

CHAPTER THREE

WHAT WORKS?

REFORM AND REPRESSION IN PRISON PROGRAMS

As the culmination of their immersion in radical political theory and prison activism, the Attica Brothers reacted to and amplified the goals spearheaded on the West Coast. In the immediate aftermath of the uprising, correctional authorities made Attica a living hell for its inmates. The uprising left eleven employees of the facility and twenty-nine inmates dead. Despite the creation of an official state commission, the only short-term change at Attica was the erection of new gun towers.[1] Over time, the uprising left another legacy: the correctional facility met several of the inmates' demands, particularly those that affected cultural and educational programs.

The Attica prisoners proposed—and the Department of Corrections agreed—to "modernize the inmate education system."[2] In the spring of 1972, one winter removed from the murders of the previous September, the New York State Council on the Arts provided funds to start a writing workshop at the facility. Hospital Audiences Incorporated, a New York City–based arts subcontractor asked if the Buffalo Black Drama Workshop (BBDW) would sponsor the workshop. Founded in the late 1960s by Ed Smith, the BBDW was part of a nationwide theater movement that grew out of the spirit of the civil rights movement. According to one estimate, almost six hundred African American theaters emerged in the 1960s and 1970s.[3] Like this movement more generally, the BBDW sought to represent African American experiences, perform in front of African American audiences, and, in many cases, serve as a cultural arm of the Black Power movement.[4]

The BBDW hired Celes Tisdale, a professor of English at Erie County Community College who had conducted successful workshops at BBDW, to make weekly trips to the prison. Tisdale himself had grown up in Buffalo's Willert Park projects and was familiar with some of the men in Attica. What's more, the political focus of BBDW was on display during the first eight-week session: in the summer of 1972, BBDW put on a play called *Angela* and Tisdale frequently brought in tapes of leading Black Arts movement writers, including Haki Madhubuti (then still known as Don L. Lee) and Amiri Baraka. Prisoner interest was so high that enrollment needed to be conducted by lottery.[5] In 1975 a group of colleges in western New York formed the Consortium of the Niagara Frontier in order to administer a program of study leading to a bachelor's of arts degree at three New York correctional facilities, including Attica. Eighty professors taught courses to approximately 350 students.[6] This was a far cry from the five teachers providing education in only basic skills prior to the rebellion.

Not all prison programming came about under such dramatic influences, however. The institutions came under tremendous pressure after the Attica uprising, although it was not entirely clear what actions these pressures demanded. Were prisons supposed to engage the demands for relevant, politically conscious programming? Or were they supposed to crack down on the political and cultural vitality emerging from the cell blocks for fear that it might lead to other uprisings? It is not surprising, then, that officials creating or shelving programming for inmates left a confusing and contradictory legacy of innovation and repression. On the one hand, the covert education networks nurtured radical political thought and inspired inmate protest movements throughout the country. On the other hand, the rising neoconservative criminal justice regime promised a future of repressive policing and sharply increased prison populations. The people who worked or lived in prisons sought ways to respond to these pressures through various degrees of accommodation and resistance. One of the primary ways they did so was by providing and altering opportunities for cultural expression and intellectual engagement. As at Attica, at times this was a direct response to inmate demands. In other cases, the Law Enforcement Assistance Administration funded the programs.

Federal and state governments, along with major nonprofit funding agencies, provided key backing for prison arts and education programs throughout the 1960s and 1970s. Between 1965 and 1973 the number of college-level programs in U.S. prisons increased more than fifteenfold, to 182. As of 1982 there were 350 programs in forty-five states, with roughly 10 percent of all inmates attending a prison college. Perhaps the biggest boost to postsecondary education in prisons came with the Pell Grant program in 1965. It provided funding to eligible prisoners for postsecondary study until 1991.[7] In addition, the National Endowment for the Arts funded the publication of prisoner works, while other organizations began major initiatives to create freestanding programs behind prison walls.[8]

Numerous state and local agencies funded creative writing or other arts programs in prisons. The New Jersey State Council on the Arts Creative Writing Program, for example, created a writing workshop at the Bordentown Reformatory in 1972 after a pilot program at another facility received an enthusiastic reception from inmates.[9] The Bordentown writing program was run by Dan Georgakas, a writer interested in the history and practice of social activism. Debra Stein, the poetry program coordinator for the Council on the Arts, saw the program's primary function as providing an "introspective creative experience." The state would eventually fund the production of an anthology so the efforts of the workshop participants could gain wider recognition. Similarly, the California Arts Council, under the leadership of Eloise Smith, included California's prisons in its Artists in Social Institutions Program, established in 1976. This would eventually grow into the Arts-in-Corrections program in 1981.[10] The Arizona Department of Corrections joined forces with the state's Commission on the Arts and Humanities to form the Writer's Workshop at the Arizona State Prison in 1973.[11] The University of California at Berkeley's Prison College at San Quentin, funded by the Ford Foundation in 1968, was among the most ambitious of a growing number of degree-granting programs in U.S. prisons.[12] In many cases, these programs sought to provide nonviolent outlets for the radical ideologies circulating in American prisons. In the aftermath of a prison riot in 1968, the Oregon State Penitentiary began a creative writing program.[13]

This proliferation of cultural and educational programming was one important direction for prison reform during the era. It was contrasted, however, by a second trend centered on an emerging argument that all prison programs should be judged primarily by the degree to which they lowered recidivism rates. Robert Martinson provided scholarly fuel for this trend in a 1974 article in the *Public Interest*. Evaluating studies of penology reform programs, Martinson famously asked, "What works?" Martinson and his colleagues argued that "with few and isolated exceptions, the rehabilitative efforts that have been reported so far have had no appreciable effect on recidivism."[14] Martinson's study has been criticized rightly for utilizing a limited definition of "what works": if a program was found to reduce the instances of a return trip to jail, it could be said to work. Furthermore, the program would need to work virtually all of the time in order to pass muster. If a program worked some times but not others, it would be judged inconclusive. Martinson's study might also be questioned for looking only at therapeutic programs, like psychological counseling and drug treatment, that have high failure rates outside of prison as well, rather than the full range of programs that included prisoner self-government, arts and cultural offerings, reading groups, journalism, and theater.

Despite these shortcomings, scholars and policymakers should not lose sight of the fact that Martinson's study is a devastating critique of prisons. It reveals that therapeutic programs in community settings tended to be more successful than those in prisons. In addition, Martinson found that probation "may make an offender's future chances better than if he had been sent to prison."[15] Martinson implied that the overall failure of therapeutic programs lay in their assumption that criminality was a kind of disease that could be cured in a prison context. Martinson stated that criminals were in fact normal people "responding to the facts and conditions of our society."[16] Martinson's article reflects his Great Society–era belief that prisons were irreparably broken artifacts of a previous era.[17] He naively hoped that his devastating critique of reform efforts would lead to greater criticism of prisons as a central feature of American criminal justice. This view harkened back to the Johnson administrations' view that prisons should be a rare feature of a revamped criminal justice system.

Martinson's study would have a quite different impact. "Law-and-order" conservatives who emphasized the deterrent and punitive value of harsh correctional institutions would embrace Martinson's study, stripping it of its implicit social critique. Much to Martinson's surprise, his relatively impressionistic conclusion would be the most influential aspect of his study. "It is possible," Martinson wrote, "that there is indeed something that works—that to some extent is working right now in front of our noses, and that might be made to work better—something that deters rather than cures, something that does not so much reform convicted offenders as prevent criminal behavior in the first place."[18] After six years of neoconservative reframing of law and order and absent an explicit iteration of Martinson's hopes, the findings of the study could be easily put to other ends. In particular, rather than focusing on reforming offenders through rehabilitative, educational, and vocational programs, some policymakers believed that if prisons became bad enough and sentences long enough, people will be deterred from committing acts that might lead to a prison sentence.

Jerome Miller wrote in the *Washington Post* that the deterrence speculation in Martinson's article made it "the most politically influential criminological study of the past half century."[19] This view that deterrence might work where rehabilitation had failed would have devastating effects on efforts to increase access to cultural and therapeutic programming in the prison system. Miller was right, but it is important to also remember that many officials and the cultural, therapeutic, and educational contractors working in prisons greeted the study with skepticism, if not outright hostility. When the study came out, for example, Miller had only recently departed as the Massachusetts commissioner of children and youth, where he famously shut down most of the reform schools in 1972 and replaced them with a system of community-based corrections and secure treatment centers. If policymakers read the results as license to do nothing more than build repressive institutions that most people would want to stay out of, those who spent their careers working in prisons did not necessarily do the same. Some of the programs they offered seemed to accommodate the increasingly punitive approach of the 1970s; others seemed to resist the neoconservative turn in the post-Johnson approach to law and order. Many of the programs and individuals seemed caught in the middle: conscious that they worked in increasingly repressive institutions, they sought new funding sources in the public and private sector to pursue scholarly and cultural projects increasingly cut off under the law enforcement regime of the era.

Individual prisons, state departments of corrections, and the American Correctional Association sometimes worked against the twin political realities of anti-intellectualism and anti-rehabilitation to recognize the positive effects of educational, cultural, and therapeutic programming. In order to maintain state and private funding for these programs, however, prison administrators needed to embrace the conclusion that programs that "work" result in a measurable drop in recidivism rates. In order to approve (not to mention fund) educational programs, prisons needed to see an objective that, as far back as a 1930s report, "is always the attainment of some well-defined end, such as changing attitudes, increasing vocational efficiency, elimination of complexes, the development of willingness and skill for cooperative living after release."[20]

Proving that a given program resulted in fewer return trips to prison, however, remained a significant obstacle. In "What Works?," Martinson noted that the uneven effectiveness of rehabilitative personnel in a single program made it difficult to judge the program's impact. Some people just seemed to be better at it than others. Those running programs faced increasing pressure to demonstrate measurable results in order to meet the demands of public and private funders. In 1980, for example, the Santa Cruz–based William James Association and the California Department of Corrections (CDC) sponsored a study of the Arts-in-Corrections Program, seeking to document the economic and rehabilitative impact of cultural programming. Arts-in-Corrections provided instruction in visual and performing arts to inmates of California prisons. Eloise Smith formed the Prison Arts Project under the auspices of the William James Association, which she and her husband, the University of California at Santa Cruz historian and administrator Page Smith, had founded to bridge the gap between philosophy and social action. The initial Prison Arts Project was at the California Medical Facility in Vacaville, a part of the California Department of Corrections. Eloise Smith secured funding through a variety of local, state, and federal agencies, including the National Endowment for the Arts and the Law Enforcement Assistance Administration. Although the William James Association and the Prison Arts Project never concealed their vision of social action, they also framed their goals in narrow terms that would speak directly to the "what works?" concerns of prison administrators and funding agencies.

The study, conducted for the William James Association by the sociologist Lawrence Brewster, found that Arts-in-Corrections saved the state money because participants had fewer disciplinary infractions, thus saving the cost of hearings and isolation. In addition, participants produced signs, furniture, and artwork that would otherwise be absent or need to be purchased by the CDC.[21] The most significant measurable outcome, however, according to the CDC itself, centered on recidivism rates. Program participants had significantly higher rates of successfully avoiding return trips to prison than those who did not participate. According to a later study conducted by the CDC, "Six months after parole, Arts-in-Corrections participants show an 88% rate of favorable outcome as compared to the 72.25% rate for all CDC releases. For the one-year period, the Arts-in-Corrections favorable rate was 74.2% while that for CDC parolees was 49.6%. Two years after release 69.2% of the Arts-in-Corrections parolees retained their favorable status in contrast to the 42% level for all releases."[22] Although the statistical relevance of this finding lacks the authority of necessary comparisons and controls, the fact that the William James Association felt compelled to draw attention to cost and benefit to continue funding their arts program says something about the skepticism such programs faced. Even their minimal funding could not survive the budget cutters in Sacramento, who eliminated legislative funding for Arts-in-Corrections in 2003.

This strong pressure to justify their work through outcomes assessment focused on cost savings and recidivism met some resistance from instructors, artists, and inmates. When recounting their experience working with inmates, prison therapists and educators described their difficulty negotiating contradictory influences. Often working simultaneously within and against the dictates of a repressive structure, they found ways to shape courses of study and cultural programming that could pass muster with prison authorities while remaining relevant to the inmates. Thus, if they were forced to describe educational and cultural programs to people who saw them as meaningful only within the rehabilitative function of prisons, they could also judge for themselves if they were relevant to their own interests and needs.

Because artists and educators who worked in prisons depended on the cooperation and often the funding of federal and state politicians and professionals, this conflict had a particularly profound impact on their ability to teach in prisons. While the teachers and arts professionals may have had other goals in mind, they knew that they needed to negotiate the attitudes and philosophies of state officials in order to continue their work. In some cases, prison administrators were particularly critical of arts and humanities education. One Massachusetts administrator told the drama teacher Jean Trounstine, "You obviously do not understand the problems you can cause by asking these women to express themselves."[23] Despite their skepticism, prison officials allowed a number of jazz musicians, college professors, painters, directors, and poets into the prisons to teach classes and run workshops throughout the decade. Their decisions to do so were always tempered by concerns for security and the political mandate that they replace rehabilitation with deterrence. Thus, they were more likely to fund these programs or allow access to those artists and teachers able to articulate a tangible benefit.

These structural challenges were ongoing and seemingly always in motion. A sense of disorientation overwhelmed many beginning teachers as they learned that they occupied a kind of third status in the institutions' ongoing struggles. Whether these struggles were internecine struggles among convicts or prison workers or interminable battles between correctional staff and the convicts, teachers and artists could never be quite sure where they fit. Because of this complexity, it is difficult to generalize beyond the fact that teachers in prison often described their place as a middle ground between the convicts and the keepers. They were often not fully trusted by either convicts or keepers in a place structured by this binary opposition. Sooner or later, most teachers came to recognize their primary responsibility to the facility and to the concerns of the correctional staff with one caveat: they generally had a greater concern for the interior lives of the incarcerated people than other prison employees. Some teachers came to empathize with their students. Trounstine, who taught drama at Framingham Women's Prison in Massachusetts, was stunned when a correctional officer ordered her to "turn around and face the wall" as if she were an inmate. Trounstine quickly learned that "college teacher or not, you have to follow rules."[24]

Even though they were aware of their third status, during the 1960s and 1970s many teachers viewed themselves as "on the side" of the inmates based on political, emotional, or aesthetic sensibilities. Some, like the sociology instructor Paul Goodman, then a doctoral candidate at Berkeley and an instructor at San Francisco State, empathized with the students in their courses. Of his course in the late 1960s in San Quentin, Goodman wrote, "Not *less* than for the teacher as an outsider, their experience is frightening to themselves. Ignore that and you ignore the student. Deal with it and, interestingly enough, you find their greatest strength toward learning: they want out."[25] Carol Muske and Gail Rosenblum, who ran workshops at a women's prison in New York City in the early 1970s, wrote of the chapbook of prison poems they edited: "In this sense, this anthology is a crime. A crime of conspiracy, an informed, fully-consenting adult decision to commit poetry, an invention of the imagination that will never tear down the bars or break the system's back, but *has* ripped off some room for people to 'breathe together' (another definition of 'conspiracy') and pulled off a heist of institutional supermind, liberated the space as a continuum."[26]

Others, however, did not share Goodman's views of the interior lives of inmates or the professed complicity of Muske and Rosenblum. W. Reason Campbell wrote in the mid-1970s that he saw virtually every inmate as manipulative. His hostility became evident when a student lit a wastebasket on fire. Pushing the wastebasket into the center of the room, walking out, and locking the door behind him, Campbell recalled that he said to the inmates—many of whom were from Los Angeles, "I know how homesick you all are for a little smog. Breathe it in and be happy."[27] While racial and gender identity did not predetermine the experience of people who worked in prisons—both Goodman and Campbell self-identified as white men—feelings of connection or alienation from the prisoner population could be exacerbated by issues of race and gender. For example, some African American and Latino teachers reported that they felt they faced more frequent frisks or requests for proof of identity than did white men. In addition, some women of various racial backgrounds reported having to deal with flirtatious or sexually aggressive inmates and correctional officers.[28]

Despite administrators' preference for courses in basic or vocational skills, visual artists created some of the most significant prison programs of the 1970s. These programs were largely created and run by noncorrections professionals and typically depended on private funding, university support, or volunteers for their success. The Prison Art Program, created by the Black Emergency Cultural Coalition (BECC), worked with incarcerated artists in New York as an expression of its political and aesthetic agendas.[29] Among the most ambitious programs of its kind, the BECC drew on the talents of leading artists like Benny Andrews and Faith Ringgold.

In the late 1960s and early 1970s, Andrews and Ringgold were already key figures in publicizing the racist assumptions and practices in fine arts museums and galleries. At the same time, they were increasingly involved in civil rights, feminist, and prison advocacy organizations. In 1972 Ringgold installed a painting at the Women's House of Detention in New York's Greenwich Village.[30] The painting, eight feet by eight feet and titled "For the Woman's House," features images of women doing what were then typically male professions: a white woman drives a bus bound for "Sojourner Truth Square," a Puerto Rican mother gives her daughter away at a wedding officiated by a woman priest, an African American woman speaks as president (Shirley Chisholm was seeking the Democratic nomination at the time), women professional basketball players play ball years before the WNBA, a doctor sees patients at "Rosa Parks Hospital," among others. The square is divided into eight triangles, inspired, according to Ringgold, by the Kuba people of the Congo (then Zaire).[31] In an interview about the piece, Ringgold stated her belief that women would be better suited than men for most of these jobs. Women are well-suited to driving a bus, for example, because they "are accustomed to being asked silly questions."[32] The image suggests both that women are capable of doing these jobs and the social restrictions that prevent them from doing so. Although Ringgold did not work with incarcerated artists on the painting, her hanging it at the facility was part of a growing commitment to artists behind bars.[33] She did, however, consult with incarcerated women about the subject matter; they asked that it include women of all races. Ringgold wanted an uplifting, feminist painting "to give the women some reason to be proud of themselves and to believe in themselves."[34]

While Ringgold would later work with incarcerated artists, up until that point her activism centered on expanding the very limited exposure given to African American artists by museums and galleries. In 1968, she joined a distinguished group of artists in picketing the Whitney Museum of American Art's exhibit "The 1930s: Painting and Sculpture in America." The Whitney remarkably failed to include any works by African American artists. This picket resulted in the Studio Museum in Harlem's mounting a second show, "Invisible Artists: 1930," that same year.[35]

In January of the following year, the Metropolitan Museum of Art opened an exhibit titled "Harlem on My Mind: Cultural Capital of Black America, 1900–1968." Although the Harlem Cultural Council initially endorsed the show, it withdrew its support before the show opened because of a lack of African American participation in the curatorial process and because the show used photographs rather than works of painting and sculpture. Although many of the photographs were by James Vanderzee, a then relatively unknown photographer, some observers took issue with a museum of fine arts' choice of a sociological and historical approach in its first show to ever focus on African Americans. In an art world providing few opportunities for African American fine artists or curators, "Harlem on My Mind" was a missed opportunity.

After meeting with officials from the museum and the New York State Council on the Arts, many of the veterans of the Whitney protests gathered at the lower Manhattan studio of the artist Benny Andrews and formed the Black Emergency Cultural Coalition.[36] The BECC found offensive the lack of African American participation in the design of the show and the curator's decision to show few works by African American painters and sculptors.[37] The BECC staged pickets at the Met, at the Whitney, and worked with another organization, Artists and Writers Protest Against the War in Vietnam. In 1972 the BECC and Artists and Writers Protest collaborated on *The Attica Book* in solidarity with the inmate uprising the previous year.[38] Proceeds from this book would be used to support a program begun in November 1971 in conjunction with the Junior Council of the Museum of Modern Art. The administration of the Manhattan House of Detention—also known as the Tombs—invited Benny Andrews to hold a drawing demonstration for inmates.[39] His two-hour demonstration led to the creation of the BECC's Art in Prison program, which eventually grew to thirty-seven programs in fourteen states.[40]

In the autumn of 1977, Andrews curated a show called "Echoes: Prisons, U.S.A." at the Studio Museum in Harlem. Opened in 1968 in the heart of the nation's most famous African American neighborhood, the Studio Museum, like the BECC, created a venue for African American artists while also showing that white artists' creation of art historical narratives at highly visible institutions like the Whitney and the Met helped solidify the artists' reputations.[41] Andrews avoided this appearance of using incarcerated artists to advance his career by carefully putting himself in the position of student rather than expert when developing inmate skills and promoting inmate work. Andrews believed that "the accomplishments of these men, women, and children serve to educate us all."[42] Andrews emphasized the effect he hoped the works would have on what viewers considered to be "art": "Along with losing many of their basic rights, it seems that prison artists have also lost their right to be considered fine artists, regardless of their artistic accomplishment. The public has been reluctant to be open minded in its approach to art created behind prison walls."[43] This hope for inclusion grew out of Andrews's efforts to open up the art world's most visible institutions to the products of African American creativity. The Studio Museum show, like the museum itself, created opportunities for artists who would not otherwise have access to the general public. Through much of the 1970s, members of the BECC gave slide lectures on the history of art; led workshops in painting, drawing, and sculpture; organized exhibitions of work by incarcerated artists; empowered inmates to teach classes for each another; and began a postrelease program for artists wishing to continue their studies. The New York City Department of Corrections cooperated with the BECC's efforts and helped organize shows for the general public.[44]

Ringgold's feminist politics led her to participate in other prison projects as well. Feminists took note that many of the programs being offered in the wake of Attica focused exclusively on male inmates. Little had changed since Kate Richards O'Hare, a socialist sentenced to the federal penitentiary in Jefferson City, Missouri, in the 1920s for violating the espionage act, observed that the women's prison did not have a library but that the facility for men did. In 1972 the cultural critic Michele Wallace noted that despite the significant attention to the politics of incarceration by the Left, sexism among male artists and funding agencies prevented this from benefiting women prisoners: "There is no structure set up to rehabilitate women in or outside of the prisons. There is nothing nothing nothing happening for women prisoners: I repeat—nothing."[45] When Wallace contacted the Fortune Society, an organization aiding former prisoners, she was told that they did not help women. Wallace knew of the work of the Women's Bail Fund, founded in 1970 to raise money to free women political prisoners, but she was intent on helping women whose crimes did not grow out of their leftist activism. While Wallace was essentially correct in her observation, a small handful of programs did exist in women's facilities. In Wallace's native New York, a few programs taught English to Puerto Rican and other Spanish-speaking prisoners, and the Bedford Hills Correctional Facility in nearby Westchester County had an education program, funded by the New York Community Trust and a number of private family foundations.

The kinds of arts and education programs becoming increasingly common in men's facilities simply did not exist in women's prisons during the early 1970s. Seeking to fill this gap, Wallace founded Art without Walls with a number of other writers and artists, including the painter Faith Ringgold and the poet Carol Muske (now Muske-Dukes). They applied for and received a ten-thousand-dollar grant from the New York Foundation and began offering "rap sessions" and workshops in art, poetry, dance, and yoga.[46] Over time Art without Walls provided a range of opportunities for women who participated in their workshops to distribute their work, including a chapbook and a video.[47] The work ranged from Gloria Jensen's comic "Ten Ways of Looking at Prison Lunch" to Assata Shakur's charged homage to Rema Olugbala, who, after being arrested with Shakur and Ronald Myers in 1971, was killed during an escape attempt while awaiting trial. Shakur and Myers were later acquitted, and the poem appeared in her 1984 autobiography.[48] Although there were ideological conflicts between Art without Walls, corrections officials, and prisoners—as well as among the members of Art without Walls—the group persisted in prisons for many years, offering academic lectures, dance workshops, and art and writing classes. It also created the Creative Learning Center for Children of Women in Prison in its current incarnation as Art without Walls/Free Space.

Although scores of other programs were organized around the United States, the one at New York's Auburn Correctional Facility achieved national attention when the Smithsonian Institute's National Collection of Fine Arts displayed work by inmate artists who participated in its program, organized by Everson Museum of Fine Arts in nearby Syracuse. The works in the exhibition came from a fifteen-month class conducted by James Harithas, the Everson Museum's director. The works recalled a broad range of twentieth-century styles, including German expressionism, abstract expressionism, and natural realism depicting street and prison life. In the fall of 1971, the museum began the program with an enrollment of sixty inmates. Harithas found that the class served as one of the few opportunities for inmates to create and talk across racial lines, engaging in discussions of aesthetics, religion, music, and various art genres.[49] For several participants, their coursework led to postrelease jobs. Harithas had a strong track record of hiring parolees who had participated in the program. "Richard Simmons became artist-in-residence at the Everson Museum in 1972, and the third parolee from the class to join the museum staff. His classmates, John McCluney from Bedford-Stuyvesant and Melvin Metcalf from Harlem, assumed executive positions in the Education Department of the museum and are now involved in exhibitions, community programs in art, and prison reform activities."[50] Thus, opportunities to study ideas and images, exhibit at the Smithsonian, and get postrelease employment made the BECC and Everson-Auburn programs results tangible to both prison administrators and the inmate artists.

The Everson's goal of introducing prison artists and writers to the broader public was an important feature of what would become one of the most prominent and long-standing prison programs. The PEN American Center's Prison Writing Program, begun in 1971, conducts writing workshops, mentors writers, distributes a free writing guide to all inmates who request one, and holds an annual writing contest. Both the international and U.S. chapters of PEN have worked since the 1920s to free writers from prison and to protest prison censorship. With the founding of the Prison Writing Program, PEN became an advocate for playwrights, poets, novelists, and essayists seeking to hone their craft and reach audiences beyond prison walls.[51]

If the historical trend of the 1970s pointed toward a deterrence-based system openly hostile to rehabilitative programs (not to mention social and political transformation), the actual practice was much more complex. Two prison programs from the late 1970s demonstrate the contradictory ways correctional systems responded to the competing pressures of the era. The first, the Juvenile Awareness Program—known popularly as Scared Straight!—amplified a political thirst to strengthen the deterrence function of prisons. The second, the Sesame Street Prison Project, more modestly showed how prisoners could transform their lives and, in the process, intervene in cycles of abuse and crime.

While artists, educators, and therapists faced an uphill climb in securing a permanent place in the correctional institutions, programs that emphasized the new mantra of deterrence were enthusiastically embraced. Rahway State Prison (since 1988 officially named East Jersey State Prison) received national exposure during the 1970s both as the prison that held wrongly convicted boxer Rubin "Hurricane" Carter and as the setting for the Juvenile Awareness Program, a program created by long-term inmates eager to help keep future generations out of prison. Begun in September 1976, the Juvenile Awareness Program counseled young people to avoid doing things that could land them in prison. In included a range of intervention activities, including therapeutic discussions with young people and a crisis hotline for their parents. However, its most visible—and ultimately most notorious—element was a dramatic and abusive session where long-term inmates threatened and bullied teens in the belief they could scare the young people into a future of positive behavior.

The Juvenile Awareness Program hoped to show that prisons were so horrible that one day of exposure could "scare straight" any juvenile. The initial idea for the program grew from the Lifers' Group, a group of long-term inmates of Rahway who resented the stereotypes of inmates as either pathological and immoral or, just as disturbing to them, as heroes that young people sought to emulate.[52] They felt that by working to keep young people out of jail, they could make a positive contribution to the communities many of them had harmed. Frank Bindhammer, a founder of the Lifers' Group, believed that "there was no such thing as rehabilitation in our penal system."[53] In a long interview with the criminologist James Finckenauer—a prominent critic of the program—Bindhammer made clear that "our intention was to destroy that Hollywood stereotype image of criminals and gangsters being cool, tough people, of prisons being the in thing—to attack these young people's own self-image, destroy that image of being a cool, tough person so that when they return to their respective communities they would be more susceptible to opening themselves up to their counselors—the professional people."[54] Given this intent, it is ironic that the core of the program centered on violence, sexual assault, suicide, and prison slavery. The prisoners felt that simply talking about their lives in prison and counseling the young people to stay in school and learn a trade would not have the desired effect. Instead, the prisoners' goal was to "make [themselves] appear to be the most despicable people imaginable" and thus turn the adolescents forever away from the very kind of people talking to them.[55]

The Juvenile Awareness Program reached a national television audience in 1979 with the documentary *Scared Straight!*, which first aired on March 8, 1979. According to WNEW-TV, which broadcast the documentary in New York, more than 3 million people viewed the program, which earned it the top rating during its 10 P.M. time slot. This was an astounding accomplishment for a nonnetwork broadcast of a docu-

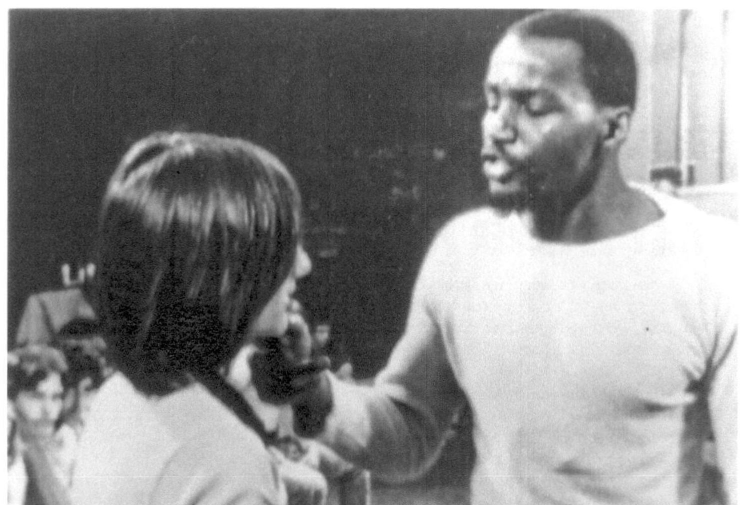

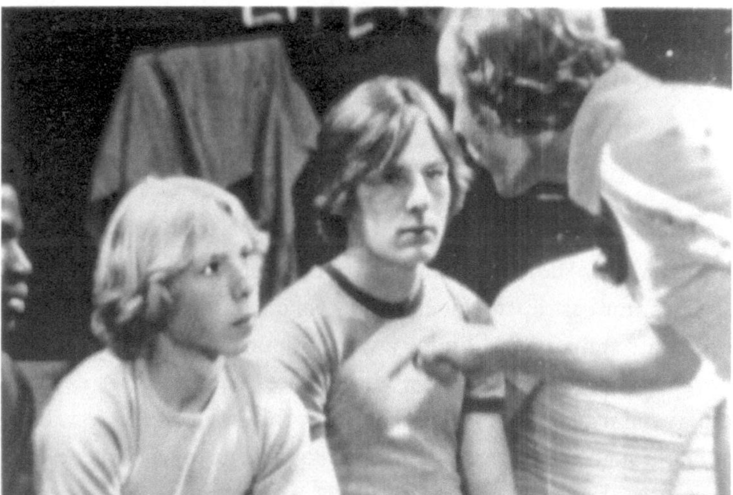

Film stills from Scared Straight!, *a 1978 documentary about the Juvenile Awareness Program at New Jersey's Rahway State Prison that went on to win Oscar and Emmy awards. Courtesy of Arnold Shapiro, ASP Productions, Inc.*

OVER THREE MILLION PEOPLE SPENT LAST THURSDAY NIGHT IN RAHWAY STATE PRISON.

THEY LEARNED A LESSON THEY'LL NEVER FORGET.

The lesson was taught by convicted murderers, rapists and thieves in a one-hour documentary entitled, "Scared Straight!" It was part of a project designed to portray the brutal realities of prison life to habitual juvenile offenders, in an effort to "scare the crime" out of them.

Thanks to you, our viewers, "Scared Straight!" was the highest rated show in its time period last Thursday with a 26 rating*. That means 39% of the total viewing audience* watched it.

Thanks to The Signal Companies and Golden West Television, Channel 5 was privileged to present "Scared Straight!" Thanks too, go to The Lifers and The Administration and The Officers of Rahway State Prison.

Due to the overwhelmingly positive response by viewers and reviewers alike, the program will be rebroadcast in the near future.

Once again WNEW-TV gave you a choice.

WNEW-TV
Metromedia
We give you a choice
5

WNEW-TV advertisement in the New York Times, *May 16, 1979. The station took out the ad after receiving the highest rating during its time slot for* Scared Straight! *Courtesy of WNYW News, Fox Television Stations, Inc. All rights reserved.*

mentary.[56] The show received an outpouring of acclaim, winning both an Oscar for best feature documentary one month after its television broadcast and a special Emmy award for outstanding informational program that September. Most news outlets trumpeted the extraordinary claim by prison officials that "more than 10,000 teen-agers have gone through the lifers program, and 80 percent to 90 percent have been 'scared straight.'"[57] This statistic, along with the national attention brought by the program, led to consistent funding for the program and expansion to other institutions in eleven other states.

The enthusiasm quickly began to die down. When a teacher from the Bronx brought a fifth-grade class to the Queens Correctional Facility for a *Scared Straight!*-style program, a parent complained after four inmates surrounded her child and one asked, "If we decided to take you into the bathroom and rape you, what could you do about it?"[58] A team of researchers then scrutinized the program's claims. It turned out that the astronomical success rate came from an anecdotal survey of the seventeen young people featured in the film—not the thousands who had participated in the program since its inception. David Rothenberg of the Fortune Society pointed out that race may have played a role in the success rate of the cohort chosen for the film. Fourteen of the seventeen were white and middle class, leading Rothenberg to observe, "These are the top candidates for probation in any criminal justice system."[59] This criticism became public in a *New York Times* feature and in a national broadcast of CBS's *Magazine*, an investigative show based on the *60 Minutes* format, questioned the success rate and claimed that the producers had fictionalized the biographies of some of the juveniles.[60] A Rutgers University team of criminologists found that, in sharp contrast to the claims made in the film, program participants actually had a higher rate of recidivism than nonparticipants.[61] Shockingly, a comparison of juveniles with similar risk factors found that people who had no contact with the criminal justice system prior to attending the Juvenile Assistance Program were more likely to commit a serious offense than those in a control group who did not attend the program.[62] For those in the control group who did commit crimes, they tended to be less serious than those committed by young people who had attended the program. In response, the U.S. Congress launched an investigation and the New Jersey commissioner of corrections demanded that only juveniles with arrest records participate in the program, resulting in the number of weekly participants dropping from two hundred to twenty-five.[63] In keeping with Robert Martinson's conclusion, however, this study found that no juvenile intervention could be said to work any better than Scared Straight![64] Arnold Shapiro, the producer, director, and writer of *Scared Straight!*, believed that the marshaling of data to prove the ineffectiveness or harm of the Juvenile Awareness Program obscured the important work that took place. Commenting on the program at Rahway and a similar program founded at San Quentin in 1964, Shapiro argued that the best judge of their effectiveness was their continued appeal to criminal justice and social service professionals: "Counselors, police, probation, social services and other agencies would not keep sending young people through the programs if they were not seeing results in some of the kids."[65]

Shapiro was right: the Juvenile Awareness Program was effective, particularly in the eyes of the criminal justice professionals who needed to respond in some way to the growing expectation that prison programs emphasize deterrence over rehabilitation. The program—and especially the documentary about the program—underscored two messages: first, teens should not look up to prisoners. Presenters continually emphasized that whatever pleasure or reward came from their previous criminality was illusory. An inmate with a missing eye explained to a group of teens: "See, I was like you when I came to prison. I was wild. Nobody could tell me a motherfucking thing. I didn't want to hear it. But you know how they showed me? By taking my motherfucking eye right out of my head. . . . Stabbing me all up the front and the motherfucking back. Tell me, how motherfucking tough could I have been? Tell me? See, you have that fucked up attitude that you want to be like me." In the end, the "system"—the state, the police, the correctional facility—would define prisoners as nothing more than a number in need of long-term warehousing. The same inmate explained, "They make us move by bells. I hear so many motherfucking bells, that when they don't ring, I still hear them ring. Why? Because I was that tough guy." Second, the program emphasized that prisons were terrible places where prison authorities and powerful inmates took advantage of the vulnerabilities and weaknesses of others. This was dramatized in the documentary in a variety of ways. Inmates would force the teenagers to take off their shoes. The inmates would either pick a pair they liked and keep them or arbitrarily throw them in the corner. Individual teenagers would be picked out of the lineup and held up for scorn. Boys and girls faced repeated threats of sexual assault.

The extraordinary critical and popular response to the film led CBS to broadcast a fictional made-for-television "docudrama" based on the Scared Straight! program. Called *Scared Straight! Another Story* and again produced by Arnold Shapiro, the fictional version grotesquely emphasized only the most sensational themes from the already selective first film, with prison rape and suicide featured prominently.[66] Furthermore, since the fictional film could not be subject to the kind of empirical criticism as the documentary, the ideological message that traditional rehabilitation efforts are futile could not be countered with facts.[67] The criticism by the Rutgers study and the emphasis on the most sensational aspects of the program embittered members of the Lifers' Group. Over time interviewers would discover that the lifers knew that their program could not solve the social issues influencing criminal activity. One inmate reminded a reporter who questioned the success rate that prisoners had never claimed the high numbers championed by the criminal justice system, repeated in the film, and endlessly reported in the news. Furthermore, James Landano, a member of the Lifers' Group, noted that the filmmakers "got what they wanted, and they left us hanging on the fence," failing to discuss the work they do to support parents of juveniles facing trouble with the law or their hotline for troubled teens.[68]

If Scared Straight! came to exemplify the growing trend toward deterrence, the Sesame Street Prison Project provided clear evidence that there was still some room for innovative rehabilitative programming. The Children's Television Workshop (CTW) organized and publicized its prison effort around its best-known show. The CTW worked with inmates throughout the federal prison system during 1977 and 1978 organizing screenings of *Sesame Street* shows that would be hosted by prisoners for children visiting the facilities. First begun as a pilot project in Fort Worth, Texas, the program soon spread to Seagoville near Dallas and then to other states. Still a relatively young organization, the Children's Television Workshop had been founded in 1968 by Joan Ganz Cooney and quickly revolutionized children's television with its signature show. Inspired by the optimistic vision of Lyndon Johnson's Great Society and well-funded through the Carnegie and Ford Foundations, the show used a daily television broadcast to enrich the literacy of preschoolers as a kind of "television equivalent of Head Start."[69] In keeping with these social reform ambitions, the CTW soon created its community education division, according to Cooney, to "reach children from disadvantaged homes with our educational programming."[70] Just as the CTW was seeking new ways to fulfill its mission, the Federal Bureau of Prisons was looking for a way to entertain children who were visiting incarcerated parents and who "were obviously bored and causing problems" for prison staff, according Norman Carlson, director of the Federal Bureau of Prisons.[71] According to Peter Rosen, the documentary filmmaker who produced, directed, and photographed a documentary for the CTW about the project, the Sesame Street Prison Project filled a need for the Federal Bureau of Prisons, particularly in minimum-security facilities that had generous visiting policies and relatively large numbers of children visiting relatives.[72]

The success of the program at two federal penitentiaries in Texas led the CTW and the Federal Bureau of Prisons to expand to other prisons.[73] The basic structure of the program remained similar: children visiting an inmate would be asked if they wanted to go to the *Sesame Street* program. Those who chose to participate would be led up a corridor painted with images of Big Bird and other characters from the show. The children and inmates gathered on the floor and watched an episode of *Sesame Street*, then inmates followed up with activities reinforcing the lessons of the episode. The simplicity of the program was the result of careful preparation, ongoing training, and, most important, a revision of expectations for inmates of correctional institutions. If Scared Straight! was based on the premise that only fear—or in the social scientific language of policymakers, deterrence—could reduce incarceration rates, the Sesame Street Prison Project demonstrated an alternative logic. One inmate reflected that he participated primarily to show that "these men up here are not something to be afraid of."[74] Aggression was seen not as a tool of deterrence but as a normal part of children's behavior that could be worked through with effective strategies.

Rosen's film, *"Sesame Street" Goes to Prison*, focused on the Child Development Program at Seagoville Federal Correctional Institution, near Dallas. The program barred people known to have committed sexual crimes or crimes against children but welcomed all others. The inmates in Seagoville's Child Development Association wanted to maintain strong relationships with their families. Some felt guilty for the vacuum their incarceration created in the lives of their children. Prior to their incarceration, many had drug habits that created significant obstacles to effective parenting. Some noted that they had themselves been first incarcerated as children in part because of their

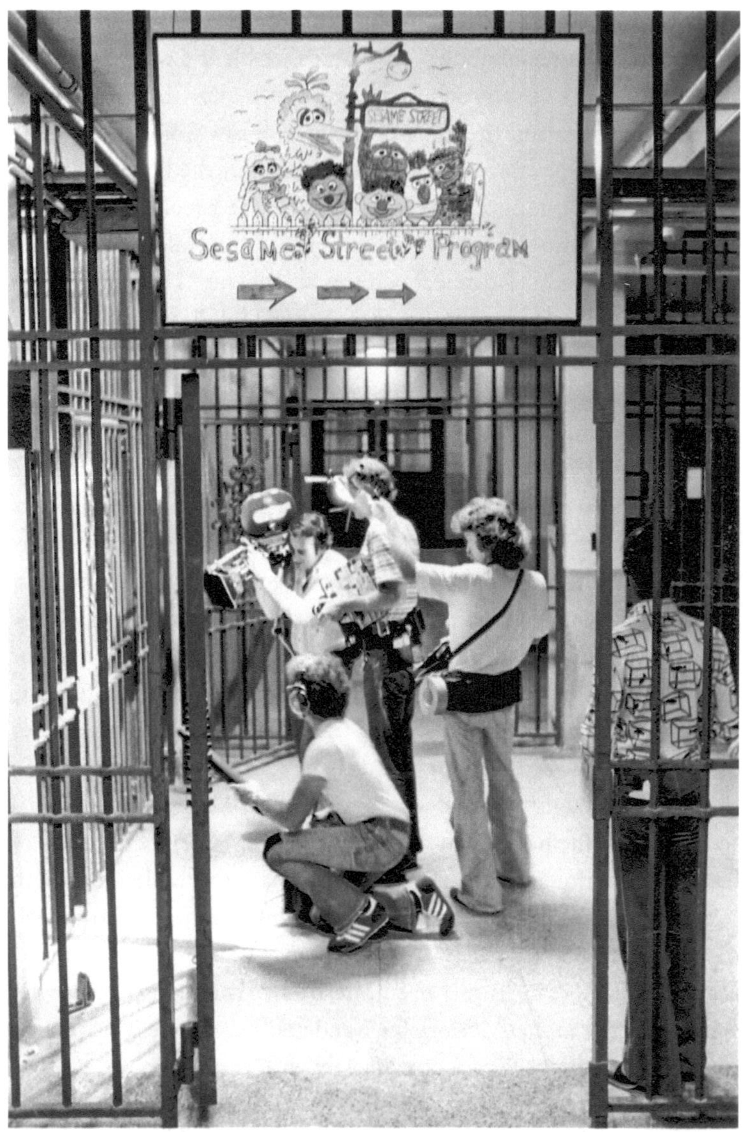

Peter Rosen filming "Sesame Street" Goes to Prison *at Seagoville Federal Correctional Institution in 1977. Courtesy of Peter Rosen Productions.*

own parents' inability to form strong, healthy relationships with them. These outcomes would not have been measurable in a way that would challenge Robert Martinson's findings, but it is clear that the Federal Bureau of Prisons and the inmates themselves saw tremendous value in the program. Norman Carlson, the director of the Federal Bureau of Prisons, told one interviewer that "there are excellent programs which help inmates by involving them in helping children."[75] An inmate interviewed by Rosen echoed this sentiment: "They have needs that I can fulfill and I have needs that they can fulfill."[76]

This result of the Sesame Street Prison Project sheds important light on the debate between deterrence and rehabilitation during the 1970s. As prison administrators worked to meet the institutional needs of their prisons, prisoners sought programs relevant to their life goals and social concerns. Meanwhile, politicians and social scientists engaged in ideologically charged policy debates. Prisoners who participated in the programs consistently defended them despite data showing that they had no positive—and may have had a negative—impact on participants' future ability to avoid returning to prison. For example, many of the prisoners in the Lifers' Group claimed that the program had significantly benefited them. Chris DeLuise, a member of the Lifers' Group who will spend the rest of his life in prison, said that Scared Straight! created a sense of peace for him after the initial sense that his life had ended with his sentence.[77] Despite their use of fear, the criminologist Robert L. Keller saw a measurable increase in self-esteem and social status within the prison for inmates who participated as counselors in the Juvenile Assistance Program. Furthermore, they became more nurturing over time, both to the young people who were subjected to their performance and to other inmates.[78] Although Martinson's study was concerned solely with recidivism rates, other researchers and people in the criminal justice system might define the parameters differently, focusing instead on the meaning of a program to the inmates or to the ability of prison administrators to run their institutions effectively. The parameters of debate shifted throughout the 1970s, with ideology often playing a key role in how one determined what worked.

WE TOOK THE WEIGHT

INCARCERATED WRITERS AND ARTISTS IN THE BLACK ARTS MOVEMENT

During the 1970s prison rehabilitative efforts seemed to narrow to the point where trying to scare people straight was the most visible prison program in the country. At the same time, alternative visions of prison life found numerous venues for expression and distribution. The work of prison writers appeared in small distribution publications like the Fortune Society's *Fortune News* and Joseph Bruchac's *Greenfield Review*. Some found their work picked up by specialty houses like Dudley Randall's Broadside Press, major university presses, and even some trade publishers. Perhaps the greatest incubators and benefactors of prison culture during the 1970s, however, were the movements for cultural nationalism among African Americans and Latinos. To public policy officials, a program would be deemed useful if it reduced recidivism. To people who championed rehabilitation, resources and measurable outcomes could lead to the creation of education and therapeutic programs. To those who championed deterrence, programs like Scared Straight! that highlighted the fearsome qualities of prison life won the day. For prisoners who highlighted the racist underpinnings and impact of the criminal justice system, however, any program originating from state departments of correction or other state agencies was suspect. As notions of liberation and black and brown cultural nationalism achieved increasing currency, African American and Latino prisoners and their advocates turned away from deterrence or rehabilitation. Instead, liberation became the new touchstone for relevancy and the Black Arts movement the ascendant force in the culture of American prisons.

In particular, the cultural life of American prisons became intertwined with the Black Arts and Black Power movements in shared ideological goals, aesthetic principles, and institutional arrangements throughout the 1970s. By the end of the decade, the two movements would symbolically embrace the plight of incarcerated African Americans as symptomatic of the broader black experience in the United States. In addition, major theoreticians and artists from the movements would spend time behind bars, either while facing criminal charges or as scholars and teachers in prison arts and education programs. The radicalization of American prisoners—and especially African American and Latino prisoners—led many to consider all inmates of color to be "political prisoners." The criminal justice system unfairly targeted African Americans, Native Americans, and Latinos and then denied them access to a fair trial. Many African American prisoners turned to cultural nationalism by changing their names, adopting African anticolonial revolutionary names for their organizations, and connecting their freedom to the broader movement for black liberation. Finally, the literary, visual, and performing arts were explicitly politicized by the Black Power movement inside and outside prison walls just as prison authorities, universities, and government and nongovernment funding agencies began experimenting with ambitious arts and education programs in major U.S. correctional facilities.

Artists from the Black Arts movement took an active role in fostering the artistic and literary ambitions of incarcerated people while including the plight of prisoners as subject matter in their work. Faith Ringgold painted a mural and worked with women prisoners at New York's Rikers Island. Benny Andrews curated a show of prisoner artwork at the Studio Museum in Harlem. The poet Gwendolyn Brooks mentored Etheridge Knight when he was still writing from a prison cell. Similarly, arts organizations provided funding and vision for numerous prison projects. Throughout the country, an impressive array of artists and writers ran workshops, published chapbooks at their own expense, taught music classes, and did the daily work of mentoring incarcerated artists.

Much of this legacy has been obscured or forgotten. The links between incarcerated people and the Black Arts movement were forged by individual and institutional commitments inside and outside of correctional facilities. What impact did the institutional context have on this key arts movement? What was the significance of the image and idea of "the prisoner" to the Black Arts movement? What did incarcerated writers contribute to the Black Arts movement? By remembering the institutions, images, and inmates that influenced the movement, we gain new insight into the politics and aesthetics of the era. While those who created these programs hoped that access to the arts and education would help reform convicts, the incarcerated artists themselves believed that they were artists in service to a revolution. Incarcerated people were central to the revolutionary aims of the Black Arts movement both in the works they wrote and in the symbol they provided of "imprisonment" in a racially oppressive society.

The political content and goals of the Black Arts movement gave it particular relevance to incarcerated people. Some African American prisoners sharply criticized the content in non–Black Arts movement classes and writing workshops that emerged during the 1960s and 1970s. They viewed the teachers as too compromised by the system in which they worked to teach anything that would bring about personal transformation or advance the political and economic goals of the various liberation movements of the time. Juno Bakali Tshombe, an inmate in Massachusetts, not only believed that the programs lacked a useful political perspective, he saw them as methods of ideological control and psychological warfare: "Clearly the administration is thinking in terms of 'let them niggers put on some plays describing their condition to each other or write poetry that no one gives a damn about, but under no circumstances whatsoever let them produce anything with political overtones.'"[1] Confirming at least part of this critique, prison educators often spoke of "rehabilitation" rather than the liberation sought by many movement activists.

But not all programs could be swept aside with Tshombe's critique. He made an exception for the Elma Lewis Technical Theater Training Program at the Massachusetts Correctional Institution in Norfolk. Elma Lewis was a central figure in the Boston-based National Center of Afro-American Artists, an organization with firm ties to the Black Arts movement. When Lewis entered the prison to teach her class, she discovered that inmates were already familiar with the political rhetoric and aesthetic sensibilities of the Black Arts movement. She described her entry into the prison as a learning experience: "The men . . . are my brothers, they are my sons, they are my students, and in a very real sense, they are also my teachers."[2] The prisoners in the Norfolk program hoped to teach not only Lewis, but also African American communities outside of prisons. According to Lewis, "They would like their children, their brothers, their sisters, their mothers and fathers to sidestep the trap before it's sprung. They teach the development of alternatives. They no longer see through a glass darkly. They would like to see their communities move toward ownership and control. They hope to pass along the revelation to blacks in all black communities."[3]

The unique purpose of Lewis' program made a difference to the inmates. At the time, Norfolk contained programs in everything from oil burner repair to GED and college-level courses. In fact, Norfolk had been founded as the Norfolk Prison Colony in the 1930s as the physical manifestation of the "new penology." It had created an innovative system of cooperative houses, inmate education, and limited self-government. Nevertheless, the emphasis on reform of the inmate—rather than ending the oppression of racism—indicated to the 1970s generation that Norfolk needed to be changed. But even Tshombe, a participant in the Norfolk theater program, made an exception because of the political and aesthetic sensibilities of Lewis's course: "There is no program other than Elma Lewis's here that is working towards attaining some degree of thinking and a positive direction that will relate to the confined black prisoner and offer him a productive analysis needed for self-awareness and racial awareness."[4] The artists and writers in the program called themselves "the Norfolk Prison Brothers," linking them not only to each other but also to the then famous "Soledad Brothers" in California. When the publisher Little, Brown released a collection of writings from the Norfolk program in 1972, the prisoners dedicated the book to "Jonathan Jackson and the Soledad Brothers & to the brothers in Attica, who gave their lives in order for us to live! A little longer."[5] Many of them adopted Swahili or Islamic names, and some were active in the Nation of Islam. Malcolm X, who been incarcerated in Norfolk decades earlier, described its debating program as his "baptism into public speaking."[6] The connection to Malcolm X was central: he had converted to Islam in 1947 while at Norfolk, and the Nation of Islam continued to have a profound influence on the religious, political, creative, and intellectual development of incarcerated African Americans. Elijah Muhammad served a four-year prison term for draft resistance during World War II. Muhammad's time in prison led him to believe that spiritual conversion to the Nation of Islam could transform black felons. After his release, Muhammad devoted substantial time and money to converting incarcerated people. By the 1970s Malcolm X was an icon of the Black Arts movement.[7]

Incarcerated artists and writers gained access to talented and experienced teachers because of a growing momentum for change within the system. While uniquely situated in a Black Arts movement organization, the Norfolk Program was one of many new initiatives throughout the 1960s and 1970s. Even the teachers and artists without the political motivations of Lewis contributed to the aesthetic and political sensibilities of prisoners. At times, the institutional context made it difficult for prisoners to pursue their more militant goals through the arts. Because of the widespread use of indeterminate sentencing, many inmates carried long sentences with parole determined by state officials who did not look kindly on political activities.[8] The Black Arts movement, however, often provided an energizing visual and literary rhetoric to pursue shared goals. To some prisoners, the Black Arts movement helped them determine whether a program was a tool of psychological warfare meant to "tame" them or a route to individual or collective liberation. In turn, prisoners would become a key symbol for a growing number of African American artists outside of prisons.

The theorist Ron Karenga wrote in 1968 that "black art must expose the enemy, praise the people, and support the revolution."[9] Prisoners would become important symbols and contributors to this new aesthetic. The political and aesthetic sensibilities of the audience—particularly the movement that had recently transformed from the "civil rights movement" to the "black liberation movement"—saw an iconic significance in the plight of incarcerated African American men and women. Rather than being outcasts from African American communities, incarcerated people provided evidence of the ongoing oppression of all African American people throughout U.S. history. Inspired at times by their own experiences with the justice system or by the writings of Malcolm X, Angela Davis, George Jackson, and Eldridge Cleaver, these artists would use police officers as metaphors for white oppression. In poetry and drama, convicts became potential revolutionaries; in sharp contrast, guards and police officers became storm troopers for the white power structure.

To be sure, prisons have often served as catalysts for social change. The prison experiences of Henry David Thoreau gave rise to his inspirational "Civil Disobedience" in the mid-nineteenth century. Eugene Debs, Kate Richards O'Hare, Jimmy Hoffa, and Martin Luther King Jr. are just a few of the many Americans who used their prison experiences as evidence of their oppression and as opportunities to inspire their movements. This tradition became more pronounced with the events of the late 1960s and early 1970s. While many people knew that Malcolm X had done time in a Massachusetts prison, the publication of his autobiography made clear that his time in Norfolk was the catalyst in his religious and political transformation. Huey P. Newton, George Jackson, and Ericka Huggins would join Malcolm X and Angela Davis in the belief that incarcerated people could play central roles in the liberation of not only themselves but all Black people. On the East Coast, the Attica uprising became the best known of the approximately three hundred prison riots in the United States between the late 1960s and early 1980s. Forty-eight of these occurred between 1968 and 1971.[10] Rather than being dismissed as the evil deeds of the worst among us, these uprisings—called a "war behind walls" by the convict Edward Bunker writing in *Harper's Magazine* in 1972—became emblematic of the increasingly volatile racial politics in the United States as a whole.[11]

The politics of black power included arguments by some activists—artists and otherwise—that there was little if any distinction between political and nonpolitical crimes. Zayd Shakur, the deputy minister of information for the New York State chapter of the Black Panther Party, argued that life behind bars was merely an "extension of our communities": "The penitentiaries, as they call them, and the communities are plagued with the same thing: dope, disease, police brutality, murder, and rats running over the places that you dwell in. We recognize that most of the militant-dissatisfied youth are off in the penitentiaries. Eighty percent of the prison population is black, brown, and yellow people. You look around and say, 'what happened to my man. I haven't seen him for along time,' then you get busted, go to jail, and there he is.'"[12]

Insights like this led the scholar Roberta Ann Johnson to argue that prisons gave rise to the Black Power movement itself.[13] According to Johnson the same difficulties—danger of physical conflict, experience of confinement, poor health and educational services, and insufficient job opportunities—existed in correctional facilities and in African American communities. As African Americans saw the experiences and contexts common to lives lived on both sides of the wall, the rhetoric and goals of social justice movements shifted from dismantling segregation to demanding power. At this point, the liberation of all Black prisoners became a central goal of the freedom struggle. As Huey P. Newton—the founder of the Black Panther Party whose incarceration became a focus of Panther efforts—said at the eulogy for Jonathan Jackson and William Christmas, "There are no laws that the oppressor makes that the oppressed are bound to respect."[14] Jonathan Jackson's older brother George would soon become well known for his book *Soledad Brother*, in which he observed that "There are still some blacks here who consider themselves criminals, but not many."[15] These writers saw the experience of "free" African Americans reflected in the lives of prisoners. In this way, the liberation of African American prisoners and the elimination of white supremacy went hand in hand.

For some Black Arts movement writers, prisoners were more than symbols of black oppression. Amiri Baraka was one of several prominent figures in the movement who spent time in prison. Baraka, then known as LeRoi Jones, was first arrested in 1961 on obscenity charges.[16] Later, after he changed his name to Amiri Baraka and increased his participation in nationalist organizations, he became subject to persistent surveillance and harassment by the FBI and other criminal justice organizations.[17] He would be arrested twice in 1967, once during the first night of the Newark Riot and later for weapons' possession.[18] During the trial on the gun charge, Baraka was sentenced to thirty days in the Morristown, New Jersey, jail for contempt of court because of his refusal to be judged by an all-white jury.[19] At his sentencing for the initial gun charge, the judge read from Baraka's infamous poem, "Black People" (1967): "Up against the wall, motherfucker, this is a stickup!" While the judge omitted the profanity, he felt that the line justified an especially harsh three-year sentence with no parole. Convicted, as Baraka put it, "of possession of two guns and a poem," he would be sent to the Trenton State Penitentiary, where he reconnected with old acquaintances from high school and met "some real warriors and even a few scholars."[20] Baraka appealed his sentence and was released on bail after little more than a week in prison. He won the appeal, but the experience made him see that prisons' "real function is as institutions of oppression for the poor and the minorities."[21]

Baraka would draw on these experiences in several works. He wrote portions of *Raise Race Rage Raze* (1971) in the Essex Country Prison and dramatized his sharp criticism of African American police officers in *Police*, a one-act play written in 1967 and first published in 1968.[22] In it, a character named "Black Cop" murders a character named "Black Man." While "Black Man" is mourned as a brother and husband, "Black Cop" is reviled by the surviving "Black Woman": "He ain't no kin to me . . . the lousyass murderer . . . for the white folks too." The one-act play ends when "Black Cop" kills himself under orders of "Black Woman." The "White Cops" are seen "slobbering on his flesh, a few are even eating chunks of flesh they tear off in their weird banquet."[23] While inspired by his experiences with African American police officers, Baraka transformed his arrests into an archetypal encounter that showed both the mechanics of oppression and a route to liberation. Two black men—one a police officer, the other his victim—are dead; one is killed in the service of oppression, the second to achieve a temporary retribution. That the white officers do nothing to stop either death underscores Baraka's opinion of an African American police officer he met during the violence that followed Martin Luther King Jr.'s 1968 assassination: "Someone or something had created him and what I was hearing was obviously tapes running through his brain track."[24]

In addition to Baraka, other artists and writers would be incarcerated for their political views. For example, Marvin X, a San Francisco playwright and the founder of Black House, the Black Arts/West Theater, and the Recovery Theater, was incarcerated for resisting the draft. These experiences gave rise to *Take Care of Business* (1968), a play set in a jail cell.[25] Incarcerated on a trumped-up marijuana charge, Wes, described as a "do-rag nationalist," and Joe Simmons, "a typical college student," meet the devil. Joe's father does not believe his declaration of innocence and refuses to get him out of jail. While Wes gives the guard the finger and responds to racism with snide comments, Joe discovers that his polite demeanor and college enrollment mean nothing. Class differences melt as the two young men learn that their black skin defines how they will be treated.

Just as the Black Power movement saw the role of prisons in maintaining white supremacy—and the role of prisoners in dismantling it—many artists in the Black Arts movement worked with prisoners and created works that featured prisoners in roles of heroes and liberators of Black people. Moreover, these works manifested the belief that, as Larry Neal wrote in 1968, the Black Arts movement was the "aesthetic and spiritual sister of the Black Power concept."[26] Neal mined African American folklore and blues in his "Shine" poems. These traditions had long highlighted struggles against the criminal justice system, and many texts had been written and sustained in the prison farms of the post-Reconstruction South.[27] In "Shine Goes to Jail" (1974), we see the mundane indignities of life in jail transformed into a story about collective experience and kinship ties:

> There was no toilet to speak of. And they gave us old newspapers to wipe our asses with. There was only this rut running through the cell. It was flushed three times a day with water from a special pump. The water was mixed with pine oil disinfectant. There is this cell. It's supposed to accommodate three men, but there are four of us here right now. Woody Neal from Georgia, down around Atlanta; Silas T. Washington, over here, he's near Titusville, Alabama; I know his folks. Blind Jack, sitting yonder with his guitar; well he from Florence, Tennessee, same as Handy. And me? I'm from everywhere.[28]

In contrast to the tendency to see incarcerated people as pariahs, Neal drew on a tradition that saw prisoners as connected to one another and to their communities outside prison walls.

The fact that these connections remained intact provided hope that the violence and exploitation convicts used for personal gain while on the streets could be constructively channeled toward their political aims. The fact that violence could be destructive and oppressive or productive and revolutionary signaled that its meaning lay in its context. Writers would come to play a key role in reshaping the meaning of violence away from exploitation and toward transformation. This made the Black Arts movement a key participant in the politics of Black Power. Larry Neal argued that poetry "is a concrete function, an action. No more abstractions." His writings were "fists, daggers, airplane poems, and poems that shoot guns."[29]

This revolutionary poetics would explicitly create a space for prisoners via an explicitly sexualized violence. The concrete action, in this case, was a phallic masculinity in service of revolution. Baraka's "Black Art" (1969) clearly makes this connection between male virility and violence:

> Fuck poems
> and they are useful, they shoot
> come at you, love what you are,
> breathe like wrestlers, or shudder
> strangely after pissing.[30]

The "shooting" of semen signals both virility and violence, as in Baraka's *Police*, when the paper gun that "Black Cop" holds in his hand is cut in the shape of a penis.[31] While sexualized violence would prove to be an important theme in the Black Arts movement, Neal was careful to denounce same-sex intimacy as a "rejection of the body"[32] when practiced by women or as simply "sick" when practiced by men.[33] In the homosocial culture of prisons, this hostility would take on increased significance.

If penises could be transformed into guns, the men who possessed them would need to undergo a political transformation in order to use them in service of the revolution. Here, too, sexuality would serve as the primary symbol of political change. Rather than consider the potential for same-sex intimacy as a route to building political alliances, Neal felt that pimps were better suited to serving as symbols of the potential for revolution among the criminals. In order to do so, however, pimps would need to undergo a political transformation. Without this transformation, they would be intermediaries in white exploitation. In "Brother Pimp" (1966), Neal wrote,

> You help the beast make whores out of black women,
> only you yourself are a whore.
> you and your brother pimps kill each other
> for the right to destroy our women.
> would-be heroes. would-be black men.
>
> JOIN THE STRUGGLE
> FOR REAL MANHOOD
> LINK YOUR NATURAL LIFE-SENSE
> TO THE REAL SOUL-THING[34]

In what capacity would "Brother Pimp" join the struggle? Neal hoped that he would

> become a new kind of pimp. yeah, brother, pimp for the
> revolution. I say pimp for the revolution,
> not pimp on the revolution.

Neal dedicated this poem to Iceberg Slim, a former pimp whose *Pimp: The Story of My Life* would be released the following year.[35] Neal's dedication of this poem—and his numerous poems about Malcolm X—indicate that he sought to create role models for the transformation of outlaws into revolutionaries. This image of the pimp—alongside other criminals and convicts—provided a hypermasculine, sexualized image that could be used (once transformed) to serve the revolution.

In his introduction to the 1969 anthology, *The New Black Poetry*, Clarence Major argued that poetry could be an important tool in transforming pimps into revolutionaries. Just as Larry Neal hoped that incarcerated African Americans would become "pimps for the revolution," Major argued that the new poetry signaled "death cries to the pimp par excellence of the recent capitalistic stages of the world."[36] Juno Bakali Tshombe, a participant in Elma Lewis's program in Massachusetts, plumbed this theme in a dialog he imagined between two Los Angeles pimps. The first pimp asks the second, "Have you dug this new black awareness thing going around?" They contemplate the effect of cultural nationalism on their careers after someone who threatens to rip the first pimp off if he doesn't "quit that counter-revolutionary stuff" confronts him. He then explains that earlier that same week, the nationalists castrated and killed three pimps and put a sign around their heads with a warning that "there ain't going to be any more pimping, shooting dope, and other counter-revolutionary activity in the nationalist community." As he laments the increasing difficulty of hiring new prostitutes, the first pimp vows to put his mother out on the street as a prostitute.[37]

As counterrevolutionaries, Tshombe explains, pimps needed to be eliminated from Black communities. However, Tshombe also felt that the lawlessness that brought him to Norfolk Prison was a key step in his political transformation. In his poem "discovering myself" (1972), he noted:

in order
to become a black man
instead of a nigga,
I would first
have to be a nigga.
in order to become that black man.[38]

Although Tshombe recognizes that his lawlessness and incarceration would not be a permanent solution, he also feels that it would be a necessary step toward becoming a strong patriarch. James A. Lang, a Muslim poet in Norfolk, asked in a 1972 poem to his son if his incarceration is a

disservice
To the struggle? Or, have I contributed to
The intensification of the struggle
By breaking the genealogical

Progression of paternal submission
To the oppressor's blueprint
For eternal enslavement?[39]

Answering his own question, he acknowledges his prison conversion to Islam as a necessary step in restoring "Harmony and tranquility / To our be-deviled planet." Rather than making them pariahs or parasites, prisoners' previous criminal activities showed their commitment to resistance. This, they argued, would be an important characteristic for future revolutionaries.

Lang creates a character in the short story "The (Un?)Making of a Revolutionary" who undergoes a religious and political transformation in prison.[40] Unsatisfied with the options of being unemployed, underemployed, or deployed to Vietnam, Eddie turns to robbing banks. Once in prison, "the total liberation of black people" became his "only concern." Prison gives him "the opportunity to examine the plight of black people in America from a much broader viewpoint."[41] His dedication to this cause leads him to conclude that the elimination of drug dealers and pimps "in whatever manner necessary" would be his first priority. When he is released, however, he is tempted by his brother—a pimp driving a new Cadillac Eldorado and dressed in a "white long-haired-beaver hat with a six-inch brim and a blue band"—with heroin and two prostitutes.[42] The story ends with the reader left wondering if Eddie will give in to temptation or follow through on his violent solution. Will he shoot heroin or his brother? Will this be the "unmaking" of a revolutionary or a fulfillment of his mission?[43]

As intermediaries between white customers and African American prostitutes, pimps were vulnerable to criticism from radicals that they were complicit in oppression. At the same time, the extraordinary popularity of the tawdry paperbacks by Iceberg Slim and Donald Goines and the clichéd black masculinity featured in the blaxploitation films like *Shaft* and *Sweet Sweetback's Badasssss Song* turned the pimp and drug dealer into a cultural icon for a new kind of black male hero that proved compelling to some incarcerated African American men.[44] This question about the role of pimps, thieves, and drug dealers in both the oppression and ultimate liberation of African American communities was articulated in the novels of Slim and Goines, the two most widely read novelists ever to emerge from prison. Critics tend to measure the success of these writers by the number of books sold or their influence on rap musicians. Although it is difficult to get precise sales figures, Slim's sale of 6 million books and Goines's well over 5 million place them among the top-selling writers in U.S. history. Over time their lives and characters have been featured in countless songs and several films. Their works do not fit easily into the Black Arts movement—they are sometimes linked instead to the stereotypical blaxploitation films or to gangsta rap—but their stories of pimping, drug dealing, and the racial politics of the criminal justice system are important explorations of the key themes developed by incarcerated writers like Etheridge Knight or the Norfolk Prison Brothers. Their lack of literary pretension helps explain their relative obscurity to literary and cultural critics who otherwise examine the Black Arts movement. As the *Village Voice* critic Greg Tate noted, Iceberg Slim "occupies a peculiar niche between the serious naturalism of the heavyweights (Wright, Himes, Baldwin, Ellison, and Morrison) and garish ghettocentric fabulism." Tate praised one of Slim's novels as "trash to the core."[45]

Slim and Goines center many of their novels on drug dealers and pimps. But unlike the writers of the Black Arts movement, Slim did not seem to think the move from pimp to writer represented a transformation at all, once expressing the view that "writing is just pimpin' on paper."[46] Born in 1918 as Robert Lee Maupin, Slim was also known as Robert Beck. He spent much of his young adulthood in and out of prison, but was released from prison in 1962 for the last time at age forty-three, intent on kicking a heroin habit and convinced he was too old to be a pimp. While working as an insecticide salesman in the mid-1960s, Slim told his story to a bug-infested college professor who took an interest in it. Instead of collaborating with the professor (which, legend has it, would have entailed sharing royalties), he became a writer. Iceberg Slim's autobiographical first novel, *Pimp: The Story of My Life*, features episodes from his more than twenty-year career as a pimp and convict. Most of the novel conveys the pleasure and pain Slim experienced on the streets and in jail. First published in 1967 and selling 1.75 million copies by 1973, *Pimp* is partially a novel about the transformation of the main character from a self-glorifying, boastful pimp who refers to himself at one point as a Christ-like "King of Kings" into a middle-aged ex-convict with a political and social conscience who increasingly uses prison life as a metaphor for the circumscribed place of African Americans.[47]

While this theme of an emerging social conscience is largely outweighed by the tawdry details and vernacular artistry of the main character's original vocabulary, social change was an important element of Slim's own hopes for his literary output. In a 1972 interview with the Los Angeles *Free Press*, an alternative weekly, Slim made clear that he sympathized with Bobby Seale and Huey Newton: "I'm in agreement with anybody that wants freedom, and who wants some sort of equality in this genocidal society." He elaborated on the role of pimps in the revolution later in the interview:

> It is counterrevolutionary for black people to prey on other black people, or upon poor white people. I recognize the necessity for crime in black America. I understand why, for survival, black people must steal. But I don't condone crime. I feel that what it takes to be a successful criminal could be used in a more constructive way. Like if the pimp has enough circuitry going in his brain to control nine women, surely he's got no business being a pimp. So if you're black, and you must be a criminal, don't steal my stuff. Go over there. Steal from affluent white people.[48]

If Slim expressed little faith that criminals would be transformed into revolutionaries, he at least hoped that pimps would be smart enough to channel their crime in ways that complemented a revolutionary movement. Slim devoted himself to writing and lecturing until his death in 1992, by then an elder statesman of the hip-hop generation.

Slim's work quickly gained popularity in American prisons and would change the literary fortunes of Donald Goines. Incarcerated on seven different occasions, ultimately spending six and a half years behind bars,[49] Goines began his short literary career with two novels written while in prison, *Dopefiend* and *Whoreson*. All sixteen of his novels were published in the last five years of his life, several of them under the name Al C. Clark. Born and raised in Detroit, Goines enlisted in the Air Force during the Korean War. He was introduced to heroin while stationed in Japan and became a lifelong addict, remaining clean only during his time behind bars. Goines became a full-time thief rotating in and out of jail throughout the 1950s and 1960s on charges stemming from a life of pimping, robbery, and drug use. While incarcerated in Michigan's Jackson State Penitentiary in 1965, Goines turned his attention to writing, with an early piece on Martin Luther King Jr. appearing in the prison newspaper.[50] Goines was released but returned to hustling and, by 1969, was again in prison, this time on an eighteen-month sentence for larceny.[51] At Jackson State, another prisoner introduced Goines to the work of Iceberg Slim, whose *Pimp* and *Trick Baby* circulated among the inmates. Goines soon completed his first novel, *Whoreson*, in 1970. Shortly after his release from prison he sent it to Holloway House, Iceberg Slim's publisher. Holloway House specialized in paperbacks, marketing them to liquor stores and newsstands rather than conventional bookstores—and selling millions.[52] Four weeks after Holloway accepted *Whoreson* for publication, he sent the publisher his second manuscript, *Dopefiend* (1971).[53] Goines's characters carry names like Whoreson Jones—the protagonist of the first novel—and animate plots that revolve around violence, sex, and drug use. His grim but straightforward prose reduces stomach-churning events to banal transactions or grim humor interspersed with moments of tenderness and self-examination. Goines created memorable characters like *Dopefiend*'s heavyset Porky, the owner of a "shooting gallery" for heroin addicts, who demands that junkies perform acts of bestial sex while he masturbates. Lest Goines's readers begin to feel pity for the dopefiends, he reveals that the addicts view Porky with a mixture of horror and hope, knowing that when "Porky felt freakiest, he might set enough dope out for everyone."[54] Goines's early works are devoid of redemption or revenge: dopefiends are destroyed while Porky remains slobbering and in charge at novel's end.

After his release from prison, Goines continued to write at a frantic pace each morning while feeding his heroin habit in the afternoon. His books remained vividly violent but also offered a fictional reflection of some of the key political questions of the day. *Black Gangster* (1972), for example, includes a farcical riff on the Black Power movement. Prince Walker, the novel's ex-con protagonist, starts the Freedom Now Liberation Movement as a front for a wide range of criminal activity. In 1974 and 1975 Goines published a series of four novels about a protagonist named Kenyatta, whose name honored the Kenyan president instrumental in that country's achieving its independence from Great Britain in 1963. African Americans, including African American prisoners, looked on with pride as Kenya, Tanzania, and other African states successfully fought for their right to self-determination throughout the 1950s and 1960s. After the Black Panther Party set up a chapter in Algiers in 1970, some Panthers fled there to avoid criminal charges. Algeria did not have an extradition treaty with the United States and, according to Kathleen Cleaver, afforded the Black Panther Party "quasi-diplomatic status."[55] By the late 1960s and early 1970s, African politicians and activists—including Kenyatta, Amilcar Cabral, Patrice Lumumba, Kwame Nkrumah, among others—served as inspiring examples of African nationalism and, for some, as models for a revolution in the United States. The pulp version of Kenyatta is a vigilante out to rid Detroit's African American neighborhoods of drug dealers and pimps. In *Crime Partners* (1974), the first book in the series, Kenyatta forms a small gang intent on killing ordinary drug dealers and pimps preying on black neighborhoods. As the series proceeds, Kenyatta's power grows. He relocates to Los Angeles's Watts neighborhood (as had Goines himself by that time). There he expands his vigilante targets to include police officers and develops a broad plan to figure out who is behind the narcotics industry.

The sensationally violent storyline includes the unmistakable message that Kenyatta is simply replacing government institutions that fail to provide for the health, welfare, and safety of black communities. In the final book of the series, *Kenyatta's Last Hit*, the protagonist describes Los Angeles County General Hospital as a "death trap" and creates an impromptu intensive care unit in his house when a key member of his organization is burned. Growing disillusionment among previously hopeful workers in Great Society programs like the Office of Economic Opportunity leads bureaucrats to pass tips and files on to Kenyatta in the hope that he can succeed where the policies of liberalism have failed. No longer focused on the descent of promising young African Americans into lives lost to addiction, Goines, like Iceberg Slim, paints a portrait of a "rising ghetto king with the idealism, along with the force, to make a difference."[56] But even with this more broadly political perspective, Goines's plotlines still do not allow his readers to see the evolution of his characters, from "Whoreson" to "Kenyatta," as leading to the kinds of transformations hoped for by revolutionaries: just as the drug dealer Porky is left standing at the end of *Dopefiend*, the financier behind the attempted destruction of African American communities remains alive while Kenyatta is killed at the end of *Kenyatta's Last Hit*. By the time the book came out, Goines had returned to Detroit. There he and his wife, Shirley Sailor, were shot and killed in October 1974 in an unsolved murder. He was sitting at his typewriter.

If the transformation of the pimp into a revolutionary was fraught with ambivalence in the works of Iceberg Slim and Donald Goines, this is not to say that others writers did not attempt to represent African Americans as nurturing men and strong women who together could shape a new path toward self-determination. Several incarcerated writers took the lesson of Goines's Kenyatta series—that the individual exploitation African American prostitutes by African American pimps had roots in the broader exploitation of black communities by white financiers—but did not flavor it with the ambivalence of the murdered protagonists or the man who created them.

The Kenyatta series implicitly acknowledged the embrace of African and African American cultural and political nationalism behind bars. The possibility that African culture could foster new political and cultural communities in the United States can be seen in the ideas and visions of incarcerated artists of the Black Arts movement. As in the case of Goines and Iceberg Slim, cultural and political nationalism was articulated in gendered terms. In "Stride, Strut Lady," Imani Kujichagulia, a convict in the Florida State Prison, tells a prostitute to "Come in out the cold, lady / give me your hand . . . tell me / your problems . . . lady, / i'll be your man."[57] Kujichagulia offered more than a warm room and a kind ear; in his name he indicated a devotion to the seven principles of Maulana Karenga's U.S. organization. In the

Kwanzaa tradition, *imani* (a Kiswahili term) means faith: "To believe with all our heart in our parents, our teachers, our leaders, our people and the righteousness and victory of our struggle." *Kujichagulia* stands for the principle of self-determination: "to define ourselves, name ourselves, and speak for ourselves, instead of being defined, and spoken for by others."[58] If one principle united the cultural politics of African American prisoners and activists outside prison walls it was *kujichagulia*. The goal of shaping cultural practices and community institutions free from white intervention became a hallmark of African American activism throughout the late 1960s and the 1970s. The period saw cultural nationalism influence the creation of academic fields like black studies, theological interpretation and church congregations, struggles for local control in schooling, museum exhibitions and theater performances, book publishing, and political campaigns. Self-determination had been a central touchstone of the Nation of Islam throughout the postwar period and in the Black Power movement since the mid-1960s. So when incarcerated African Americans increasingly looked to cultural nationalism as a model for relevant social and personal transformation, the principle of self-determination took on greater significance. It is telling that Imani Kujichagulia chose the principal as his surname.

Instead of the prostitute's objectification, commodification, and exploitation of her body, the poet offered her his faith and self-determination as an alternative value system based on spiritual and cultural nationalism. Other poets displayed more ambivalence about the role they could play in protecting black women. Etheridge Knight was perhaps the best-known poet to emerge from prison during this period. Knight became addicted to heroin while on active Army duty during the Korean War. After his discharge from the military in 1951, Knight moved to Indianapolis, where he turned to robbery to finance his habit. In 1960 Knight was sent to the Indiana State Prison on a robbery conviction. With a ten-to-twenty-five-year sentence in front of him, Knight took great pleasure in his expert ability to tell tall tales, and he began writing and sending poems to established writers and publishers. Knight's first published poem, an homage to the jazz vocalist Dinah Washington, was published in *Negro Digest* in 1965. This led to an enthusiastic embrace by luminaries of the Black Arts movement, including Gwendolyn Brooks, Dudley Randall, Sonia Sanchez, and Haki Madhubuti. Brooks drove from her Chicago home to visit Knight in prison and serve as a mentor. Randall's Broadside Press published Knight's first book, *Poems from Prison* (1968). Sanchez and Knight briefly married after his parole in November 1968.[59] Knight's style both embraced and transformed the spoken-word traditions through which he first came to poetry. They also demonstrate a complex relationship to his use of drugs and how that compromised his desire for revolutionary change. Knight explores the sexual exploitation of black women by white men in "The Violent Space (or when your sister sleeps around for money)": "O Mary don't you weep don't you moan / O Mary shake your butt to the violent juke / Absorb the demon puke and watch the white eyes pop."[60] While men defile his seventeen-year-old sister—cast in the role of the Virgin of the original spiritual on which the poem is based—the narrator can only watch and descend into drug addiction.

Like Neal and Baraka, Knight also believed that poetry should represent and transform Black communities, but here he reveals that he cannot protect his sister with a poem:

> I sit counting syllables like Midas gold.
> I am not bold. I can not yet take hold of the demon
> And lift his weight from your black belly,
> So I grab the air and sing my song.
> (But the air can not stand my singing long.)[61]

Perhaps because he has not conquered his own addiction or simply because "counting syllables" is too self-centered, Knight implies that his song can only provide temporary comfort, but not end his sister's exploitation. Who, Knight asks, is the real criminal? Is it the seventeen-year-old prostitute or the "demon" on top of her? Is it her incarcerated, drug-addicted brother or those who imprison him? Elsewhere, Knight showed that his crimes pale in comparison to the larger crimes that plague African American communities: "When a people set out, with a gun in one hand and a Bible in the other, to exploit and enslave and imprison all the other peoples of the world (and succeed), and then the exploited and enslaved are called the criminals—it is time to redefine terms. It is time to put the proper shoe on the proper foot."[62]

Prostitutes represented both the willingness of some African American men to exploit African American women and the impotency of others to protect them.[63] At the same time, many prison collections from the period paid homage to "Black Queens." These idealized figures represented the ongoing oppression of all Black people. At the same time, some writers could draw on literary traditions that used women as allegories for nations and freedom struggles. This could be used to describe a public figure, as in Michael Thomas Sr.'s "Poem to Angela":

> Tomorrows Black Queen who guerrilla Sisters today
> from yesterdays unidentified image.
> Spread the words of Revolution
> via pain & suffering
> us all b
> chanting.[64]

Here, the "Black Queen" is Angela Davis—an actual revolutionary who appears in the works of many prison writers during the Black Arts movement—but she bears characteristics of the more common usage of the "Black Queen" as an archetypal figure of black suffering.[65] Where the pimp stood in for the potential revolutionary inside all prisoners, the Black Queen was the suffering "voice of humanity" who could also be the harbinger of revolution.

In contrast to the actual Angela Davis, who drew attention to the masculinist discourse and practice of the revolutionary movements within which she played a key role, the literary Black Queen was usually placed on a pedestal far from the front lines.[66] This queen inspired Black men to lead and fight; but more than anything, she was a source of love that fueled, as Willi X wrote in California's Folsom Prison in 1975, "the soul of our people": "I write these lines for love, out of love, my love for your love. Love for your being, and love that reflects the soul of our people, love that saved our lives and kept our vision intact through four hundred years of long struggle, the love that gives us the will to survive with the hope that our love will carry us to the promised land."[67] Contained in a collection called *Captive Voices*, Willi X's work merges the struggle to survive his incarceration with the collective struggles of black men and women. In invoking "the promised land," he connects the modern struggle for liberation and power to the longer struggles against slavery, Jim Crow laws, and ongoing oppression. Black women, of course, were central to all of these struggles. The Black Queen, however, provided food for a hungry soul and an ideal for a lonely man.

If the connection between guns and penises provides one window into the relationship between masculinity and Black Power, then the trope of the "Black Queen" offers insight into the relationship between masculinity and Black nationalism through its elision of femininity and the "motherland." If pimps needed to be transformed into revolutionaries, women needed to become queens. Like many Black Arts movement writers in and out of prison, James Lang invokes the image of the Black Queen in the opening of "For My Ex-Wife" (1972): "To the most heavenly mother / In all of creation / The beautiful black queen / Of our glorious black nation."[68] Lang's nationalism had clear gender lines: women served as mothers of the black nation. It is unclear in this poem if the nation Lang hopes to possess will be patriarchal. In replacing the familiar Christian invocation of "the heavenly father" with a mother, Lang nods to the variety of kinship, religious, and national structures that would be possible in the "black nation." As little more than an object, however, the "Black Queen" becomes the personification of the "motherland" he hopes to inhabit.

As he indicates in his title, the symbolic queen of Lang's opening is also his ex-wife. Lang reminds his readers that his incarceration made it impossible for this couple to maintain their relationship: "Like a fool I have allowed myself / To be taken away from you, / And now all that we once had is gone— / Our dreams may never come true."[69] Lang understands that his incarceration is a product of his own actions and the larger social context. He was "taken away" by an oppressive system, but he also acted in some foolish way to allow this to take place. The central point of this poem is similar to Etheridge Knight's "The Violent Space": the helplessness felt behind bars. While images of the Black Queen appear throughout the writings of the Black Arts movement, incarcerated writers were clearly anguished that these Black Queens were left to fend for themselves while the men served their time.

At a time when leading policymakers explained that high African American poverty rates could be attributed to female-headed households and black nationalists emphasized the importance of restoring the central role of the "black man" in a patriarchal society, the perspectives of incarcerated artists stand out.[70] At first glance they offer little real counterpoint to the patriarchal assumptions of the society as a whole. Writers like James Lang make clear, however, that the absence of black men from African American communities resulted from a web of individual, kin, and structural conditions. Lang must answer for his own absence, but that absence also occurs within an unequal and racist society that continues to exploit his community.

The prison writings of Ricardo Sánchez and Raúl Salinas complemented the work of the Black Arts movement, playing key roles in shaping Chicano cultural nationalism while also exploring the possibility that creating the new nation would also involve rethinking gender roles. Literary analysis of Salinas's prison poems emphasized that "a Chicano *pinto* (convict) . . . can serve as a representative and spokesman against the repressive reality of America within and outside the prison walls."[71] Incarcerated in state and federal prisons between the late 1950s and early 1970s, Salinas founded two literary and political journals while incarcerated in Leavenworth Penitentiary in 1970 and 1971. *El Aztlan de Leavenworth* included works dedicated to George Jackson and evocations of Salinas's intensifying radicalization in the late 1960s and early 1970s.[72]

Ricardo Sánchez would emerge as the most widely published pinto poet. First incarcerated while in the Army in the late 1950s, Sánchez began writing at Soledad State Prison in the late 1950s and early 1960s. His early work appeared in mimeographed Bay Area beat magazines.[73] In an early poem, "Soledad Was a Girl's Name," Sánchez draws his readers' attention to the multiple meanings of "soledad": a California prison, "solitude," and a girl's given name. In the poem, Sánchez draws attention to the ironic connection between the name of an attractive high school classmate and his current prison:

this soledad
that I am leaving soon,
this callous nation
of bars and cement and barbarity,
it seems strange
that a name can call out to me
and mesmerize me,
yet repel me,
one a girl, now a woman,
and the other
a jagged prison world.[74]

Written in Soledad Prison in 1963, Sánchez's poem recalls the "sadness and longing" in the prison without offering a solution. The men in prison simply pretend to be tough, even as they crave connections with each other.

By the time he awaited release from a second prison term in 1969, however, Sánchez turned his attention to Chicano Power but realized that if he joined the movement it would once again make it impossible for him to connect with his son. Just as prison hindered building and sustaining family relationships in Lang's poems, participation in the movement would also create distance. Sánchez's poems from the late 1960s signal the shifting politics of art in prison. For example, where *pinto* meant simply "prison" in his poems from the early 1960s, by the late 1960s it had come to mean Chicano prisoners. The presence of a political and cultural movement gave Sánchez's poems a completely different feel:

whatever
we have to do
to make our freedom real,
i am ready,
and so are the other pintos.[75]

This poem, "Three Days to Go," speaks directly to the revolutionary movement, embracing its rhetoric of revolution while acknowledging the central role of the arts in cultural transformation. Like "Soledad

Was a Girl's Name," "Three Days to Go" reveals Sánchez's thoughts as he awaits an imminent release, but he now contemplates the political role of an artist. The poem names, for example, Lalo Delgado, whose poems became touchstones for Chicano activists from the 1960s onward. But Sánchez also seems wary of the movement he is poised to join:

> but if the movement is a game
> and hucksters are hustling
> all our people
> just to make themselves look big
> or get more money
> by pimping off the people,
> then i'm also ready
> to just go back to criming.[76]

Sánchez is committed and skeptical, ready to go and ready to retreat into familiar patterns at the first sign of hypocrisy. He concludes this transformative poem by noting another change: where "Soledad Was a Girl's Name" highlighted the hard exteriors and soft, hidden interiors of prison life, "Three Days to Go" signals that the revolutionary movement could also be understood as gendered. In it, he embraces the "raza chicana," requesting her trust and promising his own in return as precursors to building "a new nación."[77] Sánchez acknowledged the repair work necessary because of prior betrayals, lending intimacy and urgency to the nationalist project. The feminine gender of the collective—raza chicana—is further underscored in the embrace of two people previously separated by the prison walls. The pinto and the Chicano will leave the nation—the English term is used to describe the concrete and steel of Soledad Prison in the first poem—and together build the new nación.

If African American and Chicano prisoners emphasized the role they would play in the revolution using examples drawn from histories of shared struggle and intimacy, this did not necessarily also seek to eradicate patriarchy. In 1979 Michele Wallace argued that much of the Black Power movement "was nothing more nor less than the black man's struggle to attain his presumably lost 'manhood.'"[78] Obtaining "manhood," according Wallace, also meant constructing myths about emasculated men unable to take their rightful place as patriarchs in black families. Wallace implied that if successful, African American men would not extend the freedom they obtained to African American women. Her insight also helps explain why myths of resurrected pimps and Black Queens do not appear in the writings by incarcerated women. It should come as no surprise that incarcerated Chicanas and African American women envisioned other futures for themselves since, as Wallace wrote elsewhere, "a lot of women might be in prison because of something their man told them to do."[79] The writings by incarcerated African American women and Chicana writers do not, as a rule, seek the coronation of kings or soldiers as a desirable revolutionary alternative to white racism and economic exploitation.

Carolyn Baxter would eventually win some public attention for her 1979 collection of poems, *Prison Solitary and Other Free Government Services*.[80] Baxter's first poems appeared in print after she participated in the Art without Walls/Free Space writing program at the New York City Correctional Institution for Women, the Rikers Island facility now known as the Rose M. Singer Center that replaced the Women's House of Detention in the mid-1970s.[81] Baxter's "Toilet Bowl Congregation" strives for documentary authority by providing an address: "Holding cell in Criminal Courthouse, 100 Centre St." This portrait of two prostitutes arguing about "who's pimp will show / up with bail money first" demonstrates little faith in either the prostitutes or the men on whom they have pinned their hopes:

> "Fas'll be here first!"
> "Uhhahh! Smokey will."
> "Bitch, you trying to say my niggah ain't good as yours?"

The two devolve into a fight amid a swirl of fake eyelashes and micro miniskirts before being revealed as "blk, bloody, bald, a 90 lb knock-kneed deception of a cheap prostitute." The person observing the action seems to know that the pimps will not arrive. In a humane gesture, she tosses some toilet paper to help stanch the bleeding. The bleeding prostitute curses at her before they are joined together in chains: "Another slave's blood christened cement . . . Again!"[82] Baxter uses images of a church congregation, here the African American women in a holding cell waiting for a pimp. Instead of hoping that these men will arrive to save them, Baxter implies, the women might be better off supporting one another. Significant barriers remain, however, even as the women are chained together in a shared fate.

These barriers that divided African Americans were also the subject of the Black Panther Ericka Huggins's poems from her time in a Connecticut prison.[83] Huggins was the leader of the New Haven chapter of the Black Panther Party. She was arrested and imprisoned on charges related to the murder of a suspected informant. The trial attracted national attention and sparked a student strike at Yale University before her acquittal. It was in the context of the arrests in New Haven that J. Edgar Hoover famously said that the Black Panther Party is "without question, the greatest threat to the internal security of this country." Huggins's work was included in Angela Davis's collection—written and edited while Davis was incarcerated in the Marin County Jail—*If They Come in the Morning*.[84] Huggins's writing reflects her commitment to social change but also emphasizes a desire to bring down all the walls dividing African Americans:

> if only all barriers could be removed
> and we could walk/talk/sing
> be . . .
> free of all psychological, spiritual
> political, economic
> boundaries
> all of us all the freedom lovers of
> the world but especially
> right now—prisoners.[85]

She wanted all barriers removed, but she also knew that prisoners needed to get past the walls of steel and concrete before tackling the political and economic boundaries. In an attempt to begin overcoming the kinds of barriers both she and Baxter recognized, Huggins wrote to Angela Davis about creating a "Sisterlove Collective" to overcome divisions among African American women at Niantic State Farm, the Connecticut women's prison where she awaited trial.[86] Davis responded that this was a good idea but also noted more broadly that the male-oriented movement, like the society in which it took shape, incorrectly saw women's incarceration as less brutal than that of men. Davis called for "campaigns to uncover in their entirety the abominable conditions prevailing in women's institutions, from the inhuman circumstances of prison existence in general to the fascist techniques to which officials have recourse in attempting to create political neutrality and homogeneity."[87]

These efforts to divide women from one another are described at length by the sociologist Juanita Díaz-Cotto. Díaz-Cotto describes the patterns of abuse, racism, gang activity, drug use, and victimizing that preceded incarceration of the Chicana prisoners in her study: "Once the women were incarcerated, institutional personnel sought to make them conform to traditional heterosexual gender roles that demanded submission and docility on the part of women, particularly poor and working-class women."[88] Rather than conform to these expectations, the prisoners experimented with many different types of relationships with other women, including sexual relationships, fictive kinship networks, and parent/child relationships.[89] While these efforts did not end the subordination of women of color in prison or out, they fostered an alternative to both the male-dominated revolutionary movements and the patterns of inequality and exploitation in the society at large.

While emphasizing the injustice and the grinding monotony of life behind bars, the Chicana poet Judy Lucero seeks to connect her experience to broader struggles for social change. In Lucero's writings, however, the prison is a site of racist and patriarchal authority, one that must be resisted by fostering solidarity with women in new kinds of networks. While Lucero wrote out of similar political sensibilities of Chicano cultural nationalism and describes the new nación as feminine, this similarity leads to a significant contrast: where some men emphasized black queens or a raza chicana, Lucero juxtaposes her own body with the landscape. Her embrace of the new nación is that of a mother, not a lover or ruler. As B. V. Olguín argues, Lucero "omnisciently proposes her *historia* as the historia of La Raza, and vice versa." In "Ocho poemas de amor y desperación," published posthumously in

1976 in the Chicano cultural nationalist publication *De Colores*, Lucero accepted her place within the collective:

A mi RAZA aquí les cuento
Y los quero dejar saber
Como pobres seremos para siempre
Y sin nadie que los platique porqué.

[I tell my RACE here
And want to let them know
that we will always be poor
And without anyone's ever telling them why.][90]

In articulating a connection with her people and the systemic, ongoing poverty they face, Lucero's suffering and incarceration is made collective, pointing in the end to a change. If it looks in this early poem by Lucero that "pobres seremos para siempre," her last poem foresees that "todo esto algún día va cambiar" (all of this will change someday).[91] Lucero died in prison in 1973 of a brain hemorrhage. She was twenty-eight years old.[92]

Incarcerated women like Carolyn Baxter, Ericka Huggins, and Judy Lucero provide key insights into the multiple barriers of economic, gender, and racial oppression that they hoped to bring down. At the time, Angela Davis recognized that different forms of exploitation worked hand in hand: although freeing prisoners and abolishing prisons needed to be a central goal of social change, prisons also were an "inevitable byproduct of a male-oriented society."[93] African American and Latina women continue to make up the majority of incarcerated women, whose numbers are today growing faster than those of men. Collectively, men and women in the 1970s made clear that incarcerated people could be catalysts for change. Etheridge Knight hoped his poems—along with his efforts to bring the works of other incarcerated people before the larger public—would assist in the transformation of consciousness that would ultimately liberate black people from "the larger prison outside."[94] As the literary critic Patricia Liggins Hill notes, "Knight means for his prison experiences to serve as a microcosm of the freedomless void that his people are experiencing."[95]

As Hill shows, prison artists and writers played a number of roles in the Black Arts movement: first, key figures of the Black Arts movement either did time or worked closely with incarcerated artists and writers; second, the aesthetic sensibility and ideological convictions of prison artists and writers often drew on and closely resembled their more mobile contemporaries; third, real and folk prisoners proved popular as subjects of the Black Arts movement. Perhaps most powerfully, for writers inside and outside, African American convicts could accurately be called residents of "prisons within prisons." Many intellectuals and artists struggled to show the parallels between lives lived in poor African American communities and behind prison walls: limited control, consistent physical and ideological oppression, and the daily experience of racism. Incarcerated people also served as a key metaphor for "free" writers who hoped that art would aid in the transformation of black consciousness and conditions. In addition, incarcerated writers and artists participated in the movement by fostering connections with writers and artists outside, nurturing solidarity around resistance to oppression and racism, of which prisons were the ultimate manifestation. But the presence of prisoners in the Black Arts movement was ultimately more than symbolic: they revealed that prisons could be sites of transformation and that convicts would be key participants in the revolution that followed the shift in consciousness.

CHAPTER FIVE

CELL BLOCK THEATER

ENTERTAINMENT, LIBERATION, AND THE POLITICS OF PRISON THEATER

In the spring of 1979 the Center for the Advanced Study in Theatre Arts (CASTA) at the City University of New York's Graduate Center held a conference on theater in prison.[1] The event featured a spirited and divided debate about the goals of theater programs by the founders of many of the key programs then in existence, including the heads of the Theatre for the Forgotten, Cell Block Theatre, the Family, Geese Theatre Company, and the New York City Street Theatre Caravan. Stanley A. Waren, a professor at City College and the director of CASTA, summed up the varying and contradictory ways theater professionals and corrections officials thought about the value of theater programs: to entertain; to change the social and criminal justice systems by "politicizing prisoners, those who control the prisons, and the general public"; to "habilitate" inmates to the existing social system; "to develop personal skills, including language skills, voice, body and interpersonal sensitivity"; to "stretch the imagination of the inmate"; and to train inmates for careers in the theater industry.[2] This range of goals reflected the political, humanistic, and professional contexts for theater during the 1970s.

There was some question if these different values could be reconciled, and in the end, Waren did not succeed in finding common ground. With some saying their primary goal was to entertain and relieve the monotony of life behind bars and others arguing that "any attempt to ameliorate the prisoner's conditions through the arts only served to prolong the existing system," there seemed to be little basis for compromise.[3] These practitioners would soon have a clear voice in the form of the Brazilian director Augusto Boal's *Theatre of the Op-*

pressed, published in English that same year.[4] Boal argued that the theater can be an opportunity to imagine the world anew in that at its finest, drama demands active participation rather than passive viewing. Boal identified specific workshop and performance techniques to bring this about, and these techniques and views reflected some theater workshops' attempts to empower inmates with therapeutic role-playing.

The debate at the conference did little to definitively answer the question of whether prison theater programs, or arts and education programs more generally, provided avenues for entertainment, liberation, therapy, or vocational training. The debate itself, however, is instructive. Since 1967 prison theater programs had been at the forefront of the larger national discussion about the function of prisons themselves. In a period that began with Attorney General John Mitchell arguing in 1968 that the goal of the criminal justice system was "law enforcement, not social improvement," prison theater programs developed a broad range of strategies to survive. Some simply accepted the new view, arguing that prison theater could serve as a pacifying diversion in potentially violent facilities. Others resisted, using tried-and-true theater techniques like farce and improvisation to bypass prison censorship. For much of the decade, these programs did more than survive; prison dramatists linked people across the increasingly punitive divide, capturing the imaginations of the mass media and the general public in order to highlight their views and experiences.

As is true for so much of the cultural life of American prisons, California's San Quentin prison was seminal. In 1911 a professional theater company performed a play there called *Alias Jimmy Valentine*, detailing, according to the program notes, the fall and rise of an inmate at New York's Sing Sing.[5] Most histories of prison theater begin in 1957, when the San Francisco Actors Workshop staged a production of *Waiting for Godot* in San Quentin. Samuel Beckett's masterwork was a global phenomenon in the 1950s that came to mean many things to many people, but its themes of vacuous toil and futile hopes for a constantly postponed redemption surely had particular relevance to the prisoners. In any case, the production proved popular with the San Quentin inmates, leading one of them, Rick Cluchey, to found the San

Quentin Drama Workshop. Cluchey kept *Godot* in the repertoire for many years.

San Quentin generally received negative press during the early 1950s both because of a *San Francisco Chronicle* exposé of physical brutality in the prison's psychiatric department and the wildly popular books of death-row resident Caryl Chessman.[6] The arrival of Warden Fred Dickson in 1957 transformed San Quentin into a leading cultivator of a variety of arts programs. During Dickson's tenure, which ended in 1964, San Quentin was the site of jazz concerts, art exhibits, theater productions, and arts-and-crafts shows. According to Dickson, arts activities "help break down the walls and let the people outside know what kind of people we have in here. This is a community like any other community, except that the men are locked up."[7] Dickson believed that the arts were an important opportunity to create and maintain connections between San Quentin inmates and other Californians. Dickson also made it clear that cultural programming could coexist with more brutal practices. Dickson would also oversee the execution of Caryl Chessman and the construction of the San Quentin Adjustment Center, the maximum-security unit that would house George Jackson at the time of his death.

Early forays into prison productions of classic works by William Shakespeare, Samuel Beckett, and Luigi Pirandello would join with the emergent Street Theater movement of the 1960s to inspire a wide range of prison drama programs. An influential program called Cell Block Theatre ran in the New Jersey correctional system and at New York City's Rikers Island. More broadly, the term *cell block theater* can be used to describe a range of programs and productions, including the Theatre for the Forgotten (TFTF) and the New York Street Theatre Caravan, the Guthrie Theater Prison Program in Minnesota, Geese Theatre in Illinois and Iowa, the San Quentin Drama Workshop in California, and the Family in New York, among others.

Attesting to the cultural power of prisoners during the 1970s, prison drama drew attention to the grinding banality, racial and political injustice, and simmering frustration of incarceration. It did so in contradictory ways and with competing outcomes. Many of the productions were the descendents of the agitprop that flourished during the Workers' Theater movement era of the early twentieth century. Prison theater offered more utilitarian outcomes, with the workshops, rehearsals, and productions giving therapeutic experiences, job skills, and some employment for prisoners or people recently released from prison. In providing a structure for self-exploration and, for a very few, a rewarding career, theater opened up new possibilities for prisoners. Finally, prison theater provided audiences with voyeuristic titillation tinged with violence, complete with stereotypical shower scenes, stock characters, and confrontational scenarios. The saga of Miguel Piñero's *Short Eyes* is a useful starting point not only because it became the best known and most decorated of the prison dramas, but also because it enthusiastically helped define the functions of prison and the hopes of redemption for many people during the 1970s.

"Fasten your seatbelts and take the most dizzying ride of the season!" gushed the *Daily News*, capturing much of the excitement following the opening of *Short Eyes* at Lincoln Center's Vivian Beaumont Theater. After debuting at the Riverside Church, *Short Eyes* caught the attention of the Public Theater's Joseph Papp. After Papp brought *Short Eyes* to the Public Theater, the play moved on to Lincoln Center. Other reviews attempted to capture the emotional power of Piñero's story and Marvin Felix Camillo's production, with *Newsday* describing it as "theater with the impact of a punch in the mid-section."[8] The play featured scenes of sexual violence and ended with the dramatic cellblock murder of a white man accused of child molestation. While the themes of sexual violence surely contributed to the visceral response of viewers, the play defied easy political conclusions. Although Piñero did not publicly define himself as gay and was briefly married to a woman, he did have same-sex encounters throughout his life and lived with the painter Martin Wong. Plays such as *Short Eyes*, *The Guntower* (1976), and *Paper Toilet* (1979), display a deep ambivalence about same-sex relationships, frequently switching between violence and intimacy, uncritical homophobia and repudiations of contemporary morality. *Short Eyes* sends similarly mixed messages about racial conflict, both demonstrating the possibility of interracial communities behind bars and articulating racist sentiments.[9]

The play's content certainly played a role in the praise Piñero received, but the superlative used by one critic stands out: The *Record* remarked that "*Short Eyes* is the most penetrating and trenchant prison melodrama in several seasons." The comment reminds us of an extraordinary fact: in those years, *Short Eyes* was far from one of a kind. In fact, playwrights—like artists working in other media—explored the dramatic potential of prison dramas throughout the era. With its playwright only one year out of Sing Sing, *Short Eyes* played Lincoln Center and won the New York Drama Critics' Circle Award for the Best American Play as well as an Obie for its director, Marvin Felix Camillo. This play earned high praise for the moral and intimate struggles of its characters. It artfully transforms sexuality and violence—the stereotypical issues of the prison genre—into occasions to explore morality, reform, and catharsis. Over the course of the play, the residents of the cell block find opportunities for solidarity while the guards grow apart. Although divided over whether it was justified to kill a man suspected (wrongly, it turns out) of sexually assaulting a minor, the white, African American, and Puerto Rican prisoners nevertheless find common cause in their assumption that the prison guard investigating the murder merits no cooperation. This compelling drama does more than question assumptions about right and wrong; it provides an historical window into a time when aesthetics, politics, and institutions combined to create an explosion of theater workshops.

Drawing from the tradition of political theater, *Short Eyes* asked its audience to consider the relativism of morality, the public's complicity in the prison system, and the cathartic potential of the theater. Moreover, the production company, Marvin Felix Camillo's the Family, provided a support network, income, and a rehearsal method that enhanced prisoners' chance of success after their release. For the audience, *Short Eyes* depicted a hidden world not directly experienced by most Lincoln Center theatergoers. In doing so, it manipulated a series of clichés by highlighting a hidden world of violent retribution, prison homosexuality, and vacuous stereotypes of the radical politics of some incarcerated Americans. The play's public and critical reception often expressed a condescending amazement that prisoners could produce art of this quality. But this production of *Short Eyes* was not the singular emergence of a savant from the underworld. It marked the culmination of a generation of work by nonprofit groups, individual artists, and incarcerated people.

Piñero's family migrated from Gurabo, Puerto Rico, to New York City in 1950, when the future playwright was four. Piñero did not do well in school. In his teen years he frequently clashed with authorities, leading to his detention at Otisville State Training School for Boys, now an adult prison north of New York City. In 1964 Piñero turned eighteen, entered Rikers Island, and became addicted to heroin. He would remain a heroin user for much of his life, rotating in and out of prison, drug rehabilitation, and celebrity. In 1971 Piñero was sent to Sing Sing on an armed robbery charge. Piñero told one interviewer that he started writing *Short Eyes* "for the hell of it" during this stretch in Sing Sing.[10] As was often the case with Piñero, there was more to the story. In addition to being a playwright, Piñero was a talented poet who published several important collections and helped found the Nuyorican Poets Café in New York City. He is widely acknowledged as a founding father of the Nuyorican literary movement.[11] At Sing Sing, he joined a theater workshop run by Clay Stevenson and Marvin Felix Camillo. *Short Eyes* brought Piñero acting roles in television and film, first as Go-Go in the film version of *Short Eyes* (1977), then as a strip-club owner in the cult film *Times Square* (1980) and as a drug dealer in *Fort Apache, the Bronx* (1981). He would also become a sought-after script specialist for television shows, helping write "street dialect" for a long list of 1970s and 1980s police dramas, including the series *Kojak*, *Baretta*, and *Miami Vice*, as well as the TV movie *The Streets of L.A.* In 2001 the director Leon Ichaso—who had worked with Piñero on *Miami Vice*—released *Piñero*, a biopic distributed by Miramax.

Piñero achieved this success despite a lifelong heroin addiction. He was incarcerated in New York City's Tombs prison on convictions for heroin possession and grand larceny while Robert Young was filming scenes for the 1977 film version of *Short Eyes* on location elsewhere in the complex. He would appear as Go-Go in the film, but miss the opening while in prison yet another time. Throughout much of his life, Piñero continued to live in what he described as a "concrete tomb" created by "Rockefeller's ghettocide." At the same time, he celebrated the "fancy cars & pimps' bars & juke saloons & greasy spoons" that "make my spirits fly," requesting in a 1985 poem that his admirers and friends "take my ashes and scatter them thru out the Lower East Side."[12] Piñero died of cirrhosis of the liver in 1988 at age forty-one, most likely related to AIDS.[13]

The complicated and difficult circumstances of Piñero's meeting Marvin Felix Camillo while still incarcerated proved to be a turning point in Piñero's artistic career. Camillo, founder of the Family, was a professional actor throughout the 1960s. The Family grew out of Camillo's professional experiences, which included mainstream professional productions as well as Latino and African American community theater.[14] In addition to appearing in the Lincoln Center production of *South Pacific* in 1967, Camillo participated in such community theater groups as Teatro de la Calle and Theatre du Jour in Newark. Camillo's role in the national tour of *South Pacific* coincided with his participation in the Urban Arts Repertory in New York City. Sometimes known as street theater, these groups developed a style that owed much to the agitprop performances of the 1930s. Drawing on monologue, musical performance, interconnected yet distinct set pieces, political didacticism, and dance, community theater groups derived their dramatic power from their portrayal of people and experiences not often depicted onstage. After his initial release from Sing Sing, Piñero became director of the street theater program Third World Projects for the Theater of the Riverside Church. Street theater usually encouraged interaction between the audience and the performers, at times blurring the lines between the two with audience members invited to add their own stories to the performative mix. The lines between community theater and mainstream theater would be quickly blurred, as plays like Piñero's *Short Eyes* and Ntozake Shange's *For Colored Girls . . .* (1976) emerged in community theater and then "crossed over" to the mainstream stage. In addition, community theater groups routinely performed key works by contemporary luminaries like Bertolt Brecht, Samuel Beckett, and Amiri Baraka.

Its identifiable aesthetic was not the only thing that made street theater unique. While community theater groups paid close attention to the quality of their performances, they often explicitly and primarily identified themselves as seeking to tap in to the transformative power of their form. By asking their members to perform and transform their own experiences, community theater groups provided a rare opportunity for visibility and celebration for people with few avenues for access to a broad audience. As Stephen Hart notes, "The Family helps its members to see themselves as having innate worth, creative potential, specific skills and talents that can be developed, and a place in their social and cultural milieu."[15] In his rave review for the *New York Times*, Mel Gussow echoed this message: "If the team of Mr. Piñero and Mr. Camillo could be utilized in America's prisons, they would probably work wonders of rehabilitation. This production is significant not only as a theatrical event but also as an act of social redemption."[16] Gussow focused largely on the creative talent of Piñero—and continued to be a champion and friend of the playwright—but he also marveled that "only one actor in the cast is a member of Actors Equity. Half of the others have acted with 'The Family,' Mr. Camillo's company of former inmates and former addicts. Most members of the cast have served time in prison, which explains their authenticity, but not their talent for expression."[17]

Joseph Papp, who founded the Public Theater in 1967 as a forum for new work by emerging playwrights, was attracted to a work that seemed original and powerful, but he also recognized that its language and "unnerving honesty" could alienate typical white, economically privileged theater audiences. Nevertheless, Papp saw something in Piñero's play that would attract middle-class audiences to his production. "From François Villon to Jean Genet, Miguel belongs to a tradition of writers whose devious and renegade lives paradoxically result in the most painstaking devotion to the truth and rigor of their craft."[18] Papp believed that these "renegade" writers tapped into something commonly explored in drama: "All dramatists of real value must sooner or later confront what for them is truly dangerous, either within themselves of in the outside world." The social message of *Short Eyes* and the rehabilitative hopes of the Family would ultimately meet an enthusiastic response from theater audiences. Papp rightly noted Piñero's literary merit and unique talent, but the fact that his play emerged when it did speaks to a broader movement generating and promoting cell block theater.

Rather than the latest example of "devious and renegade lives" turning out works for public consumption, *Short Eyes* was the most visible and widely celebrated example of prison theater during the 1970s. Between the late 1960s and the early 1980s, theater professionals would rapidly become an important part of the cultural life of American prisons. From the early years of actors and producers with little training or experience working with inmates to the later emergence of full-fledged social agencies providing therapeutic and job-training services for correctional facilities, dramatic arts displayed something of the "do-it-yourself" spirit of reform-minded artists during the period.

In 1967 the New York production of *Fortune and Men's Eyes*, by the Canadian dramatist John Herbert, led to a broad-ranging discussion of life behind bars and to the founding of the Fortune Society, an advocacy and service organization run by and for formerly incarcerated people. Herbert spent six months in a Canadian prison during the late 1940s, but he did not write the play until the early 1960s. *Fortune and Men's Eyes* told the story of Smitty and the three men with whom he shared his cell, all young first-time inmates.[19] Smitty navigates the institution's contradictory homophobia and pattern of sexual exploitation. He does so by agreeing to have sex with Rocky, an older, more seasoned, and violent cellmate. By the end of the play, Smitty has risen in the prison's food chain and seeks sexual favors from Mona Lisa, in prison on a pre-Stonewall morality charge. The play alternates between sensationalism and Smitty's deeply felt need to accommodate himself to a degrading and exploitative reality. In 1967 the play was produced off-Broadway at New York's Actors' Playhouse. The actor Sal Mineo later revived the play in Los Angeles and New York. Due to its sharp criticism of the prison system and the treatment of gay people, productions of the play often included a discussion forum immediately following the performance.

These discussions soon eclipsed the play itself, as the producer David Rothenberg and cast members led speaking engagements throughout the city. Late that year, Rothenberg and several others founded the Fortune Society to coordinate these discussions. According to an early history of the organization, the mission of the society changed dramatically after several founders appeared on public television's *David Susskind Show* in 1968.[20] The morning after the broadcast, Rothenberg arrived at the organization's theater district office to be greeted by fifty former prisoners looking for jobs and housing. Realizing that conversations about social attitudes would not meet these needs, Rothenberg and his organization tried to meet some of the immediate concerns of released prisoners. Although people from New York's theater industry continued to work in some of the Fortune Society's programs, the organization's commitment to the arts became just one component of its services. Over the years, the Fortune Society has grown substantially to include a range of programs impacting the lives of formerly incarcerated people.[21]

The year 1967 also saw the founding of Theatre for the Forgotten by Akila Couloumbis and Beverly Rich. TFTF began by staging professional plays in New York City's prisons. Like Rothenberg, Couloumbis came to understand that "people in jail need a hell of a lot more than just a theater performance or a workshop. It has taken years to bend them into the shape that we've got them into. It'll take an equal number of years—with care, understanding, patience—to get them straight. Therefore, I take no credit for rehabilitating anyone. Entertaining a few folks, yes."[22] Humility aside, within ten years of its founding, TFTF had given more than two thousand performances to nine hundred thousand people in thirty-two prisons and drug treatment facilities throughout the Northeast.[23]

Couloumbis's comment is further belied by the fact that TFTF developed a series of theater workshops for young people in juvenile facilities and adults in prison. Among the longest-standing programs was at the Spofford Juvenile Center in the Bronx. In addition to pretrial juveniles accused of a range of crimes, 20 percent of Spofford's residents were not charged with any crime. These "persons in need of supervision" (or PINS) received their classification because of truancy, running away from home, or conflict with authority. TFTF developed a program at Spofford and at the Lt. Joseph P. Kennedy Jr. Home, another juvenile facility in the Bronx housing "PINS." It focused on teaching acting technique, physical and imaginative exercises, and problem solving through improvisation. The workshops also led to the staging of original works written by program participants, including *King Kong in Harlem* (1975). The Family and other theater companies used many of these same techniques. TFTF would take workshop participants to plays like Ntozake Shange's *For Colored Girls . . .* and productions by like-minded organizations such as the New York City Street Theatre Caravan.[24]

A typical workshop would include relaxing and stretching exercises, building group trust by "flying" (jumping off the stage into the arms of the other participants), and sensory techniques like blocking one sense (such as sight) and trying to navigate an obstacle course. Although TFTF maintained an ambitious touring schedule and experimented with staging concerts behind bars, these workshops became a significant feature of its efforts. In part, this reflected TFTF's reliance on funding earmarked for criminal justice initiatives. By 1978 all but eight thousand dollars of its sixty-five-thousand-dollar budget came from the New York State Division of Criminal Justice Services. The agency's Criminal Justice Coordinating Council received funding from the federal government's Law Enforcement Assistance Administration. The rest of TFTF's money came from other government agencies and private foundations.[25] By placing its arts activities in the context of a therapeutic and rehabilitative workshop, TFTF could both provide those services to people who needed them and couch its activities in ways that reflected the concerns of the criminal justice professionals who funded it.

Over time, TFTF began providing other services to incarcerated people. In 1978 TFTF began a job-training program. Although Piñero was able to make a living writing and acting, and Chuck Bergansky, an ex-inmate who had gotten his start in acting with TFTF and the Family in the early 1970s, went on to play a variety of television roles in such signature TV programs as the *Mary Tyler Moore Show* and *Kojak*, theater workshops could not make a credible job-training argument to potential funders. TFTF's job-training program included some activities from the drama workshops, but it overwhelmingly focused on skills like clerk typing, bookkeeping, and building maintenance.[26]

The efforts of the Family, the Fortune Society, and the Theatre for the Forgotten provided important outlets for inmate creativity, but they also reflected the range of sometimes conflicting goals that underlie prison theater programs. Collectively, however, their understanding of the practical concerns of workshop participants after their release from prison, as well as the programs' search for funding within broader criminal justice bureaucracies, led them to stretch their goals for the arts to include providing job training, housing, and other social services. Despite this broad range of pressures and goals, theater programs helped inmates build self-confidence, explore emotionally complex issues, and express themselves creatively. One inmate who participated in a TFTF workshop at New York City's Women's Correctional Institute described it as an important release from the stresses of daily life behind bars: "You build up all these tensions but when you finally get on the stage, they're gone. I was completely relaxed by it. It gave me confidence and brought me outside of myself."[27] Other inmates said that the collaborative context of theater training both allowed them to explore personal creativity and served as a "viable means of creating community discourse."[28]

Correctional authorities understood the theater programs as providing a means of "creative, positive recreation."[29] One official of the New York State prison system believed that "good programs are our best security" and that "arts programs have played a significant role."[30] As a key creative recreational activity, theater workshops captured the interest of many incarcerated participants while providing an important service to the institutions. While many of TFTF's programs seem to contradict Couloumbis's modest claim that he could not take credit for any rehabilitation, he elsewhere suggested that his goal was "pure entertainment" and "therapy" rather than ideological or political critique.[31] Partially for this reason, TFTF rarely ran afoul of prison administrators, who echoed many of Couloumbis's goals for the program when interviewed by an outside evaluator in 1972 and 1973. The evaluator noted that virtually all prison administrators enthusiastically endorsed TFTF on the grounds that it "had a very beneficial effect on the inmate's sense of self-worth, his inter-personal relations with other inmates and COs and that it provided an opportunity for the release of tension and pressure that accumulates during the monotony and routine of incarceration."[32]

Although TFTF received overwhelmingly positive responses from prison administrators, the organization still found it impossible to avoid engaging politically charged subjects that ran afoul of some correctional administrators. In some cases, TFTF produced socially relevant works that explored themes like race relations and the history of radical politics. Although TFTF preferred comedy, it did not avoid politically charged farce or satire. For example, TFTF produced *A Day of Absence* in 1972. The play featured a reverse minstrel—a black inmate in whiteface—in the role of a southern mayor. When the mayor discovers that all the African American residents have left town, he turns to the largely African American and Latino inmate audience and offers fellatio and other favors if they return to the South. This Douglass Turner Ward play had been first produced in 1965, giving rise on some college campuses to an annual Black Solidarity Day, during which some African American students and other students of color boycott classes to highlight the misunderstood and unsung role African American laborers have played in U.S. society. It went on to inspire the Million Man March/Day of Absence in 1995.[33]

In other cases, the workshop process itself resulted in politically engaged works, including some that critiqued the radical politics and cultural nationalism of the period. Many of the workshops culminated in a variety show featuring professional actors and actresses performing works written by incarcerated workshop participants. In some cases, these shows would tour to other prisons. "Survival" was a choreopoem set to music during a TFTF variety show in 1975. Written by an anonymous poet at the Women's House of Detention, "Survival" initially seems to endorse the cultural politics of the Black Power movement: "Now that the look is Afros, dashikis, and African rings. And people not knowing why we wear all these things. Clench your fist then raise it high while you give your observer a black power cry. Teach me how to survive."[34] By the end of the performance, it is less clear if the singer endorses the views of the movement or remains puzzled as to how all of this will meet her more tangible needs: "I'll learn your Lumumba, Malcolm, and Brown," she says. "I'll even learn how machine guns and dynamite sound. Teach me how to survive." The protagonist seems divided about the meaning of cultural nationalism, never fully accepting the movement as her own. She will be a good soldier, but the chorus, "Teach me how to survive," may have left the enthusiastic audience of four hundred women wondering if Black Power contained these lessons.

It was always a difficult balancing act, remaining relevant to the inmate participants in the workshops without losing the necessary support of correctional authorities. TFTF maintained this balance in more than a decade of programs at a wide range of prisons, but it did run into some problems with content and staffing. The warden at Rikers Island, for example, placed considerable pressure to get advanced clearance of all plays presented by TFTF and believed that it was a violation of common sense to "present plays that deal only with racial themes or encourage or permitting the same in workshop productions." He believed that the plays should be "sheer entertainment rather than vehicles for social or political commentary."[35]

If some plays sent mixed political messages or embedded them in satire, TFTF could not ensure that its teaching faculty would not upset this balance. The TFTF instructor who ran the programs at both the Queens and Bronx Houses of Detention for Men seemed to foster the greatest criticism. The wardens at both facilities exhibited a great deal of unhappiness with the program, despite the fact that the outside evaluator described the instructor at those facilities as "by far the most skilled, effective, and committed" of TFTF instructors. The intensity of her commitment to the workshop participants led her to clash with the prison authorities: "Her attitudes toward the inmates—their social plights, their needs, both educational and spiritual—and toward prison functionaries, are unabashedly political." Her attitude also led her to choose, and allow the inmates to choose, workshop exercises and content that demonstrated a "cutting edge."[36]

Despite the concerns of correctional officers and prison administrators, there is no evidence that the portrayal of "racial themes" and instructor sympathy with inmates exacerbated the tense and sometimes violent prison environment. Wardens even presented evidence contradicting their view that discussing and performing "racial themes" promoted racial conflict: program participants lowered their infraction rate despite—or perhaps because of—these opportunities to express their views of race relations and the criminal justice system. Prison authorities sometimes resented the political and social ideologies of prison theater programs, but they also came to rely on them to alleviate problems in their institutions. In fact, the therapeutic model used by some prison theater workshops attracted correctional authorities who lacked other programs to deal with inmates in need of psychological counseling or with more serious psychological problems. According to its frustrated director, the arts program at New York's Bedford Hills Correctional Facility for Women became a "dumping ground for inmates who don't fit into the regular curriculum, as a form of therapy."[37]

The entertainment-driven TFTF found it difficult to avoid clashes over content or techniques, but other prison programs drew their strength from the critical stance they took toward social inequality in general and the criminal justice system in particular. New Jersey's Cell Block Theatre, New York's Street Theatre, and the Boston-based Elma Lewis Technical Theater Training Program at Massachusetts Correctional Institution in Norfolk articulated a sharper edge then TFTF.[38] Ramon Gordon, a former actor who founded Cell Block Theatre in 1972, directly confronted the entertainment-based model of TFTF, asking Akila Couloumbis in 1979, "What good is entertainment? You cannot have criminal justice until you have social justice."[39] This echoed Augusto Boal's belief that "all theater is necessarily political."[40] While Boal acknowledged that much contemporary theater avoided engaging political questions, he noted that the very desire to entertain was a disguised attempt to distract oppressed people from the task of their own liberation, precisely what some prison administrators said they feared. "Theater," Boal wrote, "is a weapon. A very efficient weapon. For this reason one must fight for it. For this reason the ruling classes strive to take permanent hold of the theater and utilize it as a tool for domination. In so doing, they change the very concept of what 'theater' is. But the theater can also be a weapon for liberation."[41] Boal developed specific techniques and structures to facilitate empowerment. If popular theater told viewers what to think and not to think, what he came to call "theatre of the oppressed" engaged people to be not spectators but instrumental parts of the process of narrating and performing the story. This "liberation of the spectator" would be less a performance than a "rehearsal of revolution."[42] Over time, Boal would adapt techniques from the longer history of radical theater like having participants make and perform a theatrical scene based on a recent piece of news. Boal hoped that this process would help demystify the ideological grounding hidden in the stance of objectivity while simultaneously generating a catharsis in theater that could be echoed when oppressed people took the means of production in the larger society.[43]

This is not to say that Gordon was engaging inmates in explicitly political dialog in order to generate a Marxist revolution. Rather, his program rested on a broader view that prisons could not meet the immediate or long-term psychological or vocational needs of inmates or the communities into which they would be released. The real work of prison theater occurred not in public performance but in the workshops themselves. It was in the techniques that engaged incarcerated people as agents of change—primarily of themselves and their consciousness—that long-term social change could be possible. Cell Block Theatre implied that prisons were the result of a variety of social forces and problems that brought individuals and groups into conflict with the criminal justice system. In many cases, these problems continued and deepened during incarceration. Prison administrators and correctional officers responded to repeated infractions with a combination of psychotherapy (which many inmates rejected) and repression (which tended to intensify opportunities for conflict and further punishment).

Theater programs disagreed on what to do differently from the existing prison-based responses, but couched their programs in terms that called into question some of the basic assumptions of existing prisons. While Cell Block Theatre provided what it called "Crucial Bridge-Gap Therapy" to inmates and people recently released from prison, the Elma Lewis program affirmed the already highly developed work of African American artists and intellectuals at Norfolk in the traditions of the Black Arts movement.

Cell Block Theatre, especially in its use of Crucial Bridge-Gap Therapy, provides the clearest application of Boal's theories to the prison setting. With support from the U.S. Department of Labor and the National Endowment for the Arts, Cell Block Theatre paid inmates at two New Jersey medium-security correctional institutions to attend therapy sessions that included improvisation training and writing workshops. These sessions would result in the production of an original play. Following essentially the same model used by the Family and TFTF, Cell Block Theatre also included the informal discussions between audience and performers that had been a key element of *Fortune and Men's Eyes*. Unlike the Family and TFTF, however, Cell Block Theatre did not employ professional actors performing for inmates.[44] Gordon, the group's founder, was not surprised that his workshops and performances were the participants' first experience with theater. In listening closely to workshop participants, however, he was struck by how many commented that this was the first time they had "fun in a straight way, and the first time they had been treated like human beings."[45] It was not simply that incarcerated people chose a life of crime; Gordon's work with inmates led him to believe that they could not even imagine other possibilities for themselves.

In response, Gordon developed a therapeutic model specifically tailored to the theater and to the problems incarcerated people faced prior to and during incarceration. Gordon learned from the director of psychiatry at New York's Roosevelt Hospital that the typical clients for psychoanalysis were "YAVIS": young, attractive, verbal, intelligent, and successful. They typically sought psychoanalysis for help with sexual problems, personal relationships, or career advancement. While these were surely issues for people in prison as much as they were for "YAVIS" people, Gordon recognized that models of therapy would need adaptation to meet the needs of prisoners. Gordon revised improvisational theater training techniques to teach new models for conflict resolution and release of stress. In one exercise, a Cell Block Theatre instructor created a conflict and asked the participants to enact a process leading to resolution without walking away, resorting to violence, or calling the police.[46] In this way, Gordon hoped that prisoners would come to experience new modes of resolving problems less likely to lead to conflicts with other prisoners, correctional officers, or the criminal justice system.

Gordon and the psychiatric advisor of Cell Block Theatre also believed that "prisoners have an inordinate need for immediate gratification."[47] In response, Cell Block Theatre instructors intentionally frustrated workshop participants by asking them to repeat the same exercise or scene multiple times, requesting subtle changes with each performance. Their goal was to help workshop participants to learn to listen and watch closely for small changes, thus coming to appreciate that rewards follow effort. Gordon claimed that this exercise enabled prisoners to see and value their own improvement and helped them psychologically adjust to the endless repetition characteristic of many jobs they might have after their release.[48]

While sharply critical of the criminal justice system, Gordon also believed that his program provided incarcerated people with the techniques they need to "play the game of the middle class power structure."[49] In contrast, the Elma Lewis Technical Theater Training Program provided an institutional structure within the prison for African American inmates to connect with the cultural nationalism then prominent among African American artists and dramatists outside prison. The theater training program was an offshoot of the Elma Lewis School of Fine Arts, founded in 1950 to provide a range of cultural programs to Boston's Roxbury and Dorchester communities. By the 1970s Elma Lewis was virtually without parallel in her ability to build arts and cultural institutions in Boston's poor African American communities. Her efforts were recognized by the MacArthur Foundation, which included her among its first class of "genius" fellows in 1981. She also received a medal from the President's Committee on the Arts (later renamed the National Medal of the Arts) in 1983.

In 1968 Lewis founded the National Center for African American Artists. While it ultimately outlasted the Elma Lewis School, the National Center was originally part of it. The school provided training in music, dance, and theater to young people in the community and in 1970 founded a program teaching all aspects of theater production at the Norfolk prison. The Norfolk program, like the Elma Lewis School more generally, articulated an ethic of pride, self-determination, and empowerment. Lewis saw that the program, in addition to mirroring her programs for the wider community, could play a unique role in the lives of incarcerated African Americans by giving them an opportunity to express pain, suffering, or guilt while committing themselves to positions of leadership and change.

A remarkable series of plays emerged from the Norfolk program soon after its founding. One play, *Justice or Just Us, Part 1* by the incarcerated writer Hugh M. Johnson, offered a dramatic analysis of the cumulative effect of bias in the criminal justice system. While many legal scholars and policy analysts made clear that racial bias existed in the criminal justice system during the 1970s, it was only in the 1990s that outside observers of criminal justice came to fully acknowledge what Johnson described in 1972. At each point of contact with the criminal justice system—creation of laws, police policy and practices, prosecution, sentencing, and parole—racial disparities compound creating a significant overrepresentation of African Americans in the criminal justice system.[50]

Set in a court's holding area and courtroom, *Justice or Just Us, Part 1* features a five-year veteran of the Vietnam War, (also named Hugh M. "Scooter" Johnson) who is awaiting trial on drug charges. Unable to afford a lawyer, Scooter must rely on the services of a public defender. In the holding area, Scooter and two drug addicts discuss their experiences with police harassment and looking for work. The men tell how, after arresting them, the police continually inquire if they are members of the Black Panthers and beat them when they are unsatisfied with the answer. A bail bondsmen arrives with what Johnson describes as an "Amerikkkan flag" on his lapel, symbolizing the history of racial exploitation and violence that underlies the financial wealth of the nation. Like the police before him, the bail bondsmen asks, "Say kid, you aren't one of those Communist Black Panthers, are you?" If the slave trader Simon Legree of Harriet Beecher Stowe's *Uncle Tom's Cabin* stood in for the commodification of African Americans during slavery, Johnson's bail bondsman plays that role in *Justice or Just Us, Part 1*. Worse, when Johnson answers, "It's none of your motherfuckin business what I am," the bondsman condescendingly advises Scooter, "That's the trouble with your kind today, never appreciate what decent people try to do for you."[51]

Continually asked to "play along" with a transparently unfair process, Scooter explodes at the public defender who has never met him before the moment of his probable cause hearing: "How in the hell can you insure me adequate representation in this fascist courtroom?" The judge is more concerned with superficial respect for the proceedings then with a fair and complete trial. When he predictably finds probable cause, setting bail at twenty-five thousand dollars, the judge repeats and amplifies the sentiment of the bail bondsman, "That's the problem with your kind today, always complaining in one form or another. One must be willing to work for what one gets." Scooter lectures back, "You know something, Judge, you are a miserable living example of what Fanon refers to as psychopathological fratricide." In the final rebuke of what Johnson refers to as "Massa's Golden Rule," the play ends with a comment from the courtroom's janitor, "Few more years, I can retire. This job sure can get tiresome. Course, I reckon the judges really have a hard time with them damn Communist militants and all."[52]

Johnson's play communicates a number of key messages: the criminal justice system offers leniency to those who do not demand fairness while harshly punishing those who point out the system's contradictions. In this context, intelligence and critical consciousness become handicaps to success. Furthermore, the system simultaneously promises and betrays impartial deliberation. At each contact point with the criminal justice system, Scooter's chances for a fair hearing seem to dwindle. His incarceration is a foregone conclusion. The janitor shows us the ultimate reward for playing along: pushing a broom in the courthouse.

Johnson's ideas and approach would be echoed in other writing workshops. For example, the active Creative Writers' Workshop at California's Folsom Prison focused on poetry and fiction, but the poet Gordon Kirkwood-Yates composed one dramatic poem that reflects the flip side of the story Johnson tells. Unlike Johnson's Scooter, Kirkwood-Yates's protagonist seems to hope for a better outcome. *An Accurate Account of My First Arrest: A Comedy in IV Acts* describes the arrest and trial that follows an assault on the protagonist by four FBI agents and two beatings by arresting officers.[53] Unlike Scooter, this drama's protagonist is white and able to afford a private defender described as "the best in Texas." Nevertheless, when he tries to explain that he was trying to stop the agents from killing him, he is repeatedly told that "we'll take care of it" and "don't worry about it" before receiving six years in Leavenworth. Both Johnson and Kirkwood-Yates emphasize that people accused of crimes are asked to conform to the demands of the criminal justice system while the system seems to make no accommodation to its own avowed principals of deliberation and fairness. These writers confirm Malcolm X's 1964 view that "what is logical to the oppressor isn't logical to the oppressed. And what is reason to the oppressor isn't reason to the oppressed."[54] When police officers, bail bondsmen, attorneys, and judges request that they "play by the rules," the characters in these plays ultimately describe a very different reality. They are not simply being unreasonable or ungrateful, they are refusing to accept the reasonableness of the request.

On these stages, the whole process of criminal justice seems more like a self-justifying parody rather than the mandated providing of fair-minded, impartial trials. These plays clearly did not have entertainment or alleviating stress as their central goals. They were not therapeutic or even liberatory in the ways that Boal and similar practitioners expected. They did reveal that some prison theater programs provided space and guidance for inmates to articulate their experience that the criminal justice system lacks the integrity to abide by its own provisions.

Prison drama played several unique roles in the cultural life of American prisons. It provided a diversion, a forum for therapy, opportunities for social and political critique, and even job skills. If these outcomes occasionally led to sharp disagreement among theater professionals working in prisons, they largely went unseen by the general public. There were some opportunities for free theater audiences to see cell block theater, as in the cases of *Fortune and Men's Eyes* and *Short Eyes*, but the more visible and popular dramas bore little resemblance to the prison workshops. One popular effort poked fun at how criminal justice had been politicized during the decade and thus undermined many of the efforts taking place on prison stages. Perhaps seeking to capitalize on the recent popularity of *Short Eyes*, the ABC television network featured the story of another Latino inmate, the fictional Héctor Emilio Fuentes, in *On the Rocks*, a situation comedy that aired in 1975 and 1976. *On the Rocks* treads some of the same terrain as prison drams, featuring storylines that explore the political and cultural world of prisoners. The episodes ultimately see inmate efforts to be heard through the arts as little more than a confidence game. For example, when asked by another inmate what he is in for, Fuentes responds with political indignation, "I'm only here due to a tragic circumstance. . . . I got caught."[55] But the show also featured some satire of official morality reminiscent of the work of Piñero or Kirkwood-Yates. Fuentes tells a self-pitying inmate on his cell block "there are worse places to be. Look at the state of this once great nation of ours: energy crisis, economy crisis, unemployment, pollution. It could be worse. We could be free." In an ironic twist, after the show was cancelled, José Pérez, who played Fuentes, went on to play Juan, the lead, in the film version of *Short Eyes*.

Within the admittedly limited range of a half-hour comedy, the show ultimately rejected the view that inmates are themselves victims. While Scooter quoted Fanon on the stage at Norfolk prison, *On the Rocks* laughed at the notion that the criminal justice system was the brutal front line of a racist society. Sullivan, a white liberal prison guard, continually cleans up after the prisoners and serves as an accommodating target of prisoner con games, much like the character of Sergeant Schultz in another unlikely sitcom, the late 1960s *Hogan's Heroes*, set in a Nazi prisoner-of-war camp. But *On the Rocks* also featured a second guard, the hard-nosed Gibson, an African American officer who sees Sullivan as naive and makes few concessions to the prisoners. Sullivan is clearly out of his league and an easy mark, while Gibson sees the inmates for who they really are. *On the Rocks* provided a few laughs but little in the way of new insight into the criminal justice system; nevertheless, its view that white liberals were no match for more crafty inmates would ultimately help publishers and prison authorities justify their broad retreat from mentoring and distributing work produced by incarcerated people.

CHAPTER SIX

RADICAL CHIC

JACK HENRY ABBOTT AND THE DECLINE OF PRISON PROGRAMMING

On a Wednesday evening in 1970, ninety New Yorkers gathered in a Park Avenue apartment for an event that would presage the decline of prisoners' cultural influence. George Jackson had not yet been killed or the Attica rioters massacred; Angela Davis had not yet been put on trial or Miguel Piñero's play staged at Lincoln Center. Already, however, concerns that twenty-one members of the New York chapter of the Black Panther Party might face violations of their civil liberties in their upcoming trials led Felicia Bernstein to organize a fundraiser for their legal defense. Unable to make bail on conspiracy charges stemming from an alleged plot to dynamite department stores, police precincts, railroad stations, and the New York Botanical Garden, thirteen members of the Black Panther Party had remained in jail since their arrest the previous April.[1] According to a society reporter for the *New York Times*, the event at the home of Felicia and Leonard Bernstein, the recently retired director of the New York Philharmonic, raised nearly ten thousand dollars.[2]

Two days later, Daniel Patrick Moynihan submitted his now infamous memorandum to President Richard Nixon suggesting that "the time may have come when the issue of race could benefit from a period of 'benign neglect.'"[3] As proof that the administration should not engage radical activist rhetoric, Moynihan drew Nixon's attention to the *New York Times* story. Moynihan wrote, "The Panthers were apparently almost defunct until the Chicago police raided one of their headquarters and transformed them into culture heroes for the white—and black—middle class. You perhaps did not note on the society page of yesterday's Times that Mrs. Leonard Bernstein gave a cocktail party on

Wednesday to raise money for the Panthers. Mrs. W. Vincent Astor was among the guests."[4] In the margin of the memorandum, Nixon criticized the Bernsteins as the "personification of the American 'upper class' intellectual elite."[5]

Wealthy liberals of all racial backgrounds, including celebrities, had long been a key source of funding and publicity for social movements. Indeed, the House Committee on Un-American Activities made great hay of the remaining Hollywood veterans of the Communist Party in the late 1940s. In 1963 Martin Luther King Jr. left the front lines of his nonviolent army in Birmingham to fundraise in New York City, and in 1972 Jane Fonda took a turn as "Hanoi Jane." Economic and rhetorical support of the Panthers by white liberals and civil rights establishment figures like Roy Wilkins and Bayard Rustin intensified with Nixon's election and his appointment of John Mitchell as attorney general. In December 1969, as Moynihan indicated, the Illinois State Police, with help from the Chicago Police Department and the FBI, killed two members of the Chicago chapter of the Black Panthers, including Fred Hampton, its charismatic young leader. When a commission found that police claims of a "gun battle" were false, liberal attorneys, educators, and students began to look more closely at the killings of nearly thirty additional Panthers by the police since 1967 as well as at judicial and prosecutorial conduct in Panther trials. The chaplain of Yale University, William Sloan Coffin, helped inspire half of the student body to go on strike in support of fourteen New Haven Panthers on trial for murder. Kingman Brewster, Yale's president, then authorized the university to fund monitors to measure the trial's fairness.[6]

In an article that shone a glaringly uncomfortable light on the often unquestioned racism of white liberals while making no apologies for his own self-conscious bigotry, Tom Wolfe famously chronicled the Bernsteins' fundraiser in a special issue of *New York* magazine nearly fully devoted to the topic. At times uproarious in his pillaging of wealthy white liberals, Wolfe constructed elaborate fantasies of some of the wealthiest people in the world lamenting over the racial politics of servants or wondering, "What does one wear to these parties for the Panthers or the Young Lords or the grape workers?"[7] He went on to compare the fundraiser to a recent *Vogue* magazine column teaching

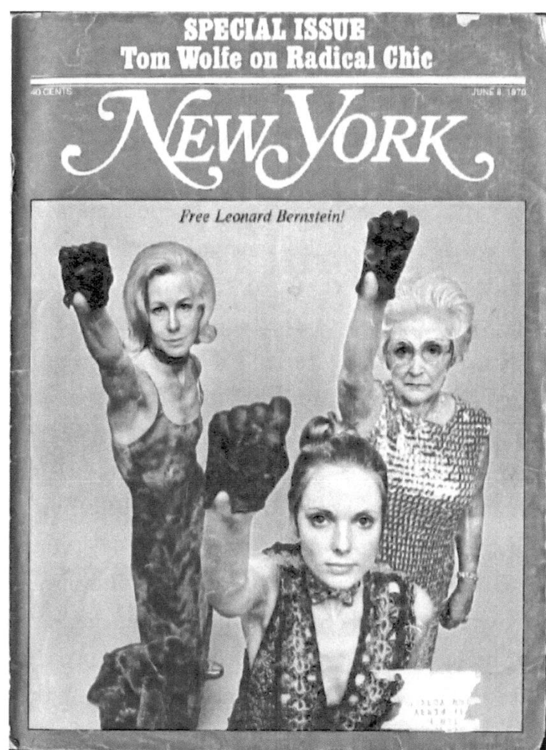

Writing for New York *magazine, Tom Wolfe coined the phrase "radical chic" to describe a fundraiser for the Black Panther Party at the Manhattan apartment of the conductor and composer Leonard Bernstein. Courtesy of* New York *magazine.*

its fashionable readers a new recipe for "Sweet Potato Pone," implying, perhaps, that the white liberal elite had come to consume African American culture in ways that resembled white hipsters' interest in jazz during the 1950s.[8]

More specifically, Wolfe believed that the new rich—particularly if, like Bernstein, they were Jewish—harbored a nostalgia for the poverty of their fathers and mothers and used the Panthers to assuage a deep-seeded anxiety about their recent wealth while simultaneously claiming a mantle of noblesse oblige. Although these caricatures of upper-class angst provided effective, if easy, punch lines, Wolfe also argued that the Black Panthers preyed on the sexual titillation of wealthy whites in raising money at the Bernsteins. "Shootouts, revolutions, pictures in *Life* magazine of policemen grabbing Black Panthers like they were Viet Cong—somehow it all runs together in the head with the whole thing of how *beautiful* they are. *Sharp as a blade*. The Panther women—there are three or four of them on hand, wives of the Panther 21 defendants, and they are so lean, so *lithe*, as they say, with tight pants and Yoruba-style headdresses, almost like turbans, as if they'd stepped out of the pages of Vogue."[9]

Comedians of the 1950s and 1960s similarly lampooned white wealthy supporters of civil rights as hopelessly naive and self-involved, but there is little doubt that Wolfe captured some of the sexually inflected longing, objectification, and resentment endemic in the multiracial, cross-class struggles of the period.[10] These have been insightfully described and analyzed in works like Ann Moody's *Coming of Age in Mississippi* (1968) and Alice Walker's *Meridian* (1976). The cultural theorist Robert Reid-Pharr argues that Black Panther Party Chairman Huey P. Newton used seduction in his own political organizing and that the Party "actively promoted the fact of its' leaders' physical beauty, not to mention the physical beauty of all black persons."[11] Wolfe was not wrong to note the sexual energy in the Bernsteins' apartment, but he seemed to see its presence as evidence that the white liberals were victims of a con. In the months and years that followed, Bernstein became a stock character in conservative efforts to discredit liberalism.[12] J. Edgar Hoover approved a COINTELPRO—the FBI's secret Counterintelligence Operation—effort against the conductor that included sending forged letters describing Black Panther anti-Semitism to the attendees of the Bernstein fundraiser (signed "A Concerned and Loyal Jew") and a failed attempt to place stories in Hollywood trade papers alleging that Bernstein had a "fondness for young boys."[13] These efforts reached an almost comic level when the board of the Kennedy Center for the Performing Arts—led by Jacqueline Kennedy—commissioned Bernstein to compose a piece for the center's opening in 1971. According to Alex Ross, music critic for the *New Yorker*, Nixon chose not to attend after J. Edgar Hoover warned the president that Bernstein could use the occasion to "embarrass the United States government" by coercing him to clap at a performance with an antiwar theme. The piece in question was the Latin Mass.[14]

In 1970 and 1971 Tom Wolfe satirized liberal interest in radical politics, the FBI generated letter-writing campaigns and picketing, and the president stayed away from the opening of the Kennedy Center for the Performing Arts. But these efforts would not eliminate an otherwise strong and growing movement to rethink the relationship between racism, economic inequality, and the American criminal justice system. In fact, in the weeks after the Bernstein fundraiser and the negative publicity that followed, attendees quickly defended their actions as necessary to protect the civil liberties of all Americans rather than as support for the Panthers's revolutionary politics. The New York Panther Twenty-one would be acquitted on all charges in May 1971. Fundraisers and meetings continued at a fairly steady clip throughout the decade, despite ongoing efforts to shame liberal supporters into silence.[15] There would also be a widespread rejection, however, of the reform-minded (not to mention revolutionary) assumptions underlying much of the critique of prisons. The criminal justice establishment would increasingly need to justify all arts and education programs during a period when Robert Martinson's "What Works?" (1974) and James Q. Wilson's *Thinking about Crime* (1975) announced the failure of reform. Over time, conservatives would convince enough people of Wolfe's argument that supporters of fair trials and humane treatment in prisons were dupes. In the early 1980s, when another symbol of cultural liberalism embraced the cause of an incarcerated critic of the criminal justice system, charges of "radical chic" would have a more decisive impact.

Born in Oscoda, Michigan, in 1944, Jack Henry Abbott rose to national prominence in 1981 when Random House published his *In the Belly of the Beast*, a collection of autobiographical, political, and philosophical writings. The book is grounded in his interpretations of his time behind bars. Abbott had spent only nine and a half months of the previous twenty-five years outside of prison, first entering a youth detention facility—the Utah State Industrial School for Boys—at age twelve after numerous failed attempts to place him in foster homes. He described himself as a "state-raised convict," which he defined as anyone who is "reared by the state from an early age after he is taken from what the state calls a 'broken home.'"[16] Abbott did not know his father, and his mother was too impoverished and in trouble with the law to care for Abbott and his sister, Frances. Abbott believed that his being "state-raised" implicated the state itself in his crimes and provided a way for him to interpret his experience.

Abbott moved on to an adult prison after leaving the juvenile system. In 1963 he was sentenced to a maximum of five years in the Utah State Penitentiary in Draper after being convicted of check forgery. He had stolen some checks from a shoe store and made them out to himself. This five-year sentence would extend to more than seventeen years, except for a brief period in the spring of 1971 when he escaped from a Utah prison. In 1966 Abbott knifed to death James Christensen, a fellow inmate who Abbott alleged made sexual advances to him. He received a twenty-year sentence to run concurrent with his forgery sentence. In addition, during his 1971 escape, Abbott robbed a savings and loan association in Denver. After his capture and conviction, Abbott entered the federal prison system to serve a nineteen-year sentence.[17]

Despite never finishing the sixth grade and refusing to attend prison schools, Abbott read widely in European philosophy, especially communist political and economic theory. Like many convicts of the 1970s, Abbott was convinced by Marx's arguments and by the deep commitment of communists to the plight of incarcerated men and women. Communists, he wrote, "do everything legally possible to help reform these prisons and to rescue prisoners from insanity, injury, death. . . . No one else does a thing."[18] During the 1970s this education in radical politics and philosophy helped him develop the critique of the prison system that appears in *In the Belly of the Beast*. In it, he critiqued the justice system as irrational: "A system of justice that does not instruct by *reason*, that does not rationally demonstrate to a man the error of his ways, accomplishes the opposite ends of justice: oppression."[19]

His politics also made him disinclined to cooperate with prison administrators or correctional officers, earning him numerous disciplinary charges during his incarceration. "So long as classes are not equal," he wrote, "men are not equal, and there is no way I can reach any agreements with the enemies of my class—particularly since these enemies hold the power of life or death over us."[20] Because of Abbott's frequent participation in political resistance and his history of violence toward correctional officers and other inmates, he spent fourteen years of his sentence in solitary confinement reading books received from his sister and from the PEN American Center, a writer's organization committed to human rights and free speech based in New York City.[21]

During the 1970s Abbott began corresponding with many American writers, first with Jerzy Kosinski, then the president of PEN. Later, he would correspond with the Pulitzer Prize–winning author Norman Mailer. His relationship with Mailer would prove central to later events in Abbott's life. Well known for such works as *The Naked and the Dead* (1948), *Advertisements for Myself* (1959), and *Armies of the Night* (1968), Mailer announced in 1978 that he would write a nonfiction work about the life and execution of Gary Gilmore, a Utah man who was to be the first person executed since the Supreme Court suspended the practice in 1972 (*Furman v. Georgia* [408 U.S. 238]). Abbott saw an item in the newspaper about the project and wrote a letter to Mailer offering to help. This project would become Mailer's Pulitzer Prize-winning *The Executioner's Song* (1979). Abbott believed that he could offer unique insight into the experiences and mindset of Gilmore, who, like Abbott, was a state-raised convict.[22]

Mailer encouraged the correspondence and received, according to his own estimation, a thousand pages of letters over a two-year period.[23] Mailer found the information helpful for his writing project. He also felt strongly that Abbott was the best convict writer since Eldridge Cleaver, known for *Soul on Ice* (1968). In an effort to make Abbott's work more widely available, Mailer showed the letters to Scott Meredith, his literary agent.[24] At Meredith's urging, the *New York Review of Books* published several excerpts from these letters in 1980.[25] The letters would also serve as the basis of much of *In the Belly of the Beast*.

In addition to citing Marx and Lenin, *In the Belly of the Beast* contains references to such philosophers as Jean-Paul Sartre, Albert Camus, Fyodor Dostoyevsky, Benedict de Spinoza, Søren Kierkegaard, and Carl Jung. Abbott's second book, *My Return* (1987), coauthored with the philosophy professor Naomi Zack, shows a continued interest in continental philosophy as well as a new familiarity with classical drama. *In the Belly of the Beast* was released in early 1981 to great fanfare. Random House heavily promoted its new author, and early reviews of the book ranged from favorable to raves. Abbie Hoffman reviewed the book in the *Soho News*, linking the book to literary giants like Aleksandr Solzhenitsyn and Jacobo Timmerman.[26] The *Nation* featured Abbott's contention that the American prison system was worse than the Soviet gulags. In the *New York Times Book Review*, Terence Des Pres offered perhaps the most positive and prescient critique: "Now that his letters have been published, we have before us the most intense, I might even say the most fiercely visionary book of its kind in the American repertoire of prison literature. *In the Belly of the Beast* is awesome, brilliant, perversely ingenuous; its impact is indelible, and as an articulation of penal nightmare it is completely compelling."[27] While he was deeply moved by Abbott's account, Des Pres made clear that Abbott's experience left him completely unprepared for life outside of prison. Abbott's precision about "evil and human ugliness" did not allow for the kind of romanticized attention to violence that his work was sure to engender. While Des Pres did not think that Abbott's anger would lead to future violence, he did point out that "in Abbott's view, convicts kill to gain respect, to establish moral superiority," a worldview that could have tragic consequences inside and outside prison.[28]

As the book was nearing release, Abbott was nearing the end of his sentence on the federal bank robbing charges. He applied for and received early parole in 1981, expecting to be returned to Utah to finish his state sentence for the 1966 murder of Christensen. Mailer, along with Random House's Erroll McDonald; the *New York Review of Books* editor Robert Silvers; and Mailer's literary agent, Scott Meredith, wrote letters to the Utah Board of Pardons attesting to Abbott's literary talents and potential for full-time work as a writer. According to Thomas R. Harrison, then serving as chairman of the Utah board, these letters testified to Abbott's "sensitivity, talent, goals, and accomplishments."[29] Harrison was convinced that Abbott had "a great deal going for him" and that he no longer posed a violent threat. On June 5, 1981, with the prospect of a lucrative and productive writing career in front of him, Abbott was placed in a halfway house in New York City, pending his full parole date of August 25.

Abbott's parole from the federal prison in Marion, Illinois, would normally have been to Denver, the location of the 1971 savings and loan robbery that resulted in his federal conviction. However, because of the promise of a job paying one hundred and fifty dollars a week as the research assistant for Mailer, who was based in Brooklyn, federal authorities agreed to parole Abbott to a halfway house run by the Salvation Army on New York's Lower East Side. In a flurry of activity, Abbott was interviewed on *Good Morning America*, featured in *People* magazine, and feted by well-known writers and the editorial brass of Random House. He also made a point of learning to dance, something he never had the opportunity to do in prison. Early in the morning of July 18, 1981, after a night of dancing, Abbott and two women—Susan Roxas and Veronique de St. Andre—went to the Binibon Restaurant on the corner of Second Avenue and Fifth Street, several blocks from his halfway house at Third Street. Abbott was involved in an altercation that resulted in the death of Richard Adan. Terence Des Pres's review of *In the Belly of the Beast* appeared in the next day's *New York Times*.

The altercation between Adan and Abbott is clouded by competing versions of the story. Abbott, media accounts, and trial testimony agree on some details. Abbott entered the Binibon restaurant with Roxas and St. Andre. Adan, a 22-year-old Cuban-born dancer and actor, was working as a waiter and night manager at the restaurant, which was owned by his father-in-law, Henry Howard. After several tense exchanges between Abbott and Adan, Abbott asked to use the bathroom. According to some accounts, Adan explained that because the bathroom was through the kitchen, it would be a violation of health codes to allow customers access. According to Abbott, Adan merely told him that he could not use the bathroom. Depending on who told the story, either Adan or Abbott asked the other to step outside. The two men then left the restaurant and went around the corner. In the midst of a brief altercation, Abbott stabbed Adan once in the heart with the knife he began carrying after seeing several muggings in the neighborhood. Adan staggered, slumped to the pavement, and died.

Abbott fled the scene, phoned Mailer (who asked that he call back at a later hour), and then returned to the halfway house for the daily

7:30 A.M. "face-to-face" roll call. Later that morning, he ate brunch at the apartment of the French writer Jean Malaquais but made no mention of the altercation with Adan. He then fled New York, traveling to Philadelphia and Chicago before crossing the U.S.-Mexico border at Nuevo Laredo with the goal of going to Cuba, which had no extradition treaty with the United States. Unable to gain work on a ship destined for Cuba and with funds running low, Abbott hitchhiked to New Orleans, where he worked in a series of odd jobs before gaining employment as a roustabout for offshore oil rigs near Morgan City, Louisiana. After several weeks, an informant contacted New York Police Detective William J. Majeski with information about a man with the letters "J A C K" tattooed across the fingers of his left hand. Federal authorities arrested Abbott on September 24.[30]

Abbott was quickly transferred to New York City to face charges of murder in the first degree. The trial lasted from January 9 to January 21, 1982. Under heavy media scrutiny, James H. Fogel, a New York City assistant district attorney, argued the case for the prosecution. Ivan S. Fisher defended Abbott, arguing that the death was an accident occasioned by Abbott's attempt at self-defense. On the first day of the trial, Fogel asked the judge, Acting Justice Irving Lang, if he could introduce excerpts from *In the Belly of the Beast* as a partial explanation of Abbott's motive.[31] Lang ruled against the prosecution, but when Abbott chose to take the stand in his own defense on January 15, the judge allowed the prosecution to use previously agreed-upon excerpts in questioning as long as no passage referred to any of Abbott's previous crimes, including the 1966 stabbing. However, when Abbott took the stand, Henry Howard, Adan's father-in-law, shouted from the observers' seats, "It's just like in the book, Abbott, just like in the book!," presaging the prosecution's own strategy.[32] The judge barred Adan's family from the remainder of the trial.

Under questioning from his attorney, Abbott described Adan's death as a "tragic misunderstanding" brought about by paranoia. Adan, he admitted, was probably just leading him to a hidden spot around the corner so that Abbott could relieve himself. Abbott testified that he mistakenly interpreted all of Adan's benign gestures as hostile and when Adan approached him, he pulled out a knife. Instead of pulling away, as Abbott expected, Adan leaned into the knife and unluckily walked into a fatal stabbing.[33] During his cross-examination, Fogel read several excerpts from *In the Belly of the Beast*, including Abbott's discussion of the importance of using deadly force when behind bars: "Here in prison the most respected among us are those who have killed other men, particularly other prisoners. Beneath all relationships in prison is the ever-present fact of murder. It ultimately defines our relationship among ourselves."[34] Abbott insisted that, while based in fact, the book was a fictionalized account of his experiences and views.[35] In one sense, the trial acknowledged the importance of Abbott's writing in the murder of Adan. The prosecutor and the family of Richard Adan directly implicated Abbott's writing in his murderous acts. They did not argue that his writing made him a violent person; however, they did use his published work as proof that, as Fogel remarked after sentencing, Abbott was a "killer by habit, a killer by inclination, a killer by philosophy and a killer by desire."[36] The writing, then, became a key context to understand Abbott's beliefs and motivation.

The jury members had five options. They could acquit Abbott of all charges. They could convict him, as the prosecution wished, of murder in the first degree. This would require evidence of premeditation. In addition, Lang gave the jury several other options: second-degree murder (causing a death with intent to kill), first-degree manslaughter (causing a death, but where blame is mitigated by "extreme emotional disturbance"), or second-degree manslaughter (causing death because of recklessness). After deliberating for two days, the jury found Abbott guilty of first-degree manslaughter on January 21, his thirty-eighth birthday. Lang handed down a sentence of fifteen years to life, although he could have given Abbott a life sentence under New York's "persistent violent felon" law.[37]

The manslaughter conviction can be seen at face value: Abbott killed Adan while in a state of paranoia. His history in prison, including long periods of solitary confinement and periods in the early 1970s, when he was prescribed heavy doses of Valium, Prolixin, and Mellaril, a tranquilizer, made it impossible for him to see Adan's actions as anything but a threat.[38] However, perhaps the jury saw Abbott's experience as much as his mental state as a mitigating factor. Abbott's lawyer argued as much in his appeal of his sentence: in it, he wrote that prison "is the only 'society' that the defendant has ever known."[39] As a state-raised convict, Abbott was acting within the rules of his society rather than the new context of a restaurant.

Because his altercation with Adan was also a violation of his parole, Abbott returned to Marion, Illinois, to complete his federal sentence for the 1971 bank robbery conviction. After completing this sentence, he was transferred to the New York State Department of Corrections with little public attention. In 1987 he and Zack released *My Return*. The book includes a play, *The Death of Tragedy*, about the altercation with Adan and the trial that followed. The play refutes the idea that either Mailer or Abbott's prison experience played any role in the altercation with Adan. In her introduction, Zack made an assertion that proved particularly offensive to Adan's family. Arguing that it "takes two to tango," Zack contended that "Had [Adan] known to be more careful with strangers, he would probably not be dead today. But from his appearance, his words, his behavior, the night manager must not have realized any problem existed and that he could not handle the man in the manner he did."[40] In addition to holding Adan partially responsible for his own death, *My Return* raised many objections to the prosecution's use of Abbott's writings during the cross-examination and summation, reiterating his comment at the time of the trial that *In the Belly of the Beast* was a fictionalization of his life rather than an autobiography. "The Leader," a character in *The Death of Tragedy* based on a traditional role in Greek drama, says, "Abbott had been tried for writing a book. His book has been used as evidence against him. But Abbott and his book are two different things. Abbott's ability with a pen should not be taken as ability to kill."[41]

Despite Abbott's continued reluctance to connect his literary creations with the altercation with Adan, the two would remain intertwined inside and outside the courts. In December 1981, Ricci Adan, Adan's widow, filed a ten-million-dollar wrongful death suit against Abbott. A jury found Abbott liable for damages in 1983, but it would take until June of 1990 for a civil court to decide damages. In the interim, Abbott's two books had earned more than one hundred thousand dollars in royalties and film rights and he had signed a contract worth one hundred and fifty thousand dollars to write an autobiographical film script. While Abbott had hoped that his sister would benefit from these earnings, the New York County Sheriff and the New York State Crime Victims Board held the money under the state's "Son of Sam" law, which prevented convicted felons from profiting from their crimes. Abbott and Zack married in 1989.[42] The jury awarded Ricci Adan 7.5 million dollars, ensuring that she would receive all future royalties from the sale of Abbott's work.[43]

In March 2000, while incarcerated in Attica, Abbott was severely beaten by fellow inmates. After recovering from seven hours of surgery, he was transferred to Wende Correctional Facility, near Buffalo. He was denied parole at his first hearing in August 2001 and continued to have difficulty behind bars. According to letters to Michael Kuzma, his lawyer at the time, Abbott faced continued harassment from correctional officers and fellow inmates through early February 2002. Abbott was found dead in his cell at Wende on February 10, 2002, an apparent suicide. Correctional authorities refused to release his last work of writing, a suicide note.

According to the media coverage of Abbott's trial, Abbott was the beneficiary of "radical chic" and Adan its victim. Wolfe's 1970 lampooning of efforts by wealthy and influential people to support radicals or the oppressed served as a primary way to understand Abbott's release and Adan's murder. Mailer's mentorship of Abbott could be compared to Bernstein's sponsorship of the Black Panthers, Bob Dylan's efforts to get a new trial for the boxer Ruben "Hurricane" Carter, William F. Buckley Jr.'s help in gaining the release of Edgar Smith, Jean Paul Sartre's mentorship of Jean Genet, or Nelson Algren and William Styron's mentorship of James Blake. The *Washington Post* gasped: "Jack Henry Abbott wasn't so much Mailer's literary protégé as a feather in his cap: a real live crook—one who writes with his fists!—to be put on exhibit in the salons of radical chic."[44] The paper urged readers to "keep [their] distance" and leave criminals to the penal system. The "radical chic" argument would long outlive Abbott's public visibility. The New York *Daily News*, for example, singled out Mailer and his literary agent, Scott Meredith, as "fancies and nellies and swells" fussing over a "noble savage" almost two decades after Abbott's return to prison.[45]

This theory drew on several important factors. First, many media accounts felt that Mailer and the others who wrote letters to the Utah Board of Parole should be held partially responsible for Adan's death. In their efforts to connect with an "outsider," Mailer let his passions get away from him.[46] None of the letters said that Abbott no longer posed a threat; however, Mailer did write in his preface to *In the Belly of the Beast* that "it is certainly time for him to get out."[47] A Greenwich Village dinner honoring Abbott and celebrating his release also influenced the belief that he was a beneficiary of radical chic. The dinner, attended by Jason Epstein (a Random House editor); Robert Silvers of the *New York Review of Books*; Mailer and his wife, Norris Church; and Kosinski and his partner, Katherina Von Fraunhofer, was used to cast aspersion on the literary crowd that championed Abbott's talents. His promotional appearance on *Good Morning America* attested to the extent of the publicity Abbott received in the short period of his freedom. One newspaper even transformed the early morning meal at Binibon—an inexpensive café on the then humble Lower East Side—into something more glamorous: "He walked into an East Village restaurant, a woman admirer on either arm."[48]

The implication of this theory is that Abbott should never have been released from prison and that he received preferential treatment because of his connections to literary giants. Some reporters went beyond this view by noting Mailer's literary fascination with strong men who meet tragic outcomes. From essays like "The White Negro" (1959) to *The Executioner's Song* (1979)—the book that led Abbott to him—Mailer documented his identification with marginalized men and his view of them as appealingly masculine.[49] Michiko Kakutani, the influential cultural and literary reviewer for the *New York Times*, traced the many ways Mailer's characters assert their "identity in the face of an arbitrary system of officially regulated morality" and "kill without apology." According to Kakutani, Mailer had long "equated violence not only with virility but also with creativity and moral courage."[50] She heralded the use of "the man on the fringes" as a literary device that defines "the perimeters of bourgeois society" in writers like William Blake, Friedrich Nietzsche, Charles Baudelaire, Arthur Rimbaud, Fyodor Dostoyevsky, Franz Kafka, Jean-Paul Sartre, John Cheever, and even the ex-convict Jean Genet. However, Kakutani felt that the championing of Abbott replaced literary and philosophical exploration with a dangerous experiment. In interviews with leading cultural critics and novelists like H. Bruce Franklin, Irving Howe, Joyce Carol Oates, and Richard Slotkin, Kakutani builds the argument that it was "wishful impulse to see Mr. Abbott's life as a store not just of crime and punishment, but of crime and punishment and redemption; and it was the fervently held belief that talent somehow redeems, that art confers respectability, that the act of writing can somehow transform a violent man into a philosopher of violence."[51] Kakutani stopped far short of blaming the literary establishment for Adan's death, but she used the opportunity of his death to show the consequences of romanticizing violent men with radical politics.

Mailer's attention to violent themes both predated his relationship with Abbott and outlived their connection. Many pointed out that Mailer had stabbed a previous wife in 1960 and as late as a 2000 interview Mailer revealed his continuing belief that "we are as ugly as animals in our fashion, and unless we deal with the ugliness in ourselves, unless we deal with the violence in ourselves, the brutality in ourselves, and find some way to sublimate it, just to use Freud's term, into something slightly higher, we're never going to get anywhere with anything."[52] Mailer had a literary interest in the themes explored in Abbott's letters, but he and Kosinsky also saw Abbott's talent as indicative of an inner transformation. Kosinsky, reflecting on this view, agreed with Kakutani's central point: "Maybe I share with my intellectual friend Norman Mailer the feeling that talent redeems."[53] Both men felt blameworthy for not seeing that Abbott had frequently used both philosophical and physical violence. Many of Abbott's early letters to Kosinsky were "an unremittant litany of spiritual and intellectual abuse." So Kosinsky did not so much ignore Abbott's justification of violence in *In the Belly of the Beast* as see it as evidence that the physical propensity to violence had been channeled into a literary form: "We preferred to see him as a man who is going to become an intellectual of violence."[54]

Other journalists found the sharp critiques of Mailer overly simplified. They recognized that politically engaged writers like Mailer and Kosinsky placed great importance on their relationships with convict writers for a variety of literary, political, and personal reasons beyond a simple attempt to be "chic." "It is easy to dismiss [Mailer's] efforts on behalf of Mr. Abbott as radical chic," the *New York Times* editorialized, "or the overly romantic celebration of his literary ability. But perhaps too easy. Mr. Abbott's writing may be unusual, but his state-sponsored rearing in rage and murder are not. For that, we all must bear some responsibility."[55] The attention to the "radical chic" of left-leaning elites ignored important aspects of the larger context for Abbott, *In the Belly of the Beast*, and the killing of Adan. Much of the mass media focused attention on the predictability of Abbott's violence based on his own words and criminal record. This ignored or discounted Abbott's implication of the state—and, the *Times* opined, the general readership of newspapers—in creating the conditions in which this violence occurred. In one of the more powerful passages in *In the Belly of the Beast* (and thus before the altercation with Adan), Abbott argued that "to say you are *not* responsible for the life of someone you killed in self-defense, not responsible for the circumstances that brought you to prison (and kept you there for two decades)—to say all that in the face of your accusers, accusers who also justify their mistreatment of you by those accusations, is to be really responsible for your words and deeds. Because every time you reject the accusations, you are held responsible *further* for things you are not responsible for."[56] Instead of holding himself at fault—or blaming well-meaning intellectuals—Abbott insisted that the penal system (and the capitalist economy) held responsibility for placing him in a brutalizing context for much of his life. Des Pres, in his *Times* review, found this view compelling but thought that Abbott's interpretation of society as a whole was limited by his confinement: "Abbott uses Marxist theory to generalize his own experience, assuming that what happens in American maximum security prisons must be a sort of paradigm for oppression everywhere."[57]

According to Des Pres, prisons were oppressive but could not be used to broadly generalize that America is a prison as well.

Media coverage of the crime and trial paid close attention to the role of Abbott's talent in misleading well-meaning, if naive, writers and editors. The larger subtext of this critique called into question the charge that the prison system was emblematic of a racist society. The very idea of "radical chic" connoted a critique of the embrace of the Black Panther Party by the white conductor and composer Leonard Bernstein. Wolfe coined the phrase to cast cynical aspersion on the alliance between moneyed New Yorkers and Black radical activists. While Abbott was, in contemporary terms, biracial, no mention was ever made of his Chinese or white ancestry in any coverage of his saga. For that matter, Abbott seems not to have written about this aspect of his background. Instead, he was frequently compared to African American radical writers and activists. Abbott's politics placed him closer to the incarcerated African Americans Eldridge Cleaver, George Jackson, and Angela Davis than to incarcerated white writers like Caryl Chessman or, for that matter, the imprisoned Nixon coconspirator Charles Colson. Abbott would have been comfortable with Black Panther Chairman Huey P. Newton's claim that "there are no laws that the oppressor makes that the oppressed are bound to respect."[58] Abbott was part of a political and cultural renaissance behind bars that had deep and lasting connections to political activists without the elite pedigree of Mailer, Bernstein, or Kosinsky. Nevertheless, the charge that Abbott's release from prison and Adan's death resulted from "radical chic" would prove damning. The financial and political support of wealthy or well-connected whites rapidly dried up.

The historical period provides evidence of a more complicated link between Abbott's celebrity and the killing of Richard Adan. Mailer was not alone; there was a profound fascination with prison writers and intellectuals during the 1970s. Many incarcerated people benefited from the sharp rise in writing and artistic opportunities available in correctional facilities. In addition to Cleaver, Jackson, and Davis, writers like Etheridge Knight, Jimmy Santiago Baca, and Miguel Piñero won widespread acclaim for their creative works. Less literary-inclined incarcerated people exposed a legacy of injustice in penal institutions by rioting. During the years leading up to *In the Belly of the Beast*, many incarcerated people sought to participate in social and political debates occurring in the "free" world despite their incarceration and need to overcome obstacles like illiteracy or poor writing skills. Learning to write, for many incarcerated people, became a political and cultural act as much as one of individual betterment.

Abbott's politics and literary talents, while not in the mainstream of American political life, were representative of a period of tremendous upheaval in U.S. prisons. Leonard Munker, the attorney who represented Abbott at his 1981 parole hearing, pointed out that "the '70s were a turbulent time in prisons and Jack was leader of the pack."[59] Abbott's time in solitary, Munker observed, should be seen in relation to the political nature of his violence. For example, in 1975, to protest the heavy doses of tranquilizers the prison administered, Abbott punched a doctor in the face. This led to a long stint in solitary confinement. Munker asked readers to consider whether this was an example of a violent nature or an act of political and personal resistance. For most readers, this would require an interpretive leap they were not ready to take. But Abbott provided an opportunity to ask this, and far more difficult, questions about how Americans understand criminality and incarceration.

The crime, trial, and media coverage of Jack Henry Abbott's release and return to prison sparked a debate about the relationship between art and redemption, prisons and reform, and "radical chic" among the cultural elite. According to the critics, prison writers and activists were no more than gifted con artists; and liberal reviewers, teachers, and readers were their easy marks. As Abbott's prosecutor pointed out, clues to their deceptions and the true threat they posed could be found in their own writings.

Few media accounts noted Abbott's critique of the prison system, instead choosing to find fault with the literary establishment in general and Norman Mailer in particular for mentoring, publishing, and celebrating Abbott. They used the killing of Adan as an opportunity to call for the further marginalization of incarcerated people. The *Washington Post* urged an imaginary "Author's Guild" to stick to their typewriters: "The rehabilitation of convicted criminals is for the penal system, not for the city desk or the book-review department."[60] Others, like Terence Des Pres, observed that many of the conditions that Abbott wrote of were eliminated only after a series of reforms in the 1960s and 1970s. Abbott had himself been active in the Marion Prisoners' Rights Project, an organization founded during the period of reform.[61] These reforms, as the *Christian Science Monitor* noted, did not occur because of a self-critique by correctional facilities. Prisoners, activists, and, eventually, the courts, demanded that torture, extended solitary confinement, and many of the other practices described by Abbott be stopped. In fact, the *Monitor* reported in 1981, Chief Justice Warren E. Burger urged that these reforms needed to go further. The *Monitor* also argued that Abbott needed to remain part of the debate about prison reform. To at least one observer, Abbott's continued violence did not negate the brutality of his experience, nor did his re-incarceration prevent others from going down that path.[62]

But 1981 also signaled how far the tide had turned since the mid-1970s. That year *Saturday Night Live* ran a mock documentary titled "Prose and Cons" that poked fun at liberal elites who viewed prisoners as victims. "Prose and Cons" began with a Handel score recalling the PBS series *Masterpiece Theater*. A British-accented voice-over asks, "Where are tomorrow's Hemingways and Faulkners coming from?"[63] The answer, provided by Terry McDonnell, managing editor of *Rolling Stone* magazine: "Prisons." The parody continues with the noted literary agent Swifty Lazar remarking on the commercial success of several prisoners: "Without a doubt, anything by a prisoner is an automatic bestseller. I tell aspiring writers, if you commit a crime, we'll talk." The warden of a fictional Rockland Prison beams with pride at the literary merits of his inmates: "You can talk Leavenworth, you can talk Attica. You can even talk Folsom. But none of them—none of them—has the sterling literary tradition we have here at Rockland."

After a series of short scenes featuring inmates typing, talking to agents, and being taken to solitary confinement for plagiarism, the camera settles on Tyrone Greene. We are told by the voice-over that Greene, played by the *Saturday Night Live* star Eddie Murphy, won that year's Rockland poetry festival. Murphy stares into the camera, "angrily intense," according to the script, and recites his prize-winning poem:

"Images," by Tyrone Greene . . .
Dark and lonely on the summer night.
Kill my landlord, kill my landlord.
Watchdog barking—*Do he bite?*
Kill my landlord, kill my landlord.
Slip in his window,
Break his neck!
Then his house
I start to wreck!
Got no reason—
What the heck!
Kill my landlord, kill my landlord.
C-I-L-L . . .
My *land—lord* . . .
Def!

The wide gap between the narrator's literary pretension and Greene's doggerel is clearly meant to provoke laughter. The senseless violence also stands in obvious contrast to the more politically minded content of much of the work emerging from prisons during the decade that preceded the sketch. Interest in Greene's output stems not from the work itself but from a voyeuristic "slumming" by an elite literary crowd. The source of this perception is made clear in the fictional credits that roll up the screen at the conclusion of "Prose and Cons." The credits facetiously inform viewers that the documentary was written, produced, and directed by Norman Mailer, with research assistance provided by Jack Henry Abbott.

By the beginning of the 1980s this parody both reflected the heightened visibility of prisoners' creative output and called into question the motives of their audience. As funding for the arts in prison dried up in the early 1980s, this parody also revealed a cultural and political shift in the public mood. While the relationship between Abbott and Mailer revealed the hopes of many during the 1970s that the arts were therapeutic and that artistic success was a marker of rehabilitation, the tragic outcome of Abbott's release heightened a shifting mood that saw the arts as just another con.

Few discussions of Norman Mailer fail to mention his connection to Abbott. *In the Belly of the Beast* has remained in print since 1981. In addition to these impacts on popular culture, Abbott had a long-term influence on the prison system in a way rarely mentioned. In 1972 he was the lead plaintiff in a class action lawsuit seeking to reform prison regulations of mail delivery. With support from the National Prison Project of the American Civil Liberties Union, the suit prompted prison authorities to provide inmates increased access to personal correspondence. While Abbott never shook his reputation as a misguided prophet who did not deserve the faith of the New York literary crowd, his reputation as a reformer and self-defined troublemaker is also not forgotten.

CONCLUSION

In 1924 Huddie Ledbetter played a concert at the Sugar Land Prison Farm for the governor of Texas. Ledbetter, who would go on to international celebrity as "Lead Belly," was doing time as "Walter Boyd," the name he assumed after escaping from a previous prison. This time, Ledbetter was arrested after he murdered a relative during a fight in 1917, receiving a sentence of seven to thirty-five years at Sugar Land, a former plantation near Houston. Ledbetter cut sugar cane on the prison farm and entertained other inmates and the prison staff with ballads and blues songs. Ledbetter was particularly good at reworking the lyrics of well-known prison songs to include references to the exploits of other prisoners, prison staff, or notorious Houston police officers.[1] In January 1924 a captain at the prison asked Ledbetter to perform for Pat M. Neff, the Texas governor who was then on a tour of the state's prisons. Ledbetter danced a demeaning number he called the "Sugar Land Shuffle," in which he lampooned an eager and happy cotton picker. The songs included the hymn "What a Friend We Have in Jesus" and the minstrel song "Ole Dan Tucker." He also played an original ballad in which he asked for forgiveness. The plea went over well: Neff returned to the prison several times to hear Ledbetter perform and specifically requested the original ballad in which the musician asks for his forgiveness.[2] Just before leaving office in January 1925, Neff delivered on a promise he made to Ledbetter by granting him—as Walter Boyd—a full pardon.

Many years passed before Ledbetter became a fixture on the folk music circuit with songs like "Midnight Special" and "Goodnight, Irene." In the meantime, Ledbetter supported himself as a laborer and musician in Louisiana and once again ran into trouble with the criminal justice system. In 1930 Ledbetter received a sentence of six-to-ten years of hard labor for assault with intent to murder after an altercation in Mooringsport, near Shreveport. Ledbetter, then forty-three, was sent to Angola Prison Farm, also a former plantation. One observer called Depression-era Angola "probably as close to slavery as any person could come in 1930."[3] Gun-toting convict "trusties" carried out the orders of the prison staff. They had the authority and incentive to shoot people who attempted to escape. In 1933 and 1934 the famed musicologists John and Alan Lomax arrived at Angola, where they recorded Ledbetter for the Library of Congress and sent a petition to O. K. Allen, the Louisiana governor, along with their recording of Ledbetter performing "Goodnight, Irene." Although there is some disagreement about whether the petition was instrumental or coincidental to Ledbetter's release—Ledbetter had petitioned the governor himself before the Lomaxes arrived—there is no question that Allen authorized Ledbetter's release. Over time, the legend of Lead Belly's release grew: in 1937, *Life* magazine featured the story of the two pardons in a photo essay featuring a close-up of the musician's hands strumming his twelve-string guitar with the caption: "These hands once killed a man."[4] *Life* boiled down Ledbetter's story into a racist fantasy. In this telling, a violent, oversexed man—the story included often repeated stories of "Leadbelly's" sex life—became a complacent servant, entertainer, and object of professional analysis, one week driving John Lomax and his recording equipment around the South as he searched for the next diamond in the rough and the next week playing "Midnight Special" for intellectuals at a Modern Language Association conference. The article also betrayed, however, a nagging fear that Ledbetter used his grin and guitar to play a confidence game: "Amuse the public, and you can get away with almost any crime."[5]

By the late 1970s and early 1980s, the days of singing for a pardon had long passed, but the attractions, fears, and self-doubt of the Lead Belly story were still sources of conflict when attention turned to prison writings and performances. Some observers might still be tempted to view the widespread interest in the cultural and political expressions of people in prison as a con. According to this false logic, if Lead Belly needed to play the role of a "darkie" to get out of Sugar Land and Angola in the 1920s and 1930s, Jack Henry Abbott needed to play a revolutionary in the late 1970s and early 1980s in order to appeal to a left-wing elite. Although this view provides some insight into the politics of consumption, race, and prison, we would seriously misread the significance of prison culture and politics if we saw them as the expressions of jailhouse philosophers or minstrels pulling a fast one on guilt-ridden limousine liberals.

The stories of Ledbetter and Abbott still sometimes serve as convenient legends to discredit prisoner advocates as misguided people who have fallen victim to a fascination with bad men turned good. Meanwhile, other prison writers continue to face years of incarceration and isolation, as well as execution. One lesson of the 1970s is that writing and performing puts people at risk of increased trouble with the criminal justice system. Those who spoke out at Attica were targeted during the takeover; prosecutors attempted to introduce Angela Davis's writings as evidence of her guilt of murder, conspiracy, and kidnapping; Amiri Baraka received an unusually long sentence for weapons possession after the judge read from his 1967 poem "Black People." In less celebrated cases in recent years, prisoner efforts to contribute to U.S. politics, society, and culture are typically misrepresented in order to carry out punishment. In perhaps the most brutal example of this, California Governor Gray Davis wrote of the poet Stephen Wayne Anderson in 2002, "His intelligence makes the brutality and indifference of his crimes all the more reprehensible. Clearly he had the capacity to know better."[6] Davis denied Anderson's appeal for clemency, clearing the way for Anderson—a poet and playwright convicted of capital murder in 1981 while represented by a lawyer who never talked to him outside of court—to be executed three days later.

There are other important reasons to reject the view that prison culture was little more than an unholy alliance between manipulative prisoners and misguided liberals. Prisoners demonstrated the importance of free/incarcerated—as well as cross-class and cross-racial—solidarity in pushing for change during the 1970s, a period understood by some historians of the civil rights era as a balkanization of the Left. The efforts to encourage solidarity with incarcerated people through cultural and political expression should not be blamed for what later happened to American prisons, even if we acknowledge that prison writers and artists did not succeed in creating a revolutionary culture.[7] But the discrediting of these alliances did play a role in the expansion of the prison system that immediately followed. During the 1980s and 1990s, the construction of prisons skyrocketed and the prison population exploded. When adjusted for inflation, per capita spending on corrections ballooned 218 percent between 1960 and 1985, with the vast majority of that increase occurring after 1970. To put this in perspective, spending on education outside of prisons increased 56 percent during the same period, with virtually all of the increase occurring between 1960 and 1975.[8] In 1970 there were 196,429 people doing time in federal and state prisons. By 1976 that number stood at 283,000. In 2006 there were 1.7 million people in prison and another 750,000 people in jail awaiting trial.[9]

While spending on corrections increased and prisons became overcrowded the day they opened, the money went to ever more punitive structures amid growing privatization and the sense that rehabilitation was a waste of taxpayer funds. The 1990s saw the sharp reversal of a key trend that began in the mid-1960s. In 1965, in the midst of the Great Society, the Higher Education Act explicitly stated that inmates could apply for federal financial aid for postsecondary education. By 1980, when it was renamed the Pell Grant Program, the program had become the primary funding for inmate higher education.[10] This program directly led to a sharp expansion of educational opportunities behind bars. According to Michele F. Welsh, in the dozen years that followed, incarcerated people in forty-three states and in federal prisons could receive an associate's degree; thirty-one states and the federal prisons provided access to bachelor's degrees; and nine states plus the federal prisons provided access to master's degrees.[11] Pell Grants provided a way for prison education advocates to continue to provide educational opportunities for inmates in a climate increasingly hostile to their efforts. At first, it seemed like corrections reformers had succeeded in moving the criminal justice system toward a more effective and just rehabilitative regime. Furthermore, individual inmates could apply for funding and pay tuition to state community and comprehensive colleges, augmenting state education budgets. As the 1990s began, however, state governments increasingly denied funding for rehabilitation programs as either too expensive, ineffective, or both. In the meantime, corrections officials could turn to the federal government's Pell Grant program to fill the budget gap.

Even while the federal money supplemented educational and cultural opportunities in prison, there were warning signs that this did not directly benefit the inmates or the communities to which they would return. In some cases, the federal dollars proved attractive to for-profit "proprietary schools." Most notably, in the late 1980s, the Corrections Corporation of America (CCA), a politically connected private prison company, invested in the Education Corporation of America—its headquarters even adjoined CCA's offices in Nashville, Tennessee. The Education Corporation's Branell College provided certificate programs in a variety of vocational fields in eighteen CCA and public prisons throughout the country.[12] In 1994 Branell College was ordered to repay the U.S. Department of Education more than 3 million dollars after it was found that the corporation improperly disbursed federal dollars during the 1990–91 and 1991–92 award years. Pell Grant funding was a sign that corrections officials continued to find ways to provide rehabilitative programming amid the trend toward increasingly punitive criminal justice and privatization. It was also a sign that the states had largely washed their hands of rehabilitation, leaving the U.S. Department of Education to fund programs in a patchwork fashion.

Although Pell Grants were the central source of funding for inmate higher education, incarcerated people accounted for about 35 million federal dollars going to twenty-three thousand prisoners, with the average recipient granted less than thirteen hundred dollars. According to the U.S. Department of Education, total dollars granted, including incarcerated and nonincarcerated recipients, amounted to 5.3 billion dollars in 1993.[13] According to Robert Bruce Slater, total U.S. expenditures on prisons that year amounted to over 22 billion dollars.[14] Despite the fact that inmate benefits represented a small fraction of the total Pell Grant or prison budgets, between 1982 and 1993 conservative members of Congress sought to eliminate inmate eligibility. North Carolina Senator Jesse Helms drew on the resentment that a college education seemed out of reach to so many Americans when, in 1991, he urged eliminating Pell Grants for prisoners on grounds that "the American taxpayers are being forced to pay taxes to provide free college tuition for prisoners at a time when so many law-abiding, taxpaying citizens are struggling to find enough money to send their children to college."[15] The implication that impoverished inmates deprived law-abiding Americans of the chance to attend college failed to convince lawmakers that year, but in 1993 the Violent Crime Control and Law Enforcement Act—the so-called Biden Crime Bill—eliminated the provision of the 1965 Higher Education Act allowing inmates to receive Pell Grants. This bill provided an additional 9.7 billion dollars in federal funds for prisons, funding for one hundred thousand new police officers, and expanded use of the federal death penalty. Ironically, a bill named for a Democratic senator and future vice president and signed by a Democratic president gave conservatives much of what they could not accomplish during the previous twenty-four years—a period that included the punitive "law and order" and "war on drugs" approaches of the Nixon, Reagan, and Bush presidencies.[16] Just as Richard Nixon's law and order found an easy conduit in Lyndon Johnson's "Great Society" Law Enforcement Assistance Administration, the Biden Crime Bill led to more funding for punitive policing and corrections. Sadly, it went much further than even Nixon had been able to by eliminating use of the Pell Grant program to help prisoners.

The effect was catastrophic. Within one year, the number of correctional systems offering any postsecondary education programs slipped 19 percent, from thirty-eight to twenty-nine. The drop in certificate- and degree-granting programs was even sharper: whereas 71 percent of the country's prison systems offered associate's degrees in the last year of Pell funding, that figure had dropped to 50 percent one year later. More than 350 programs closed as a direct result of this legislation.[17] Among the correctional education programs that remained, Charles Ubah found, 41 percent of directors thought their programs had "completely changed" with the withdrawal of Pell monies. Only 18 percent saw no change.[18] The federal Youthful Offenders Program partially alleviated this loss of funding by providing some money for postsecondary education for inmates under twenty-six who were eligible for parole or release within five years. Even with this funding, by

2003 only nineteen states offered an associate's degree to inmates, and eleven of those also offered a bachelor's degree.[19]

If the 1970s brought to light the view that prisons were symbols of American racism and inequality, it immediately preceded policies inspired by the contradictory conviction that they were too few and too comfortable. In the end, the attacks on the cultural and intellectual lives of prisoners centered on successful links they made with foundations, liberal supporters, and state and federal agencies. Prison programming was the direct result of solidarity between politically and culturally engaged people on both sides of prison walls. Discrediting these alliances proved crucial to dismantling the programs that remained. By the 1980s, efforts by incarcerated people and the agencies that provided services to them would be devastated by charges that they were "radical chic" or "limousine liberalism," with rehabilitation made to look like an elaborate con. In more recent years, even politicians who otherwise support rehabilitation programs and vocational education draw the line at broader access to education. For example, New York State Senator Michael F. Nozzolio, who sits on the Crime and Corrections Committee and whose district includes Auburn Correctional Facility, claimed to have seen "inmates that have no chance of ever getting out of prison becoming philosopher kings at taxpayer expense."[20] Nozzolio's vision of inmate "philosopher kings" sharply contrasts the 60 percent illiteracy rate among U.S. prisoners.[21]

Despite the real destruction by the Biden Crime Bill and the trend it represents, the efforts during the 1970s to reshape the meanings of prison left an important legacy. State or federal funding for education and the arts, while welcome, was not the only goal of prisoner and allied efforts during the 1970s. In fact, some prisoners even refused to participate in programs offered by institutions. Even if the numbers of people behind bars exploded, incarcerated people brought to light the simple falsehood at the center of many assumptions about the criminal justice system. People victimized by economic exploitation and racism gained a new language to express their critical consciousness of the experience. Even at the start of the decade—before Felicia and Leonard Bernstein's fundraiser, before Attica, before *Short Eyes*, before *In the Belly of the Beast*, 80 percent of Los Angeles's black residents polled believed that Angela Davis would not get a fair trial.[22] Indeed, James Baldwin was not too far off the mark when he said, "No Black person will ever believe that George Jackson died the way they tell us he did."[23]

This critical consciousness led the veterans of the movements of the 1960s and 1970s and the generations that followed to go behind the walls, engage incarcerated people in dialog, and share what they learned. In going behind bars, they also shared their experience, skills, and viewpoints with prisoners, partially filling in for the failures of state and federal correctional institutions. As the political culture became dominated by a repressive law-and-order mentality, the institutions would come to depend on unpaid volunteers and those church-affiliated schools and organizations that include prisoner outreach in their mission.

Fine and performing artists continue to provide opportunities for their audiences to consider the impact of incarceration on individuals, landscapes, and communities. The visual artist Sandow Birk wryly recalls the dreamlike natural utopias of Hudson River Valley painters like Thomas Cole and Frederick Church in his "Prisonation" series. Birk updates nineteenth-century concerns about the impact of industrialization on the American landscape and the republican ideals the painters believed it fostered. Now, instead of images of machines in the garden, Birk paints pastoral landscapes that include razor-wire-encircled edifices of New York and California prisons. Encouraging his viewers to consider the destructive impact of these institutions, Birk includes the economic, natural, and human costs of the prison system, noting below one of his canvases, for example, that San Quentin had an annual operating budget of 120 million dollars in 2003 and had executed 420 people (215 hanged, 196 gassed, 9 killed by lethal injection) since opening in 1852.[24]

As Birk's caption testifies, increasing public concern over executions is perhaps the most tangible outcome of the recent cultural politics of criminal justice. Jessica Blank and Erik Jensen's play *The Exonerated* was performed hundreds of times in New York, Los Angeles, Washington, D.C., and Chicago before being made into a 2005 television film. *The Exonerated* used a rotating cast of celebrities performing monologues drawn from interviews the playwrights conducted with people sentenced to death for crimes they did not commit. Some had been on death row for more than twenty years before they were exonerated.

This was a crucial moment in the history of the anti–death penalty movement. In 1992 Barry Scheck and Peter Neufeld founded the Innocence Project at Yeshiva University's Benjamin N. Cardozo School of Law in order to provide broader access to DNA technology. More than two hundred people have been cleared since this project began, including more than a dozen death row inmates.[25] In addition, David Protess, a professor at Northwestern University's Medill School of Journalism, founded the Medill Innocence Project in 1999. Journalism students were instrumental in finding evidence of wrongful convictions that eventually led to the exoneration of eleven inmates, including five on Illinois's death row.[26] These revelations set off a spate of investigations and confessions revealing, among other things, flawed procedures in thousands of cases at the Federal Bureau of Investigation, false testimony in West Virginia, and negligence and misrepresentation of evidence in Houston.[27]

In 2002 the producers of *The Exonerated* staged a performance for Illinois Governor George Ryan, then considering commuting the sentences of that state's death row inmates in response to the discoveries made by the investigative journalism students at Northwestern. The next day, Ryan pardoned Gary Gauger, one of the six people featured in the play. Ryan saw the play a second time and commuted the sentences of all 164 inmates on Illinois's death row in January 2003.[28] The risk of executing innocent people played a large role in Ryan's decision.[29]

In less visible ways, the techniques pioneered by the Family and Theatre for the Forgotten remain central to prison cultural programming. For example, in 1998 the playwright Eve Ensler began leading writing workshops at New York's Bedford Hills Correctional Facility that concluded with well-known actresses Glenn Close, Rosie Perez, and Ruby Dee, among many others, performing inmate works.[30] Ensler's efforts were supported in part by a fundraiser featuring performances of inmate works at New York's Lincoln Center, where Miguel Piñero's *Short Eyes* had opened almost thirty years earlier. Furthermore, a 2006 performance by the Black Repertory Group of Berkeley, California, captured some of the activist sensibilities of the prison theater of the 1970s. The performance began at 12:01 A.M. on December 13 and starred Darby Tillis, an exonerated death row inmate from Chicago, as Stanley "Tookie" Williams. Williams had been killed by the State of California exactly one year earlier, in a case that garnered international attention. Williams founded the Crips youth gang in 1971 and had been convicted of murder in 1979. In the years he spent on California's death row, Williams became an internationally known advocate of nonviolence through youth programs and wrote an eight volume series of books providing strategies for young people to avoid gang membership.

In the end, then, as with so many lessons of the 1970s, the cultural life of prisons and prisoners leaves one with a series of paradoxes. The historian Bruce J. Schulman may have put it best when he asked, "Did [Nixon's] presidency mark the last gasp of postwar liberalism—of energetic, activist government? Or did it mark the onset of a new, more cautious era—of small government, fiscal conservatism, diverting resources and initiative from the public to the private sector?"[31] In the context of the prisons and the criminal justice system more broadly, the question might be reworded: Did the era represent the last gasp of reform-minded programming or the onset of a more repressive regime that would fully flower in the 1980s and 1990s? Both tendencies were present. In his introduction to Abbott's *In the Belly of the Beast*, the novelist Norman Mailer revealed more than his own glorification of violent men when he wrote that "not only the worst of the young are sent to prison, but the best—that is, the proudest, the bravest, the most daring, the most enterprising, and the most undefeated of the poor."[32] Mailer called this the "paradox at the core of penology." The public fascination with both the political and cultural analysis and the social deviance of Jack Henry Abbott, Judy Lucero, George Jackson, Miguel Piñero, and Carolyn Baxter, among others, allowed some to see the brutality of the criminal justice system. For others, the ongoing struggles of these writers and artists with the prison system or with drug addiction proved that nothing works. If people with talent and connections could not be redeemed, then what hope could exist for rehabilitation? Rather than a sign of redemption, talent and accomplishment became greater evidence of guilt.

While the work continues, the artists and teachers who continue to go into American prisons are little more than a skeleton crew, applying for grants to provide sorely needed and much appreciated programming. Outside of prison walls, a handful of activists, scholars, and aficionados know of the work during the 1970s. Walk into a classroom or studio inside of a prison, however, and you will find a community of artists and writers who nurture that legacy by creating new works, participating in the few programs that remain, and reminding anyone who will listen of the little-known writers who fostered a movement. Beyond this immediate impact, the cultural work of incarcerated people represents a key moment at the onset of our current era of incarceration. Since the Cold War—and especially since the War on Drugs—incarceration has become the primary response to crimes committed by poor people in the United States. Without the structures left in place by the 1970s, there would be virtually no aesthetic programming in U.S. prisons. Perhaps the most important paradox is this: the period that saw the solidification of a law-and-order response to criminality also gave rise to an extraordinary range of opportunities for prisoners to access cultural and educational programs. Artists, writers, and filmmakers continue to tell the stories of people behind bars. Prison administrators and cultural programmers find ways to encourage cultural expression. Today Art without Walls/Free Space, *Fortune News*, the PEN Prison Writing Program, the Prison Creative Arts Project, Arts-in-Correction, Arts in Prison Inc., the Children's Prison Art Project, Free Write Jail Arts and Literacy Program, pARTners Unlimited, Inside-Out, the Bard Prison Initiative, the Theater of Empowerment, the Medea Project, and Voices from the Inside are among the many programs that provide educational and arts programming to people behind bars.

Incarcerated people would write, perform, and create visual art without these programs, but the programs provide access to resources and audiences outside of prisons. This last point is particularly important because in addition to revealing the experience of prison from the perspectives of incarcerated people, these programs also show us, to quote Angela Davis, that "prison walls are not entirely unscalable."[33] Incarcerated people during the 1970s hoped that the prison walls that segregated them from the larger world might reveal unseen aspects of U.S. society. Their words crossed the wall, but they also helped many people to rethink the meaning of the walls and, ultimately, the society that produced them. More recently, the poet Easy Waters unpacked the meanings of the marble walls of Mount Pleasant Prison, the forerunner of Sing Sing. In his poem "Chronicling Sing Sing Prison" (1994), which won the PEN American Center prize, Waters animates the walls themselves by recalling the inmates from Auburn Prison who arrived on the banks of the Hudson in 1825: "the prisoners labored to build their own cells" on land named for the Mohegans, who called themselves and their village Sint Sincks. Once the prison cells were complete, the inmates' labor turned to cutting granite to build nineteenth- and twentieth-century corporate and public buildings: a courthouse in Troy, a government building in New Haven, the city hall in Albany. Designed by the leading architects of their day, these buildings would eventually land on the National Register of Historic Places with no mention of the Sing Sing marble. It was not just hypocritical that convict labor built the key institutions of government; the absence of explicit recognition of this contribution was itself a kind of admission of collective complicity. It would take prisoners like Waters to remind the country that "if you get close enough to the shore / to the granite known as Sing Sing marble / you can hear the ghosts of prisoners' past."[34]

NOTES

Introduction

1. Zayd Shakur, "America Is the Prison," in *Off the Pigs! The History and Literature of the Black Panther Party*, edited by G. Louis Heath (Metuchen, N.J.: Scarecrow, 1976), 247–80, mimeographed article, New York, N.Y., Oct. 17, 1970. Shakur attributed the insight to Malcolm X. See, e.g., Malcolm X, "The Harlem Hate-Gang Scare," *Malcolm X Speaks* (New York: Grove, 1965), 64–71. In that discussion, Malcolm X said that "our people in this particular society live in a police state" (66). New Jersey state troopers killed Shakur in 1973.

2. Angela Yvonne Davis, "I Am a Communist Revolutionary," in Heath, *Off the Pigs!*, 255, mimeographed article, Black Panther Party, Los Angeles chapter, Nov. 17, 1970.

3. Eldridge Cleaver, *Soul on Ice* (New York: McGraw-Hill, 1968), 59.

4. Fania Jordan Davis, quoted in Bettina Aptheker, *The Morning Breaks: The Trial of Angela Davis*, 2d ed. (Ithaca, N.Y.: Cornell University Press, 1997), 31.

5. Ibid., 26.

6. Editorial, *New York Times*, Oct. 16, 1970, quoted in ibid., 24.

7. Leonard Peltier, *Prison Writings: My Life Is My Sun Dance*, edited by Harvey Arden (New York: St. Martin's, 1999); Mumia Abu-Jamal, *Death Blossoms: Reflections from a Prisoner of Conscience* (Farmington, Pa.: Plough, 1997); Abu-Jamal, *Live from Death Row* (New York: Harper Perennial, 1996). Ruchell Magee and Hugo Pinell, two men associated with George Jackson, remain in prison as well. The Oakland-based Prison Activist Resource Center tracks close to one hundred political prisoners, many of whom have been incarcerated since the 1970s. For the periodically updated list, see Prison Activist Resource Center, ⟨www.prisonactivist.org.⟩

8. Angela Davis to George Jackson, June 2, 1970, letter read into the record of the *People of the State of California vs. Angela Y. Davis*; rpt. in Aptheker, *Morning Breaks*, 209.

9. "Entertainers Raise $38,000 for Angela Davis Defense," *New York Times*, Mar. 6, 1972. See also Sol Stern, "The Campaign to Free Angela Davis . . . and Ruchell Magee," *New York Times Magazine*, June 27, 1971, 8.

10. "Long John," *Negro Prison Camp Work Songs*, recorded and produced by Pete and Toshi Seeger (New York: Ethnic Folkways Library, 1956); lyrics transcribed in Harold Courlander, *A Treasury of Afro-American Folklore* (New York: Crown, 1976), 407–9.

11. See also Alan Lomax, *The Land Where the Blues Began* (New York: New Press, 2002), 256–313.

12. "Long John."

13. Lomax, *Land Where the Blues Began*, 258.

14. H. Bruce Franklin, ed., *Prison Writing in Twentieth-Century America* (New York: Penguin, 1998), 8. Franklin developed this thesis in 1978. The most recent edition of his pathbreaking study, *The Victim as Criminal and Artist*, is titled *Prison Literature in America: The Victim as Criminal and Artist* (New York: Oxford University Press, 1989). Similar arguments about the relationship between slavery and incarceration appear throughout the political, cultural, and historical literature on prisons. See, e.g., Scott Christianson, *With Liberty for Some: Five Hundred Years of Imprisonment in America* (Boston: Northeastern University Press, 1998); Neil Websdale, *Policing the Poor: From Slave Plantation to Public Housing* (Boston: Northeastern University Press, 2001); David Oshinsky, "*Worse than Slavery*": *Parchman Farm and the Ordeal of Jim Crow Justice* (New York: Simon Cand Schuster, 1997); and Charles J. Ogletree Jr. and Austin Sarat, eds., *From Lynch Mobs to the Killing State: Race and the Death Penalty in America* (New York: New York University Press, 2006).

15. Ronnie Reed, "Open Letter," in *From the Cold Jaws of Prison: By Inmates and Ex-Inmates, Musicians, and Poets from Attica, Rikers, and the Tombs*, sound recording (New York: Folkways, 1971).

16. Laws of New York, 1822, chap. 273, sec. 3; Laws of New York, 1829, Revised Statutes, part 4, chap. 3, title 2, sec. 58.

17. Laws of New York, 1846, chap. 324, sec. 7.

18. Laws of New York, 1847, chap. 460, title 2, art. 1, sec. 48, subdiv. 12.

19. Prison Association of New York, *Twenty-Sixth Annual Report of the Executive Committee of the Prison Association of New York*, Reports, 1871 to 1873 (vol. 7), New York State Archives, Albany, 187–88.

20. Larry E. Sullivan, *The Prison Reform Movement: Forlorn Hope* (Boston: Twayne, 1990), 17.

21. Wines, quoted in ibid., 18.

22. Christianson, *With Liberty for Some*, 180. See also Oshinsky, "*Worse Than Slavery*."

23. Christianson, *With Liberty for Some*, 177.

24. Ibid., 180.

25. Estelle Freedman, *Their Sisters' Keepers: Women's Prison Reform in America, 1830–1930* (Ann Arbor: University of Michigan Press, 1981), 41.

26. David J. Rothman, *Conscience and Convenience: The Asylum and Its Alternatives in Progressive America* (Boston: Little, Brown, 1980), 126.

27. Ibid., 129.

28. Freedman, *Their Sisters' Keepers*, 115.

29. Ibid., 109.

30. Rothman, *Conscience and Convenience*, 324.

31. Freedman, *Their Sisters' Keepers*, 146. Freedman goes on to point out that these shortcomings did not result in a loss of support for reforms. Opposition to reformatories, prison farms, and juvenile reform schools came largely from "those who favored more punitive measures in traditional penal institutions" (146).

32. Edgardo Rotman, "The Failure of Reform," in *The Oxford History of the Prison: The Practice of Punishment in Western Society*, edited by Norval Morris and David J. Rothman (New York: Oxford University Press, 1998), 159.

33. Sullivan, *Prison Reform Movement*, 36–37.

34. D. Ross Pugmire, *The Administration of Personnel in Correctional Institutions* (New York: Bureau of Publications, Teachers College, 1937), 2.

35. Ibid., 14–15.

36. See, e.g., Walter M. Wallack, Glenn M. Kendall, and Howard L. Briggs, *Education within Prison Walls* (New York: Teachers College Press, 1939).

37. Rotman, "Failure of Reform," 161.

38. Ibid., 165.

39. Quoted in Christianson, *With Liberty for Some*, 233.

40. Sullivan, *Prison Reform Movement*, 48.

41. Ibid., 54.

42. Nathan Leopold, *Life plus Ninety-Nine Years* (Garden City, N.Y.: Doubleday, 1958), 189–91.

43. Ibid., 261.

44. Kate Richards O'Hare, *In Prison* (Seattle: University of Washington Press, 1976), 93.

45. Jimmy Santiago Baca, *Working in the Dark: Reflections of a Poet of the Barrio* (Santa Fe, N.M.: Red Crane, 1992), 8.

46. The college program had far higher numbers of violent criminals than the prison's general population. Stuart Adams, *The San Quentin Prison College Project*, Final Report, Phase 1 (Berkeley: University of California School of Criminology, Apr. 1968), 27.

47. Michel Crozier, Samuel P. Huntington, and Joji Watanuki, *The Crisis of Democracy: Report on the Governability of Democracies to the Trilateral Commission*, Task Force Report no. 8 (New York: New York University Press, 1975), 113.

Chapter One

1. Richard M. Nixon, "Presidential Nomination Acceptance Speech in Miami Beach, Fla., August 8, 1968," ⟨http://www.presidency.ucsb.edu/shownomination.php?convid=17⟩; accessed May 31, 2007.

2. Milton Viorst, "Justice Department Is an Institution for Law Enforcement, Not Social Improvement," *New York Times Magazine*, Aug. 10, 1969, 10–11, cited in James W. Button, *Black Violence: Political Impact of the 1960s Riots* (Princeton, N.J.: Princeton University Press, 1978), 135.

3. For example, Michael Flamm argues that Nixon's law-and-order campaign rhetoric marked the key turning point in the rise of postwar conservatism. Michael W. Flamm, *Law and Order: Street Crime, Civil Unrest, and the Crisis of Liberalism in the 1960s* (New York: Columbia University Press, 2005).

4. Thomas J. Sugrue, *The Origins of the Urban Crisis: Race and Inequality in Postwar Detroit* (Princeton, N.J.: Princeton University Press, 1996).

5. Bruce J. Schulman, *Lyndon B. Johnson and American Liberalism* (Boston: Bedford, 1995).

6. Flamm acknowledges that law and order would remain a fixture of political campaign rhetoric, George H. W. Bush's 1988 use of Willie Horton being the most notable example; however, he sees a "decline of law and order in presidential races after 1968." Flamm, *Law and Order*, 178.

7. Ruth Wilson Gilmore, "The Wages of Abolition: Race, Gender and the Changing State," unpublished lecture at Vassar College, Poughkeepsie, N.Y., Oct. 2004.

8. Ruth Wilson Gilmore, *Golden Gulag: Prisons, Surplus, Crisis, and Opposition in Globalizing California* (Berkeley: University of California Press, 2007), 24.

9. Ibid., 39.

10. Ibid., 88.

11. Michael Denning, *The Cultural Front: The Laboring of American Culture in the Twentieth Century* (New York: Verso, 1996), xx.

12. Christopher P. Wilson, "'Where's Whitey?': *Black Mass*, Ethnic Criminality, and the Problem of the Informant," *Crime, Law and Social Change* 43, nos. 1–2 (2005): 177. See also Wilson, *Cop Knowledge: Police Power and Cultural Narrative in the Twentieth Century* (Chicago: University of Chicago Press, 2000).

13. Wilson, "'Where's Whitey?,'" 178.

14. James Baldwin, *The Fire Next Time* (New York: Vintage, 1993), 19.

15. A radio version of the song maintained the song's vision of a wasted life but did not include its critique of the criminal justice system. Stevie Wonder, "Living for the City," *Innervisions* (Detroit: Tamla Records, 1973).

16. Huey P. Newton, "Eulogy for Jonathan Jackson and William Christmas," delivered at Saint Augustine's Church, Oakland, Calif., Aug. 15, 1970, rpt. in *Off the Pigs! The History and Literature of the Black Panther Party*, edited by G. Louis Heath (Metuchen, N.J.: Scarecrow 1976), 322–23; Robert Chrisman, "White Racism, Black Crime, and American Justice: An Application of the Colonial Model to Explain Crime and Race," *Phylon* 36, no. 1 (1975): 14–22; George Jackson, *Soledad Brother: The Prison Letters of George Jackson* (New York: Bantam, 1970), 173–90; Angela Y. Davis, "Political Prisoners, Prisons, and Black Liberation," in *If They Come in the Morning: Voices of Resistance* (New Rochelle, N.Y.: Third Press, 1971), 19–36. For a discussion of the radical critique of American criminal justice, see Lee Bernstein, "The Age of Jackson: George Jackson and the Culture of American Prisons in the 1970s," *Journal of American Culture* 30, no. 3 (Sept. 2007), 310–23; and Eric Cummins, *The Rise and Fall of California's Radical Prison Movement* (Stanford, Calif.: Stanford University Press, 1994).

17. Katherine Beckett, *Making Crime Pay: Law and Order in Contemporary American Politics* (New York: Oxford University Press, 1997), 83.

18. Ibid., 84–85.

19. Joe McGinniss, *The Selling of the President 1968* (New York: Penguin, 1988).

20. Keith Beattie, *The Scar That Binds: American Culture and the Vietnam War* (New York: New York University Press, 2000), 79.

21. *Nixon/Wallace: 1968 TV Election Spots*, video recording (Chicago: International

Historic Films, c1985). Nixon used a similar line in his acceptance speech at the GOP convention in Miami.

22. Donald Janson, "Police Assaults on Twenty-One Newsmen in Chicago Are Denounced by Officials and Papers," *New York Times*, Aug. 28, 1968; "Churchill Grandson, Newsman, Assails Chicago Police as Brutal," *New York Times*, Aug. 28, 1968.

23. Franklin Delano Roosevelt, "Inaugural Address," Mar. 4, 1933. Full text available at John Woolley and Gerhard Peters, *The American Presidency Project* (Santa Barbara: University of California), ⟨http://www.presidency.ucsb.edu/ws/?pid=14473⟩; accessed May 31, 2007.

24. Franklin Delano Roosevelt, "State of the Union Address," Jan. 6, 1942. Full text available at John Woolley and Gerhard Peters, *The American Presidency Project*, Santa Barbara: University of California, ⟨http://www.presidency.ucsb.edu/ws/?pid=16253⟩; accessed May 31, 2007.

25. Richard M. Nixon, "What Has Happened to America?," *Reader's Digest*, Oct. 1967, 50, quoted in Button, *Black Violence*, 135.

26. Ibid.

27. Hazel Erskine, "The Polls: Politics and Law and Order," *Public Opinion Quarterly* 38, no. 4 (1974–75): 634.

28. Ibid., 633. It is important to note, however, that although a large majority of people wanted the courts to give long sentences, they also wanted prisons to emphasize rehabilitation. More than 70% of Republicans and Democrats agreed that the main emphasis of prisons should be rehabilitation of the individual offender, with less than 10% agreeing that they should primarily punish and less than 15% agreeing that they should primarily protect society. Ibid. Also, while Nixon's "law-and-order" message surely resonated with many voters, I do not mean to argue that this was the primary reason people voted for him. Nixon also tapped into the great displeasure with the Vietnam War. As William Chambliss points out, while 29% of those polled in 1968 believed that "crime, lawlessness, looting, and rioting" were among "the most important problem[s] facing the nation," this paled in comparison to the 52% who put Vietnam on their list. Chambliss believes that the moral panic was primarily a construct of the New Right, not a response to voter demand. See Chambliss, "Policing the Ghetto Underclass: The Politics of Law and Law Enforcement," *Social Problems* 41, no. 2 (1994): 188.

29. This interpretation of Nixon's employment of drug treatment somewhat contradicts that of Michael Massing. Massing tells a compelling story about the replacement of drug treatment policies by the "get tough" approach during Nixon's first term in office. Michael Massing, *The Fix* (New York: Simon and Schuster, 1998), 113–31.

30. Louis Althusser, "Ideology and Ideological State Apparatuses (Notes towards an Investigation)," in *Lenin and Philosophy and Other Essays*, translated by Ben Brewster (London: NLB, 1971), 121–73.

31. Ibid., 131.

32. Ibid., 127.

33. Ibid., 128.

34. Christian Parenti, *Lockdown America: Police and Prisons in the Age of Crisis* (New York: Verso, 2000), 3–4.

35. Paul Takagi, "The Walnut Street Jail: A Penal Reform to Centralize the Powers of the State," in *Crime and Capitalism: Readings in Marxist Criminology*, edited by David F. Greenberg (Philadelphia: Temple University Press, 1993), 542. Originally published in *Federal Probation* (Dec. 1975): 18–26.

36. William Ker Muir, *Police: Streetcorner Politicians* (Chicago: University of Chicago Press, 1977), 37.

37. Ibid., 48.

38. Ibid., 9.

39. Ibid., 112.

40. Ibid., 266.

41. James Q. Wilson and George L. Kelling, "Broken Windows: The Police and Neighborhood Safety," *Atlantic Monthly*, Mar. 1982, 29–38. Wilson's influence on contemporary policing is symbolized in part by the California attorney general's "James Q. Wilson Award for Excellence in Community Policing," given annually to "California law enforcement agencies who have successfully institutionalized the philosophy of community oriented policing." ⟨http://www.safestate.org/index.cfm?navid=28⟩; accessed July 13, 2004.

42. *The Negro Family: The Case for National Action* (Washington, D.C.: Office of Policy Planning and Research, U.S. Department of Labor, 1965).

43. Daryl Michael Scott, *Contempt and Pity: Social Policy and the Image of the Damaged Black Psyche* (Chapel Hill: University of North Carolina Press, 1997), 152. For a critique of the Moynihan Report, see Lee Rainwater and William L. Yancey, eds., *The Moynihan Report and the Politics of Controversy* (Cambridge: MIT Press, 1967).

44. Edward C. Banfield and James Q. Wilson, *City Politics* (Cambridge: Harvard University Press and the MIT Press, 1963), 295. See also Malcolm X, *The Speeches of Malcolm X at Harvard* (New York: Morrow, 1968). There is an interesting exchange between Wilson and Malcolm X.

45. Banfield and Wilson, *City Politics*, 295.

46. James Q. Wilson, *Thinking about Crime* (New York: Basic, 1975).

47. Ibid., 20.

48. Ibid., 28.

49. David J. Rothman, *The Discovery of the Asylum: Social Order and Disorder in the New Republic* (Boston: Little, Brown, 1971).

50. Wilson, *Thinking about Crime*, 39.

51. Jane Jacobs, *The Death and Life of Great American Cities* (New York: Random House, 1993), 40. As the intellectual historian Howard Brick points out, the ideal neighborhoods Jacobs saw were "places such as Greenwich Village and San Francisco's North Beach" rather than the "wastelands" and "jungles" of public housing projects containing large numbers of people of color. At the time, both Greenwich Village and North Beach were mixed-class but largely white and white ethnic communities. Brick, *Age of Contradiction: American Thought and Culture in the 1960s* (Ithaca, N.Y.: Cornell University Press, 2000), 100.

52. Wilson explicitly made the link between Jacob's earlier work and his own: "Jane Jacobs described how and to what ends informal community controls operate in

working-class Italian sections of New York and elsewhere. Middle-class black neighborhoods tend also to develop a distinctive code." Wilson, *Thinking about Crime*, 33.

53. Ibid., 37.

54. Ibid., 98.

55. Eric Monkkonen, *Police in Urban America* (New York: Cambridge University Press, 1981), 55.

56. Ibid., 62.

57. Simon Cole, *Suspect Identities: A History of Fingerprinting and Criminal Identification* (Cambridge: Harvard University Press, 2001).

58. Michael Willrich, *City of Courts: Socializing Justice in Progressive Era Chicago* (New York: Cambridge University Press, 2003), xxxv.

59. Clare Bond Potter, *War on Crime: Bandits, G-Men, and the Politics of Mass Culture* (New Brunswick, N.J.: Rutgers University Press, 1998), 13.

60. Ibid., 37.

61. Edward Escobar, *Race, Police, and the Making of a Political Identity: Mexican Americans and the Los Angeles Police Department, 1900–1945* (Berkeley: University of California Press, 1999), 158.

62. Ibid.

63. Christopher P. Wilson, *Cop Knowledge: Police Power and Cultural Narrative in Twentieth-Century America* (Chicago: University of Chicago Press, 2000), 9.

64. James Q. Wilson, interviewed by Ben Wattenberg on *The First Measured Century*, Public Broadcasting System, 2000, ⟨http://www.pbs.org/fmc/interviews/jwilson.htm⟩. The President's Commission on Law Enforcement and the Administration of Justice was created by executive order in 1965. See also *The Challenge of Crime in a Free Society: A Report by the President's Commission on Law Enforcement and the Administration of Justice* (New York: Avon, 1968).

65. Jonathan Simon, *Governing through Crime: How the War on Crime Transformed American Democracy and Created a Culture of Fear* (New York: Oxford University Press, 2007), 91.

66. *Challenge of Crime in a Free Society.*

67. Ibid., 255.

68. Governor's Commission on the Los Angeles Riots (McCone Commission), *Violence in the City: An End or a Beginning?* (Los Angeles: State of California, 1965).

69. Ibid., 28. See also Jill Nelson, ed., *Police Brutality: An Anthology* (New York: Norton, 2000).

70. In fact, the introduction to the paperback edition criticizes the commission (and by extension, police departments) for minimizing the extent of police brutality, noting that "public fear about crime encourage[s] police excesses" and that "such excesses are often obviously or tacitly approved by the political power structure." Isidore Silver, introduction to *Challenge of Crime in a Free Society*, 28. In 1968 the *New York Times* reported that 27% of police officers in three urban slums were guilty of police misconduct. "Misconduct Laid to 27% of Police in Three Cities' Slums," *New York Times*, July 7, 1968. See Ramsey Clark, *Crime in America* (New York: Simon and Schuster, 1970).

71. *Challenge of Crime in a Free Society*, 412.

72. Ibid., 415–20.

73. Ramsey Clark was one of the few people who did not underestimate the roles police brutality and discriminatory policing played in the urban riots of the late 1960s. For much of the Johnson administration, Clark represented the best hope of reformers who saw increased criminalization and incarceration as having little value in the fight against crime. Clark brought a visionary zeal to his work, arguing that crime was a product of dehumanization brought on by poverty, poor housing, racism, and all their byproducts. Clark, *Crime in America*, 5.

74. Dan Baum, *Smoke and Mirrors: The War on Drugs and the Politics of Failure* (Boston: Little, Brown, 1996), 9.

75. Malcolm M. Feeley and Austin D. Sarat, *The Policy Dilemma: Federal Crime Policy and the Law Enforcement Assistance Administration* (Minneapolis: University of Minnesota Press, 1980), 61.

76. Simon, *Governing through Crime*, 94.

77. Parenti, *Lockdown America*, 8.

78. Despite a century of reform movements, "in 1965 *only four* states mandated police training; more than twenty states did not even have *minimum* educational and literacy requirements for their recruits." Ibid., 15; emphasis in original.

79. Ronald Goldfarb, *Perfect Villains, Imperfect Heroes: Robert F. Kennedy's War against Organized Crime* (New York: Random House, 1995); See also Lee Bernstein, *The Greatest Menace: Organized Crime in Cold War America* (Amherst: University of Massachusetts Press, 2002), 180.

80. Bruce J. Schulman, *Lyndon B. Johnson and American Liberalism* (Boston: Bedford, 1995), 100.

81. Simon, *Governing through Crime*, 105.

82. Charles E. Jones, "The Political Repression of the Black Panther Party, 1966–1971: The Case of the Oakland Bay Area," *Journal of Black Studies* 18, no. 4 (1988): 415–34.

83. Button, *Black Violence*, 139.

84. Brick, *Age of Contradiction*, 163.

85. Ibid., 158.

86. Jill Jonnes, *Hep-Cats, Narcs, and Pipe Dreams: A History of America's Romance with Illegal Drugs* (New York: Scribner, 1996), 44, 47.

87. Ibid., 162.

88. Ibid.

89. Ibid., 163. In contrast to the alarm that led to these changes in sentencing laws, heroin addiction remained relatively rare—but it was rising. In 1956, the Federal Bureau of Narcotics estimated that there were 35,835 heroin addicts in the United States. By 1960, that number rose to 44,906. According the Office of National Drug Control Policy, there were between 750,000 and 1 million users of heroin in 2003. Drug Policy Information Clearinghouse, "Heroin Fact Sheet," ⟨http://www.whitehousedrugpolicy.gov/publications/factsht/heroin/index.html⟩. As of 2002, 7.1 million Americans were dependent on or abusers of illicit drugs. Of those, 3.2 million were dependent on or abusers of both alcohol and illicit drugs. Substance Abuse and Mental Health Services Administration, *Results from the 2002 National Survey on Drug Use and Health: National*

Findings (Office of Applied Studies, NHSDA Series H-22, DHHS Publication No. SMA 03-3836, Rockville, MD: SAMHSA, 2003). Computer file available online at ⟨http://www.oas.samhsa.gov/nhsda/2k2nsduh/Results/2k2Results.htm⟩.

90. Robert L. DuPont, "Heroin Addiction in the Nation's Capital, 1966–1973," in *One Hundred Years of Heroin*, edited by David F. Musto (Westport, Conn.: Auburn House, 2002), 68.

91. Eric Schlosser, *Reefer Madness: Sex, Drugs, and Cheap Labor in the American Black Market* (Boston: Houghton Mifflin, 2003), 23.

92. Jerome H. Jaffe, "One Bite of the Apple: Establishing the Special Action Office for Drug Abuse Prevention," in Musto, *One Hundred Years of Heroin*, 49.

93. Ibid., 53.

94. Egil Krough Jr., "Heroin Politics and Policy under President Nixon," in ibid., 41. Krough—a Nixon loyalist implicated in the Watergate scandal—also explains that the CIA and other government agencies sought to reduce poppy production in Turkey, Burma, and other producing countries. This is in sharp contrast to the findings of Alfred W. McCoy, *The Politics of Heroin: CIA Complicity in the Global Drug Trade* (New York: Lawrence Hill, 1991).

95. Bureau of Justice Statistics, "State and National Crime Level Estimates," computer file available online at ⟨http://bjsdata.ojp.usdoj.gov/dataonline/Search/Crime/State/StateCrime.cfm⟩.

96. Bruce J. Schulman, *The Seventies: The Great Shift in American Culture, Society, and Politics* (New York: Da Capo, 2001), 26.

97. Baum, *Smoke and Mirrors*, 1.

98. Massing, *Fix*, 119.

99. In 1968, there were fewer than 200,000 people in state and federal prisons. By 1976 there were 283,000. By the end of 2006, that number would stand at 1.7 million. Note that these figures only include state and federal prisons, omitting city and county jails. Including county and municipal jails brings the current figure to 2.5 million. U.S. Department of Justice, Bureau of Justice Statistics, ⟨http://ojp.usdoj.gov/bjs⟩.

100. Ronald Reagan, "Remarks at the Annual Conference of the National Sheriffs' Association in Hartford, Connecticut, June 20, 1984," *The Public Papers of President Ronald W. Reagan*, Ronald Reagan Presidential Library, ⟨http://www.reagan.utexas.edu/archives/speeches/1987/061287d.htm⟩; accessed May 31, 2007.

Chapter Two

1. Walter Rodney, "George Jackson: Black Revolutionary" *Maji Maji* 5 (n.d.): 4–6. The full text is available online at the World History Archives, ⟨http://www.hartford-hwp.com/archives/45a/477.html⟩. It is discussed in Rupert Charles Lewis, *Walter Rodney's Intellectual and Political Thought* (Detroit: Wayne State University Press, 1998), 177.

2. John Bergman, "Dirty Laundry: How a Theatre Company Grew Up in Corrections," in *The Arts in Prison*, edited by Stephen Hart (New York: Center for Advanced Study in Theatre Arts, Graduate School and University Center of the City University of New York, 1983), 150.

3. Mel Gordon, "The San Francisco Mime Troupe's 'The Mother,'" *Drama Review* 19, no. 2 (1975): 101.

4. Ibid., 95.

5. Rodney, "George Jackson," 4–6.

6. Bob Dylan, "George Jackson," Rams Horn Music, 1971.

7. C. L. R. James, "George Jackson," *Radical America* 5, no. 6 (1971): 54.

8. Eric Cummins, *The Rise and Fall of California's Radical Prison Movement* (Stanford, Calif.: Stanford University Press, 1994), 169.

9. Ibid., 139.

10. Raul Salinas Papers, Stanford University Department of Special Collections, box 7, folders 1–5.

11. Cummins, *Rise and Fall*, 139.

12. Ibid., 134.

13. Larry E. Sullivan, *The Prison Reform Movement: Forlorn Hope* (Boston: Twayne, 1990), 75.

14. Joy James, ed., *Imprisoned Intellectuals: America's Political Prisoners Write on Life, Liberation, and Rebellion* (Lanham, Md.: Rowman and Littlefield, 2003), 85.

15. Ibid. The Black Guerrilla Family continues on in American prisons, including some of its political orientation as a Marxist revolutionary movement. However, according to the U.S. Department of Justice, members of the group also engage in the illegal drug trade and other illicit activities. U.S. Department of Justice, National Institute of Corrections, *Management Strategies in Disturbances and with Gangs/Disruptive Groups* (Washington, D.C.: U.S. Department of Justice, 1991), 4.

16. Ibid.

17. George Jackson, *Soledad Brother: The Prison Letters of George Jackson* (New York: Bantam, 1970), 38.

18. Ibid., 167.

19. Ibid., 208.

20. Anonymous interviewee in Cummins, *Rise and Fall*, 138.

21. Lin Bao, excerpted in Timothy Cheek, *Mao Zedong and China's Revolution* (New York: Bedford/St. Martin's, 2002), 172.

22. Mao Zedong, *Quotations from Chairman Mao Tse-tung* (Peking: Foreign Languages Press, 1966), 60.

23. Mao Zedong, "American Imperialism Is Closely Surrounded by the Peoples of the World," in Cheek, *Mao Zedong*, 167–68.

24. "Riot in Gallery Halts U.N. Debate; American Negroes Ejected after Invading Session," *New York Times*, Feb. 16, 1961.

25. Cheek, *Mao Zedong*, 168.

26. Jackson, *Soledad Brother*, 221.

27. Ibid., 225–26.

28. Frantz Fanon, "Racism and Culture," speech before the First Congress of Negro Writers and Artists in Paris, Sept. 1956, in *Toward the African Revolution* (New York: Grove, 1967), 33.

29. Frantz Fanon, *The Wretched of the Earth* (New York: Grove, 1968), 38.

30. Frantz Fanon, *A Dying Colonialism* (New York: Grove, 1967), 179.

31. Fanon, *Wretched of the Earth*, 53.

32. Jackson, *Soledad Brother*, 169.

33. James, "George Jackson," 56.

34. Jackson, *Soledad Brother*, 216.

35. Luis Talamantez, quoted in Cummins, *Rise and Fall*, 196.

36. Ibid., 138.

37. Huey P. Newton, "Comments at Funeral of George Jackson," Aug. 1971, University of California at Berkeley, Social Activism Sound Recording Project: The Black Panther Party, ⟨http://www.lib.berkeley.edu/MRC/pacificapanthers.html⟩.

38. Martin Luther King Jr., *Why We Can't Wait* (New York: Mentor, 1964), 83.

39. Alvin Rudoff, "Prisons in Turmoil: An Involuntary Association" (PhD diss., University of California, Berkeley, 1964), 164. See also Bert Useem and Peter A. Kimball, "A Theory of Prison Riots," *Theory and Society* 16, no. 1 (1987): 92–93. In 1958 the Mexican Mafia was founded in Deuel with the goal of monopolizing illicit activity within the prison. U.S. Department of Justice, National Institute of Corrections, *Management Strategies in Disturbances and with Gangs/Disruptive Groups* (Washington, D.C.: U.S. Department of Justice, 1991), 3.

40. Kathleen Neal Cleaver and Susie Linfield, "The Education of Kathleen Neal Cleaver," *Transition* 77 (1998): 183.

41. Huey P. Newton, "Eulogy for Jonathan Jackson and William Christmas," delivered at Saint Augustine's Church, Oakland, Calif., Aug. 15, 1970, rpt. in *Off the Pigs! The History and Literature of the Black Panther Party*, edited by G. Louis Heath (Metuchen, N.J.: Scarecrow, 1976).

42. Courtney Morris, "Former Black Panther Recounts Prison Time," *Daily Texan*, Mar. 1, 2002. Available online at ⟨http://media.www.dailytexanonline.com⟩.

43. There were surely many more Panther chapters without formal recognition. See "The San Quentin Branch of the Black Panther Party Opens!," *Black Panther*, Feb. 27, 1971. On the Walla Walla chapter, see interview with Mark Cook, University of Washington, Seattle Civil Rights and Labor History Project, ⟨www.civilrights.washington.edu⟩.

44. Kenneth Lamott, *Chronicles of San Quentin* (New York: Ballantine, 1972), 216. In 1984, after living in exile in Europe for thirteen years, Bingham returned to the United States, where he stood trial two years later for his part in the escape attempt and was acquitted. There are many contradictory versions of this story, and I make no attempt to judge the accuracy of them here. See Jo Durden-Smith, *Who Killed George Jackson?* (New York: Knopf, 1976); Eric Mann, *Comrade George: An Investigation into the Life, Political Thought, and Assassination of George Jackson* (New York: Harper and Row, 1974); and Joy James, ed., *Imprisoned Intellectuals: America's Political Prisoners Write on Life, Liberation, and Rebellion* (Lanham, Md.: Rowman and Littlefield, 2003).

45. Georgia Jackson, quoted in Tom Wicker, "Death of a Brother," *New York Times*, Aug. 24, 1971.

46. Tom Wicker, "Surface and Core," *New York Times*, Sept. 9, 1971.

47. James Baldwin, quoted in Jackson, *Soledad Brother*, x.

48. Jack Bass and Jack Nelson, *The Orangeburg Massacre* (Macon, Ga.: Mercer University Press, 1999).

49. Roy Wilkins and Ramsey Clark, *Search and Destroy: A Report by the Commission of Inquiry into the Black Panthers and the Police* (New York: Metropolitan Applied Research Center, 1973).

50. New York State Special Commission on Attica, *Attica: The Official Report* (New York: Bantam, 1972), 40–41.

51. Ibid., 107.

52. Useem and Kimball, "A Theory of Prison Riots," 113.

53. Tom Wicker, *A Time to Die* (New York: Quadrangle/New York Times Book Co., 1975), 185.

54. Hisham Aidi, "Jihadis in the Hood: Race, Urban Islam and the War on Terror," *Middle East Report*, no. 224 (2002): 37.

55. Ibid., 40.

56. Although the Young Lords explicitly espoused Puerto Rican liberation, Iris Morales estimates that 25% of the group's membership was African American and that it included Cubans, Dominicans, Mexicans, Panamanians, Columbians, and one Japanese American. Morales, "¡PALANTE SIEMPRE PALANTE! The Young Lords," in *The Puerto Rican Movement: Voices from the Diaspora*, edited by Andrés Torres and José E. Velázquez (Philadelphia: Temple University Press, 1998), 215.

57. Ibid., 212.

58. Ibid., 214.

59. Jennifer Nelson, "'ABORTIONS UNDER COMMUNITY CONTROL'": Feminism, Nationalism, and the Politics of Reproduction among New York City's Young Lords," *Journal of Women's History* 13, no. 1 (2001): 157–80.

60. Wicker, *Time to Die*, 135.

61. Ibid., 137.

62. Donald Noble, interview, in *Prisons on Fire: George Jackson, Attica, and Black Liberation*, audio CD (San Francisco: Freedom Archives, 2001).

63. Frank Smith, interview, in *Prisons on Fire*. In fact, the McKay Commission put the number of inmates participating in that silent protest at seven hundred, out of an inmate population of 2,243. The number of inmates participating in the takeover was 1,281. New York State Special Commission, *Attica*, 187.

64. New York State Special Commission, *Attica*, 140.

65. Ibid., 76.

66. Ibid., 149.

67. Useem and Kimball, "A Theory of Prison Riots," 94.

68. New York State Special Commission, *Attica*, 234.

69. Edward Bunker, *Education of a Felon: A Memoir* (New York: St. Martin's, 2000), 265.

70. Photo of graffiti in New York State Commission, *Attica*, n.p.

71. "A Woman's Prison That Resembles a Campus," *New York Times*, Oct. 30, 1971.

72. Gloria Negri, "Robert Heard, at 57; Ex-Inmate Later Counseled Homeless," *Boston Globe*, Feb. 11, 2006, ⟨http://www.boston.com/news/globe/obituaries/

articles/2006/02/11/robert_heard_at_57_ex_inmate_later_counseled_homeless⟩; accessed June 16, 2008.

73. Jamie Bissonette, *When the Prisoners Ran Walpole: A True Story in the Movement for Prison Abolition* (Boston: South End, 2008), 69.

74. Ibid., 73.

75. "Walpole State Prison: Unrest and Reform," ABC Evening News, May 21, 1973, Television News Archive, Vanderbilt University, ⟨http://openweb.tvnews.vanderbilt.edu/1973-5/1973-05-21-ABC-14.html⟩; accessed June 13, 2008.

76. Bissonette, *When the Prisoners Ran Walpole*, 182.

Chapter Three

1. New York State Special Commission on Attica, *Attica: The Official Report* (New York: Bantam, 1972), 466.

2. "The Fifteen Practical Proposals," in Tom Wicker, *A Time to Die* (New York: Quadrangle/New York Times Book Co., 1975), 317. These were later expanded to thirty-three proposals, twenty-eight of which proved acceptable to Russell Oswald, commissioner of corrections. They also asked for, and were granted, a Spanish-language library. A side-by-side comparison of the proposals and those accepted by the Department of Corrections appears in the McKay Commission Report. New York State Special Commission, *Attica*, 251–57.

3. Errol Hill and James Vernon Hatch, *A History of African American Theater* (New York: Cambridge University Press, 2003), 387.

4. Leslie Catherine Sanders, *The Development of Black Theater in America: From Shadows to Selves* (Baton Rouge: Louisiana State University Press, 1989), 122.

5. Celes Tisdale, ed., *Betcha Ain't: Poems from Attica* (Detroit: Broadside, 1974).

6. Stewart A. Dippel, "The Attica Muse: Lessons from Prison," *History Teacher* 26, no. 1 (1992): 61–70.

7. The Pell Grant program stopped providing money for prison programs in 1991, due largely to the efforts of Sen. Jesse Helms of North Carolina. Jon Marc Taylor, "Pell Grants for Prisoners," in *Doing Time: Twenty-Five Years of Prison Writing—A PEN American Center Prize Anthology*, edited by Bell Gale Chevigny (New York: Arcade, 1999), 111. It is important to note that many of these programs were correspondence courses through the extension service of major universities. At the primary and secondary levels, other inmates routinely provided the instruction. Etheridge Knight describes how this worked in the Indiana State Prison in "Inside These Walls," in Etheridge Knight and Other Inmates of Indiana State Prison, *Black Voices from Prison* (New York: Pathfinder, 1970), 135.

8. See, e.g., Folsom Creative Writers Workshop, *Captive Voices: Echoes off the Walls III, An Anthology of Literary Works* (Paradise, Calif.: Dustbooks, 1975); Michael Hogan, ed., *Do Not Go Gentle: Poetry and Prose from behind the Walls* (Tucson, Ariz.: Blue Moon, 1977); Frank Graziano, ed., *A Season in the Hour: Poems from the Prisons of South Carolina* (Columbia: South Carolina Arts Commission, 1978); and Joseph Bruchac, ed., *The Light from Another Country: Poetry from American Prisons* (Greenfield Center, N.Y.: Greenfield Review Press, 1984). All received funding from the National Endowment for the Arts.

9. New Jersey State Council on the Arts Creative Writing Program, *Prison Poetry* (Trenton: New Jersey State Council on the Arts, 1973), copy in the Art and Architecture Collection, New York Public Library.

10. Liz Lerman, "Arts-in-Corrections: Art from California Prisons," in *Art in Other Places: Artists at Work in America's Community and Social Institutions* (Amherst, Mass.: Arts Extension Service Press, 2000). Available online at ⟨http://www.artandcommunity.com/aopcorrex.html⟩.

11. Richard Shelton, preface to *Do Not Go Gentle: Poetry and Prose from behind the Walls*, edited by Michael Hogan (Tucson, Ariz.: Blue Moon, 1977), iii.

12. Stuart Adams, *The San Quentin Prison College Project*, Final Report, Phase 1 (Berkeley: University of California School of Criminology, Apr. 1968), 1. Copy located in the Bancroft Library, University of California, Berkeley. According to Jon Marc Taylor, there were already twelve postsecondary programs in U.S. prisons in 1965. The University of Southern Illinois began its program in Stateville Prison in 1953. Taylor, "Pell Grants," 107. A fascinating account of how Nathan Leopold and Richard Loeb—the infamous, highly educated, upper-class convicted murderers—began a high school in Stateville in 1932 is in Nathan F. Leopold, *Life plus Ninety-Nine Years* (Garden City, N.Y.: Doubleday, 1958), 222–37. Prior to the founding of the University of Southern Illinois's program, prisoners—including Leopold—could take correspondence courses through many universities.

13. Faith G. Norris, preface to *Men in Exile: An Anthology of Creative Writing by Inmates of the Oregon State Penitentiary*, edited by Faith G. Norris and Sharon J. Springer (Corvallis: Oregon State University Press, 1973), 8.

14. Robert Martinson, "What Works? Questions and Answers about Prison Reform," *Public Interest*, Spring 1974, 25.

15. Ibid., 40–41.

16. Ibid., 41.

17. Rick Sarre, "Beyond 'What Works?' A Twenty-Five-Year Jubilee Retrospective of Robert Martinson," paper presented at the conference, "History of Crime, Policing and Punishment," Canberra, Australia, Dec. 9–10, 1999, 2.

18. Martinson, "What Works," 50.

19. Jerome Miller, "Criminology: Is Rehabilitation a Waste of Time?," *Washington Post*, Apr. 23, 1989.

20. W. M. Wallack, G. M. Kendall, and H. L. Briggs, *Education within Prison Walls* (New York: Teachers College Press, 1939), 19.

21. Lawrence G. Brewster, "An Evaluation of the Arts-in-Corrections Program of the California Department of Corrections," Apr. 1983. Unpublished study in possession of the William James Association, Santa Cruz, Calif.

22. California Department of Corrections, "Arts-in-Corrections Research Synopsis on Parole Outcomes for Participants Paroled December 1980–February 1987," unpublished copy in possession of William James Association, Santa Cruz, Calif.

23. Jean Trounstine, *Shakespeare behind Bars: The Power of Drama in a Women's Prison* (New York: St. Martin's, 2001), 125.

24. Ibid., 8–9.

25. Paul Goodman, quoted in Adams, *San Quentin Prison College Project*, 24.

26. Carol Muske and Gail Rosenblum, eds., *Songs from a Free Space: Writings by Women in Prison* (New York: Art without Walls, n.d.), 7.

27. W. Reason Campbell, *Dead Man Walking: Teaching in a Maximum Security Prison* (New York: Richard Marek, 1978), 30.

28. Earnest McBurrows, Deborah Gadiel, and Mary Ann Ludwig, *A Prison Art Program* (Chicago: Earnest McBurrows, Deborah Gadiel, and Mary Ann Ludwig, 1976), 8.

29. Doloris Holmes, "Interview with Cliff Joseph, 1972," Smithsonian Archives of American Art. Available online at ⟨http://artarchives.si.edu/oralhist/joseph72.htm⟩. See also Stephen C. Dubin, *Displays of Power: Memory and Amnesia in the American Museum* (New York: New York University Press, 1999).

30. The prison was demolished in 1974. Women are now housed at Rikers Island.

31. Faith Ringgold, quoted in Michele Wallace, "For the Women's House" (1972); rpt. in *Invisibility Blues* (New York: Verso, 1990), 36.

32. Ringgold, quoted in ibid.

33. Mary Schmidt Campbell, "Tradition and Conflict: Images of a Turbulent Decade, 1963–1973," in *Tradition and Conflict: Images of a Turbulent Decade, 1963–1973* (New York: Studio Museum in Harlem, 1985), 55.

34. Ringgold, quoted in Wallace, "For the Women's House," 40.

35. Julie Ault, "A Chronology of Selected Alternative Structures, Spaces, Artists' Groups, and Organizations in New York City, 1965–1985," in *Alternative Art New York, 1965–1985* (Minneapolis: University of Minnesota Press, 2002), 19. The Whitney later agreed to mount a show of African American art, but the BECC protested when the museum reneged on its agreement to include an African American curator.

36. Benny Andrews, "Benny Andrews Journal: A Black Artist's View of Artistic and Political Activism, 1963–1973," in *Tradition and Conflict: Images of a Turbulent Decade, 1963–1973* (New York: Studio Museum in Harlem, 1985), 69.

37. Doloris Holmes, "Interview with Cliff Joseph, 1972," Smithsonian Archives of American Art. Available online at ⟨http://artarchives.si.edu/oralhist/joseph72.htm⟩.

38. Benny Andrews and Rudolf Baranik, *The Attica Book* (South Hackensack, N.J.: Custom Communications System, 1972).

39. Andrews, "Benny Andrews Journal," 73.

40. Ault, "Chronology of Selected Alternative Structures," 20.

41. David Deitcher, "Polarity Rules: Looking at Whitney Annuals and Biennials, 1968–2000," in *Alternative Art, New York, 1965–1985* (Minneapolis: University of Minnesota Press, 2002), 201–47.

42. Benny Andrews, *Echoes: Prisons, U.S.A.* (New York: Studio Museum in Harlem, n.d. [1977]), n.p.

43. Ibid.

44. The BECC served as a direct inspiration for a similar program at Chicago's Cook County Jail. After hearing a speech by Andrews and meeting with Josephs, Earnest McBurrows, an art professor at the University of Illinois at Chicago Circle (now University of Illinois at Chicago [UIC]), hoped to transform what had been a small Tuesday-night

art class at the jail into a full-fledged art program. Following the example set by the New York City Department of Corrections and the BECC, McBurrows and UIC graduate student Deborah Galdiel worked within the institutional structures already in place. Earnest McBurrows, Deborah Gadiel, and Mary Ann Ludwig, *A Prison Art Program* (Chicago: Earnest McBurrows, Deborah Gadiel, and Mary Ann Ludwig, 1976), 4.

45. Michele Wallace, "A Women's Prison and the Movement" (1972), in *Invisibility Blues* (New York: Verso, 1990), 44.

46. Marjorie Fine Knowles, "Foundation Grants to Women's Groups," *Women's Studies Newsletter* 1, no. 5 (1973): 10; Wallace, "Women's Prison and the Movement," 45.

47. Muske and Rosenblum, *Songs from a Free Space.*

48. Assata Shakur, *Assata: An Autobiography* (Chicago: Lawrence Hill, 1984), 164.

49. Everson Museum of Art (Syracuse, N.Y.), *From Within: Selected Works by the Artists/Inmates of New York State Correctional Facility at Auburn (Maximum Security)*, National Collection of Fine Arts, Smithsonian Institution, Washington, D.C., Feb. 2–Mar. 25, 1973. Original catalog in New York Public Library, Art and Architecture Division, n.p.

50. Ibid.

51. Bell Gale Chevigny, introduction to *Doing Time*, xx.

52. James O. Finckenauer, *"Scared Straight!" and the Panacea Phenomenon* (Englewood Cliffs, N.J.: Prentice-Hall, 1982), 67.

53. Ibid., 71.

54. Ibid., 74.

55. Ibid.

56. "'Scared Straight!' Tops TV Network Competition," *New York Times*, Mar. 10, 1979.

57. John J. O'Connor, "TV: 'Scared Straight!,' Documentary," *New York Times*, Mar. 8, 1979. The *Newark Star-Ledger* reported similar statistics but placed the number of participants at eight thousand. Sheryl Feinstein, "Another Look at 'Scared Straight!,'" *Journal of Correctional Education* 56, no. 1 (2005): 41.

58. "The Scary Lesson of 'Scared Straight!,'" *New York Times*, Apr. 35, 1979.

59. John J. O'Connor, "Fact-Based Dramas Can Be Deceiving," *New York Times*, Nov. 2, 1980.

60. John J. O'Connor, "TV: Issues of Accuracy," *New York Times*, Nov. 1, 1979.

61. Anthony Petrosino, Carolyn Turpin-Petrosino, and John Buehler, *The Effects of 'Scared Straight!' and Other Juvenile Awareness Programs on Subsequent Offending* (Oslo, Norway: Campbell Collaboration, 2001).

62. National Center for Institutions and Alternatives, "'Scared Straight!': A Second Look," Baltimore: NCIA, 1978, ⟨http://www.ncianet.org/publicpolicy/publications/scaredstraight.asp⟩; accessed June 6, 2008.

63. United States Congress, House Committee on Education and Labor, Subcommittee on Human Resources, June 4, 1979, Oversight on *Scared Straight!*—Hearings before the House Subcommittee on Human Resources, 96th Congress, 1st sess., June 4 (Washington, D.C.: U.S. Government Printing Office, 1979); Martin Waldron, "Teen-

Agers' Visits to Prisons Criticized," *New York Times*, Apr. 26, 1979; Waldron, "Interest Is Revived in 'Scared Straight!,'" *New York Times*, Jan. 13, 1980.

64. The Juvenile Awareness Program continued to persevere through the 1980s and 1990s. New efforts to counteract the glorification of prison life included a rap record commissioned by the producers Dr. Jam and Phaze 5. In the late 1990s, two groups per day attended the program, five days a week. In 1999 HBO broadcast a follow-up documentary called *Scared Straight 99*. The following year, the New Jersey State Department of Corrections began cutting back on the program because of continued criticism of its effectiveness. Scared Straight! programs continue to operate around the country. Stephen Holden, "The Pop Life: Rap from the Inside," *New York Times*, May 27, 1991; George James, "'Scared Straight!' Takes a Detour," *New York Times*, July 9, 2000. A second program is now in operation at the Edna Mahan Correctional Facility for Women, ⟨http://www.state.nj.us/corrections/structure/html/community.html⟩; accessed June 11, 2008.

65. Arnold Shapiro, e-mail correspondence with author, June 19, 2009.

66. *Scared Straight!* would go on to become a touchstone in the "reality" television genre, with Arnold Shapiro becoming a noted producer of such shows as *Big Brother*, *Rescue 911*, and *Border Security USA*. See Jim Rutenberg, "Reality Producer Sought by CBS," *New York Times*, Feb. 21, 2001.

67. John J. O'Connor, "Fact-Based Dramas Can Be Deceiving," *New York Times*, Nov. 2, 1980.

68. Philip B. Taft, "The Lifers Program: Does It Work?," *New York Times*, Dec. 27, 1981.

69. Michael Davis, *Street Gang: The Complete History of "Sesame Street"* (New York: Viking, 2008).

70. Cheryl Smith, "'Sesame Street' Shown in Prisons," *News World*, May 25, 1977.

71. Richard Schwartz and Marsha Kranes, "Inmates Use TV to Babysit at U.S. Prison," *New York Post*, May 24, 1977.

72. Peter Rosen, interview with the author, New York, N.Y., June 2, 2008.

73. Jennifer Dunning, "U.S. Prison Inmates Tutor Visitors' Children," *New York Times*, May 25, 1977.

74. Peter Rosen, dir., *"Sesame Street" Goes to Prison*, Children's Television Workshop, 1977.

75. Smith, "'Sesame Street' Shown in Prisons."

76. Rosen, *"Sesame Street" Goes to Prison.*

77. George James, "'Scared Straight!' Takes a Detour," *New York Times*, July 9, 2000.

78. Robert L. Keller, "Some Unanticipated Positive Effects of a Juvenile Awareness Program on Adult Inmate Counselors," *International Journal of Offender Therapy and Comparative Criminology* 37, no. 1 (1993): 75–83.

Chapter Four

1. Juno Bakali Tshombe (Craig Dee Anderson), "Psychological Warfare at Norfolk Prison Camp," in Norfolk Prison Brothers, *Who Took the Weight? Black Voices from Norfolk Prison* (Boston: Little, Brown, 1972), 95.

2. Elma Lewis, foreword to *Who Took the Weight? Black Voices from Norfolk Prison* (Boston: Little, Brown, 1972), xiv. The Elma Lewis Technical Theater Training Program of the Massachusetts Correctional Institution, Norfolk, was a project of the Boston-based National Center of Afro-American Artists. This program is discussed in greater detail in chapter 5.

3. Ibid., xv.

4. Tshombe, "Psychological Warfare at Norfolk Prison Camp," in *Who Took the Weight? Black Voices from Norfolk Prison* (Boston: Little, Brown, 1972), 95.

5. Epigraph, *Who Took the Weight*, v.

6. Malcolm X, *The Autobiography of Malcolm X* (New York: Ballantine, 1964), 182.

7. Richard Brent Turner, *Islam in the African American Experience* (Bloomington: Indiana University Press, 1997), 182. These efforts continued to bear fruit. According to Asma Gull Hasnan, 90% of the estimated 300,000–350,000 American Muslim inmates in 1985 were African American. Asma Gull Hasnan, *American Muslims: The New Generation* (New York: Continuum, 2000), 75. The Nation of Islam's emphasis on economic independence, individual self-worth, and collective identity formation would fit well with both the ethics of the Black Arts movement and the needs of incarcerated African Americans. On the cultural significance of the Nation of Islam, see Lawrence H. Mamiya and C. Eric Lincoln, "Nation of Islam," in *Encyclopedia of African-American Culture and History*, edited by Jack Salzman et al. (New York: Macmillan Library Reference, 1996), 1966–69; and C. Eric Lincoln, *The Black Muslims in America* (Boston: Beacon, 1961).

8. Etheridge Knight, "Inside These Walls," 137.

9. David Lionel Smith, "Black Arts Movement," in *Encyclopedia of African American Culture and History*, edited by Jack Salzman et al. (New York: Macmillan Library Reference, 1996), 327.

10. Scott Christianson, *With Liberty for Some: Five Hundred Years of Imprisonment in America* (Boston: Northeastern University Press, 1998), 268; see also Bert Useem and Peter Kimball, *States of Siege: U.S. Prison Riots, 1971–1986* (New York: Oxford University Press, 1989).

11. Edward Bunker, "War behind Walls," *Harper's Magazine*, Feb. 1972, 39–47; rpt. in Burtono M. Atkins and Henry R. Glick, *Prisons, Protest, and Politics* (Englewood Cliffs, N.J.: Prentice-Hall, 1972), 60–76.

12. Zayd Shakur, "America Is the Prison," in *Off the Pigs! The History and Literature of the Black Panther Party*, edited by G. Louis Heath (Metuchen, N.J.: Scarecrow, 1976), 247–80, mimeographed article, New York, N.Y., Oct. 17, 1970.

13. Roberta Ann Johnson, "The Prison Birth of Black Power," *Journal of Black Studies* 5, no. 4 (1975): 395–414.

14. Huey P. Newton, "Eulogy for Jonathan Jackson and William Christmas," delivered at St. Augustine's Church, Twenty-Seventh and West Streets, Oakland, Calif., Aug. 15, 1970; rpt. in *Off the Pigs! The History and Literature of the Black Panther Party*, edited by G. Louis Heath (Metuchen, N.J.: Scarecrow, 1976), 322–23.

15. George Jackson, *Soledad Brother: The Prison Letters of George Jackson* (New York: Bantam, 1970), quoted in Johnson, "Prison Birth," 36.

16. Hettie Jones, *How I Became Hettie Jones* (New York: E. P. Dutton, 1990), 143–44.

17. Amiri Baraka, *The Autobiography of LeRoi Jones* (New York: Freundlich, 1984), 280.

18. Ibid., 263.

19. Ibid., 269.

20. Ibid., 270–71.

21. Ibid., 271.

22. Amiri Baraka, *Raise Race Rays Raze: Essays since 1965* (New York: Random House, 1971). See esp. "Newark Courthouse—'66 Wreck (Nigger Rec Room)," 3–9, and "From: The Book of Life," 49–55.

23. Amiri Baraka, *Police*, *Drama Review* 12, no. 4 (1968): 3–12.

24. Baraka, *Autobiography*, 273.

25. Marvin X, *Take Care of Business*, *Drama Review* 12, no. 4 (1968): 29–124.

26. Larry Neal, "The Black Arts Movement," in *Visions of a Liberated Future: Black Arts Movement Writings* (New York: Thunder's Mouth, 1989), 62.

27. H. Bruce Franklin, "Songs of an Imprisoned People," *MELUS* 6, no. 1 (1979): 6–22.

28. Larry Neal, "Shine Goes to Jail," in *Visions of a Liberated Future: Black Arts Movement Writings* (New York: Thunder's Mouth, 1989), 175.

29. Neal, "Black Arts Movement," 66.

30. Leroi Jones, "Black Art"; rpt. in Larry Neal, "Black Arts Movement," in *Visions of a Liberated Future: Black Arts Movement Writings* (New York: Thunder's Mouth, 1989), 65.

31. Baraka, *Police*, 1.

32. Neal, "Black Arts Movement," 75.

33. Ibid., 68.

34. Larry Neal, "Brother Pimp," in *Visions of a Liberated Future: Black Arts Movement Writings* (New York: Thunder's Mouth, 1989), 216–17.

35. H. Bruce Franklin, *Prison Writing in Twentieth-Century America* (New York: Penguin, 1998), 167.

36. Clarence Major, introduction to *The New Black Poetry*, (New York: International, 1969), 11, quoted in Patricia Liggins Hill, "'The Violent Space': The Function of the New Black Aesthetic in Etheridge Knight's Prison Poetry," *Black American Literature Forum* 14, no. 3 (1980): 115. Amiri Baraka contrasted "pimp art" with black nationalism in a 1969 *New York Times* essay. See Baraka, "Nationalism vs. PimpArt" [*sic*], in *Black Writers of America: A Comprehensive Anthology*, edited by Richard Barksdale and Kenneth Kinnamon (New York: Macmillan, 1972), 759–61.

37. Juno Bakali Tshombe (Craig Dee Anderson), "The Only for Real People (Two Pimps' View of Black People and the National Liberation Movement," in *Who Took the Weight? Black Voices from Norfolk Prison* (Boston: Little, Brown, 1972), 8–13.

38. Juno Bakali Tshombe (Craig Dee Anderson), "discovering myself," in *Who Took the Weight?*, 27.

39. James A. Lang, "A Letter for James Andrew Lang, Jr (Age Six)," in *Who Took the Weight?*, 61–62.

40. James A. Lang, "The (Un?)Making of a Revolutionary," in *Who Took the Weight?*, 133–37.

41. Ibid., 134.

42. Ibid., 137.

43. Pancho Aguila, a poet in the Creative Writers' Workshop in California's Folsom Prison noted the four steps it took to go from a convict to a revolutionary: "Convict / Ex-convict / Fugitive / Criminal / Revolutionary." Aguila, "Boomerang," in Folsom Writers, *Captive Voices: Echoes off the Walls III, An Anthology of Literary Works* (Paradise, Calif.: Dustbooks, 1975), 9.

44. Paula Massood, *Black City Cinema: African American Urban Experiences in Film* (Philadelphia: Temple University Press, 2003), 105.

45. Greg Tate, "Pimp and Circumstance," *Village Voice*, Oct 20, 1998.

46. Quoted in Douglas Taylor, "Showdown: Symbolic Violence and Masculine Performance in *The Autobiography of Malcolm X (As Told to Alex Haley)*," forthcoming in *Men and Masculinities.*

47. Iceberg Slim, *Pimp: The Story of My Life* (Los Angeles: Holloway House, 1967), 195, 309. For an overview of Iceberg Slim's life and novels, see Peter A. Muckley, "Iceberg Slim: Robert Beck—A True Essay at a Bio-Criticism of an Ex-Outlaw Artist," *Black Scholar* 25, no. 4 (1996): 18–25.

48. Helen Koblin, "Portrait of a Pimp," *Los Angeles Free Press*, Mar. 2, 1972; rpt. online at the Biography Project, Patrick Deese, ⟨popsubculture.com⟩; accessed June 1, 2009.

49. Greg Goode, "From *Dopefiend* to *Kenyatta's Last Hit*: The Angry Black Crime Novels of Donald Goines," *MELUS* 11, no. 3 (1984): 41.

50. Eddie B. Allen Jr., *Low Road: The Life and Legacy of Donald Goines* (New York: St. Martin's, 2004), 97.

51. Greg Goode, "Donald Goines," *Dictionary of Literary Biography*, vol. 33, edited by James E. Kibler Jr. (Farmington Hills, Mich.: Gale, 1984), 96–100.

52. Allen, *Low Road*, 106.

53. Goode, "From *Dopefiend* to *Kenyatta's Last Hit*," 42.

54. Donald Goines, *Dopefiend* (Los Angeles: Holloway House, 1971), 12.

55. Kathleen Neal Cleaver, "Back to Africa: The Evolution of the International Section of the Black Panther Party (1969–1972)," in *The Black Panther Party (Reconsidered)* (Baltimore: Black Classic, 1998), 230. See also Fanon Che Wilkins, "In the Belly of the Beast: Black Power, Anti Imperialism, and the African Liberation Solidarity Movement, 1968–1975" (PhD diss., New York University, 2001).

56. Donald Goines, *Kenyatta's Last Hit* (Los Angeles: Holloway House, 1975), 14.

57. Imani Kujichagulia, "Stride, Strut Lady," in *Bound and Free: The Poetry of Warriors behind Bars* (Washington, D.C.: King, 1976), 18. Copy in the Bancroft Library, University of California, Berkeley.

58. Amiri Baraka, "7 Principles of US Maulana Karenga & the Need for a Black Value System," in *Raise Race Rays Raze: Essays since 1965* (New York: Random House, 1971), 133–34.

59. Sanchez and Knight separated in 1970 after Knight proved unable to quit his heroin habit. He was arrested for possession again in 1971. Etheridge Knight, "Letters," *Callaloo* 19, no. 4 (1996): 956–64. This cycle of drug use, arrest, getting clean, productive writing, and self-doubt would continue. Jean Anaporte-Easton, "Etheridge Knight: Poet and Prisoner, an Introduction," *Callaloo* 19, no. 4 (1996): 941–46.

60. Etheridge Knight, "The Violent Space (or when your sister sleeps around for money)," in *Poems from Prison* (Detroit: Broadside, 1968), 23.

61. Ibid.

62. Etheridge Knight, preface to *Black Voices from Prison* (New York: Pathfinder, 1970), 6.

63. Maurice O. Wallace describes this contradiction as a theme in the history of African American masculinity. See "'I *Am* a Man': Latent Doubt, Public Protest and the Anxious Construction of Black American Manhood," in *Schomburg Studies on the Black Experience*, edited by Colin Palmer and Howard Dodson (Cambridge, U.K.: ProQuest, 2005), ⟨http://gateway.proquest.com/openurl?url_ver=Z39.88-2004&res_dat=xri:ssbe:&rft_dat=xri:ssbe:ft:essay:12WALL⟩; accessed June 1, 2009.

64. Michael Thomas Sr., "Poem to Angela from Black Political Prisoners," *Black Scholar* 2, nos. 8–9 (Apr.–May 1971): 50.

65. Gomvi Malik invoked both Assata Shakur and Angela Davis in a poem that critiqued the idea that African American women should be put on a pedestal at all. Malik, "Funky Nigger/Nigger Funky," in *Bound and Free: The Poetry of Warriors behind Bars* (Washington, D.C.: King, 1976), 14.

66. See, e.g., her discussion of Vietnamese, Cuban, and Algerian women in her autobiography. Angela Davis, *Angela Davis: An Autobiography* (New York: Random House, 1974), 371. See also the letter Davis wrote to George Jackson that was introduced as evidence at her trial, in Bettina Aptheker, *The Morning Breaks: The Trial of Angela Davis*, 2d ed. (Ithaca, N.Y.: Cornell University Press, 1997), 209–11.

67. Willi X, "To My Beautiful Woman," in *Captive Voices*, 203.

68. James A. Lang, "For My Ex-Wife," in *Who Took the Weight?*, 59.

69. Ibid.

70. Douglas Edward Taylor reads George Jackson's *Soledad Brother* against Daniel Patrick Moynihan's *The Negro Family: A Case for National Action* in his doctoral dissertation. Douglas Edward Taylor, "Hustlers, Nationalists, and Revolutionaries: African American Prison Narratives of the 1960s and 1970s" (PhD diss., University of North Carolina at Chapel Hill, 2002), 103–35.

71. Tomás Ybarra-Frausto, introduction to Raúl Salinas, *Un Trip through the Mind Jail y Otras Excursions* (Houston: Arte Público, 1999 [1980]), 7.

72. Raúl Salinas, "News from San Quentin," in *Un Trip through the Mind Jail*, 81–82.

73. Miguel R. López, *Chicano Timespace: The Poetry and Politics of Ricardo Sánchez* (College Station: Texas A&M University Press, 2001), 13.

74. Ricardo Sánchez, "Soledad Was a Girl's Name," in *Selected Poems* (Houston: Arte Público, 1985), 27.

75. Sánchez, "Three Days to Go," in *Selected Poems*, 43.

76. Ibid.

77. Ibid., 44.

78. Michele Wallace, *Black Macho and the Myth of the Superwoman* (New York: Dial, 1979), 32.

79. Michele Wallace, *Invisibility Blues* (New York: Verso, 1990), 42.

80. Carolyn Baxter, *Prison Solitary and Other Free Government Services* (Greenfield Center, N.Y.: Greenfield Review Press, 1979).

81. Judith Scheffler, *Wall Tappings: An International Anthology of Women's Prison Writings, 200 A.D. to the Present*, 2d ed. (New York: Feminist, 2002), 106.

82. Carolyn Baxter, "Toilet Bowl Congregation," in *Prison Solitary and Other Free Government Services* (Greenfield Center, N.Y.: Greenfield Review Press, 1979), 8.

83. Huey Newton and Ericka Huggins, *Insights & Poems* (San Francisco: City Lights, 1975); Huggins's work from this period is also in *Wall Tappings: An Anthology of Writings by Women Prisoners*, edited by Judith A. Scheffler (Boston: Northeastern University Press, 1986), 292–300.

84. Angela Davis and Other Political Prisoners, *If They Come in the Morning: Voices of Resistance* (New Rochelle, N.Y.: Third Press, 1971), 97–105.

85. Ericka Huggins, "Untitled," in *If They Come in the Morning*, 99.

86. Angela Davis, "A Letter from Angela" (to Ericka Huggins), in *If They Come in the Morning*, 109.

87. Ibid., 111.

88. Juanita Díaz-Cotto, *Chicana Lives and Criminal Justice: Voices from El Barrio* (Austin: University of Texas Press, 2006), 241.

89. Ibid., 240–56.

90. Judy Lucero, "Ocho poemas de amor y deseperación" [Eight poems of love and despair], *De Colores* 3, no. 1 (1976): 57–58; B. V. Olguín, "Mothers, Daughters, and Deities: Judy Lucero's Gynocritical Prison Poetics and Materialist Chicana Politics," *Frontiers* 22, no. 2 (2001): 63–86; Rafael Pérez-Torres, *Movements in Chicano Poetry: Against Myths, against Margins* (New York: Cambridge University Press, 1995), 114–23.

91. Poem cited in Olguín, "Mothers, Daughters, and Deities," 81.

92. Olguín, "Mothers, Daughters, and Deities," 64; Pérez-Torres, *Movements in Chicano Poetry*, 117; José E. Armas, "Memoriam: Poems of Judy A. Lucero," *De Colores* 1, no. 1 (1973): 71.

93. Davis, "Letter from Angela," 109.

94. Knight, preface to *Black Voices from Prison*, 9.

95. Hill, "'Violent Space,'" 120.

Chapter Five

1. Steven Hart, ed., *The Arts in Prison* (New York: Center for Advanced Study in Theatre Arts, Graduate School and University Center of the City University of New York, 1983). CASTA is now known as the Martin E. Segal Theatre Center.

2. Ibid., 12–13.

3. Ibid., 13.

4. Augusto Boal, *Theatre of the Oppressed* (New York: Theatre Communications Group, 1979 [1973]).

5. Cathy Russell, "Drama Programs with the Adolescent Offender," in Hart, *Arts in Prison*, 113.

6. Kenneth Lamott, *Chronicles of San Quentin, 1852–1972* (New York: Ballantine, 1972), 203. See also Barbara Mackay, "Theater behind Bars," *SR*, July 13, 1974, n.p. On Chessman, see Caryl Chessman, *Cell 2455 Death Row: A Condemned Man's Own Story* (New York: Prentice-Hall, 1954).

7. Dickson, quoted in Lamott, *Chronicles of San Quentin*, 204.

8. Fiona Mills, "Seeing Ethnicity: The Impact of Race and Class on the Critical Reception of Miguel Piñero's *Short Eyes*," in *Captive Audience: Prison and Captivity in Contemporary Theater*, edited by Thomas Fahy and Kimball King (New York: Routledge, 2003), 41–64.

9. Ibid., 44.

10. Carlos Morton, "Nuyorican Theatre," *Drama Review* 20, no. 1 (1976): 44.

11. See, e.g., Nicolas Kanellos, *The Hispanic Literary Companion* (Detroit: Visible Ink, 1997), 244–46.

12. Miguel Piñero, "A Lower East Side Poem," *La Bodega Sold Dreams* (Houston: Arte Público, 1980).

13. Leslie Benetts, "Miguel Piñero, Whose Plays Dealt with Life in Prison, Is Dead at 41," *New York Times*, June 18, 1988.

14. Steven Hart's 1981 doctoral dissertation remains the most comprehensive discussion of this crucial organization's founding, development, flourishing, and struggles. Hart, "The Family: A Theatre Group Working with Inmates and Ex-Inmates" (PhD diss., Graduate Faculty in Theater, City University of New York, 1981), 31. Marvin Felix Camillo died as a result of a car accident in 1988.

15. Ibid., 10.

16. Mel Gussow, "Short Eyes," *New York Times*, Jan. 8, 1974.

17. Ibid.

18. Joseph Papp, introduction to Miguel Piñero, *Outrageous: One Act Plays* (Houston: Arte Público, 1986), n.p.

19. John Herbert, *Fortune and Men's Eyes* (New York: Grove, 1967); Neil Carson, "Sexuality and Identity in *Fortune and Men's Eyes*," *Twentieth-Century Literature* 18, no. 3 (1972): 207–18.

20. "Fortune Society Eight Years Old," *Fortune News*, Nov. 1975, 2.

21. The Fortune Society now runs the Fortune Academy, a sixty-two-bed housing facility for formerly incarcerated people. In 2008 an off-Broadway play, "The Castle," dramatized the lives of several residents of the facility. Jim Dwyer, "Four Ex-Convicts Tell of Lives Lost and Found," *New York Times*, July 19, 2008.

22. Akila Couloumbis, quoted in Steven Hart, "Research Findings of the Theatre in Prisons Project," in *The Arts in Prison* (New York: Center for Advanced Study in Theatre Arts, Graduate School and University Center of the City University of New York, 1983), 7.

23. TFTF History, Theatre for the Forgotten Collection, Lloyd Sealy Library Special Collections, City University of New York, John Jay College of Criminal Justice, box 1, folder 6, n.d.

24. Roberta Cantow, *Theatre for the Forgotten: Children's Alternatives through the Arts* (New York: Theatre for the Forgotten, 1978), unpaginated bound xerox, Special Collections, Lloyd Sealy Library, City University of New York, John Jay College of Criminal Justice.

25. Ibid. Funding from the Law Enforcement Assistance Administration was withdrawn after 1980.

26. TFTF History, box 1, folder 9. On Chuck Bergansky, see "Fortune Flashbacks," *Fortune News*, Nov. 1975, 4. Marvin Felix Camillo emphasized that a large number of Family graduates went on to work in the theater. Hart, *Arts in Prison*, 10.

27. "Phyllis," quoted in Martin Flusser Jr., "The Exclusive Theater for the Forgotten: It's for Prisoners Only," *Newsday*, Mar. 1, 1972.

28. "Owa," quoted in Jennifer Merin, "Prison Theater—a reawakening of Values," *Christian Science Monitor*, Feb. 7, 1973.

29. William Taylor, American Correctional Association, quoted in Hart, *Arts in Prison*, 15.

30. Robert Nelepovitz, assistant deputy commissioner of security, New York State Department of Corrections, quoted in Manuel Norat, "Imprisoned Art: New Horizons and Tight Budgets in New York State," in Hart, *Arts in Prison*, 128.

31. Paul Ryder Ryan, "Theatre as Prison Therapy," *Drama Review* 20, no. 1 (1976): 38.

32. Stuart P. Fischoff, quoted in Ryan, "Theatre as Prison Therapy," 39.

33. Martin Flusser Jr., "The Exclusive Theater for the Forgotten: It's for Prisoners Only," *Newsday*, Mar. 1, 1972.

34. "Survival," Theatre for the Forgotten Collection, Lloyd Sealy Library Special Collections, City University of New York, John Jay College of Criminal Justice, box 1, folder 6, n.d.

35. Quoted in Ryan, "Theatre as Prison Therapy," 39.

36. Norat, "Imprisoned Art," 130.

37. Sophy Corwin, quoted in Norat, "Imprisoned Art," 134.

38. Other theater companies avoided politically charged content for other reasons. Performing in the Midwest during the more conservative 1980s Geese Theatre's John Bergman found that his "radical political statements" were not well-received by inmates. John Bergman, "Dirty Laundry: How a Theatre Company Grew Up in Corrections," in Hart, *Arts in Prison*, 150. There is a Geese Theatre Company in the United Kingdom, founded by veterans of the U.S. program. Clark Baim, Sally Brookes, and Alun Mountford, *The Geese Theatre Handbook: Drama with Offenders and People at Risk* (Hampshire, U.K.: Waterside, 2002).

39. Ramon "Ray" Gordon, quoted in Hart, *Arts in Prison*, 8. Cell Block Theatre closed in 1979.

40. Boal, *Theatre of the Oppressed*, ix.

41. Ibid.

42. Ibid., 155.

43. Augusto Boal, "Categories of Popular Theatre" (1973); rpt. in Boal, *Legislative Theatre: Using Performance to Make Politics* (New York: Routledge, 1998), 237.

44. Theater professionals, including the playwrights Arthur Miller, Miguel Piñero, Charles Gordone, and Santha Rama Rau, would run workshops. Ryan, "Theatre as Prison Therapy," 32.

45. Ramon Gordon, quoted in Hart, *Arts in Prison*, 9.

46. Ryan, "Theatre as Prison Therapy," 32.

47. Ibid., 33.

48. Ibid., 33–34.

49. Hart, 8.

50. See, e.g., A. Leon Higginbotham Jr., *Shades of Freedom: The Racial Politics and Presumptions of the American Legal Process* (New York: Oxford University Press, 1996); and Randall Kennedy, *Race, Crime, and the Law* (New York: Pantheon, 1997). This is not to say that similar arguments did not exist prior to the 1990s. Indeed, W. E. B. Du Bois highlighted the impact of racial bias in the criminal justice system in the early twentieth century. See W. E. B. Du Bois, *Some Notes on Negro Crime, Particularly in Georgia* (Atlanta: Atlanta University Press, 1904). In the 1970s, works such as Mary Frances Berry's *Black Resistance/White Law: A History of Constitutional Racism in America* (Englewood Cliffs, NJ: Prentice-Hall, 1971) advanced this argument. For the historiography of African Americans and the criminal justice system see Lee Bernstein, *African Americans and the Criminal Justice System*, Schomburg Studies in the Black Experience: The Black Experience in the Western Hemisphere, Colin Palmer, managing editor, Howard Dodson, series director (New York and Ann Arbor, Mich.: Schomburg Center for Research in Black Culture and the ProQuest Co., 2009).

51. Hugh M. Johnson, *Justice or Just Us, Part 1*, in Norfolk Prison Brothers, *Who Took the Weight? Black Voices from Norfolk Prison* (Boston: Little, Brown, 1972), 144.

52. Ibid., 147.

53. Gordon Kirkwood-Yates, *An Accurate Account of My First Arrest: A Comedy in IV Acts*, in *Latitude Pain, Longitude Anger: Poems from Folsom Prison*, edited by Gordon Kirkwood-Yates and John Oliver Simon (Berkeley, Calif.: Aldebaran Review, 1976).

54. Malcolm X, "Speech at the Leverett House Forum of March 18, 1964," in *The Speeches of Malcolm X at Harvard*, edited by Archie Epps (New York: Morrow, 1968), 133. In 1995 Paul Butler drew on this same view in his essay on jury nullification, "Racially Based Jury Nullification: Black Power in the Criminal Justice System," *Yale Law Journal* 105 (1995): 677–725.

55. John Rich, dir., *On the Rocks* (pilot), aired Sept. 11, 1975, ABC. *On the Rocks* aired in 1975 and 1976. It was loosely based on a long-running British comedy, *Porridge*.

Chapter Six

1. Charter Group for a Pledge of Conscience, *The Black Panther Party and the Case of the New York Twenty-One* (New York: Committee to Defend the Panther 21, 1970).

2. Charlotte Curtis, "Panther Philosophy Is Debated at the Bernsteins," *New York Times*, Jan. 15, 1970.

3. "Text of the Moynihan Memorandum on the Status of Negroes," *New York Times*, Mar. 1, 1970. This memorandum argued that African Americans had achieved real social progress during the previous decade and that the administration should continue

to monitor this progress but avoid engaging radical activists (or turning them into martyrs).

4. Ibid.

5. Alex Ross, "The Legend of Lenny," *New Yorker*, Dec. 15, 2008, 86.

6. Lesley Oelsner, "Panthers Find Some Odd Person's Crying 'Right On!,'" *New York Times*, Apr. 26, 1970. One of these monitors was Hillary Rodham, the future secretary of state, then a law student at Yale.

7. Tom Wolfe, "Radical Chic: That Party at Lenny's," *New York*, June 8, 1970. Later published in revised form as *Radical Chic and Mau-Mauing the Flak-Catchers* (New York: Farrar, Straus, and Giroux, 1970), 13. All quotes from book.

8. See, e.g., Norman Mailer, "The White Negro: Superficial Reflections on the Hipster," in *Advertisements for Myself* (New York: Putnam's, 1959), 337–58.

9. Wolfe, "Radical Chic," 8; emphasis in original. For discussion of Jewish American angst, see ibid., 39.

10. See Stephen E. Kercher, *Revel with a Cause: Liberal Satire in Postwar America* (Chicago: University of Chicago Press, 2006).

11. Robert Reid-Pharr compellingly argues that Newton "was unusually aware of the manner in which sex and sexuality operated in not only the functioning of his organization, his movement, but also the articulation of his community and race. That is to say, Newton understood that his ability to seduce us all involved his remaining focused on the many important political uses to which his self-consciously constructed image was being put while leaving off consideration of the many blunt silences that underwrote this same image." Reid-Pharr, *Once You Go Black: Choice, Desire, and the Black American Intellectual* (New York: New York University Press, 2007), 137.

12. See, e.g., William F. Buckley Jr., "Lenny Explains," *National Review*, Jan. 27, 1989, 71.

13. Barry Seldes, *Leonard Bernstein: The Political Life of an American Musician* (Berkeley: University of California Press, 2009), 116; Curt Gentry, *J. Edgar Hoover: The Man and the Secrets* (New York Penguin, 1991); Ward Churchill and John Vander Wall, *The COINTELPRO Papers: Documents from the FBI's Secret Wars against Domestic Dissent* (Boston: South End, 1990), 159.

14. Ross, "Legend of Lenny," 86.

15. Charlotte Curtis, "The Bernsteins' Party for Black Panther Legal Defense Stirs Talk and More Parties," *New York Times*, Jan. 24, 1970.

16. Jack Henry Abbott, *In the Belly of the Beast* (New York: Random House, 1981), 10.

17. Myron A. Farber, "Killing Clouds Ex-convict Writer's New Life," *New York Times*, July 26, 1981.

18. Abbott, *In the Belly of the Beast*, 96.

19. Ibid., 118.

20. Ibid., 98.

21. Richard Cohen, "A Killer Who Writes or a Writer Who Kills," *Washington Post*, July 30, 1981; Farber, "Killing Clouds Ex-convict Writer's New Life."

22. Norman Mailer, preface to Abbott, *In the Belly of the Beast*, ix.

23. Jack Henry Abbott, "In Prison," *New York Review of Books*, June 26, 1980, 27.

24. Myron A. Farber, "Convict-Author Known by Mailer Is Being Sought in Fatal Stabbing," *New York Times*, July 20, 1981.

25. Abbott, "In Prison," 37.

26. Hoffman, cited in Michiko Kakutani, "The Strange Case of the Writer and the Criminal," *New York Times Book Review*, Sept. 20, 1981.

27. Terrence Des Pres, "A Child of the State," *New York Times Book Review*, July 19, 1981.

28. Ibid., 14.

29. Myron A. Farber, "Freedom for Convict-Author: Complex and Conflicting Tale," *New York Times*, Aug. 17, 1981.

30. Myron A. Farber, "The Detective vs. the Fugitive: How Jack Abbott Was Found," *New York Times*, Oct. 11, 1981.

31. Paul L. Montgomery, "Murder Trial of Jack Abbott Is Begun," *New York Times*, Jan. 9, 1982.

32. Paul L. Montgomery, "Abbott, on Witness Stand, Admits Fatal Stabbing," *New York Times*, Jan. 16, 1982.

33. Ibid.

34. Jack Henry Abbott and Naomi Zack, *My Return* (Buffalo, N.Y.: Prometheus, 1987), 59–60.

35. Paul L. Montgomery, "Abbott Rejects Account of Him as Violent Man," *New York Times*, Jan. 19, 1982.

36. Paul L. Montgomery, "Abbott Is Sentenced to Fifteen Years to Life in Slaying of Waiter," *New York Times*, Apr. 16, 1982.

37. Ibid.

38. *New York v. Jack Henry Abbott* (Apr. 15, 1982), Supreme Court of New York, New York County, 113 Misc. 2d 766; 449 N.Y.S. 2d 853; Lexis 3378. Retrieved Nov. 15, 2003, from Lexis/Nexis database.

39. Ibid.

40. Abbott and Zack, *My Return*, 10.

41. Ibid., 61.

42. Ronald Sullivan, "Author Facing Damages for Murder," *New York Times*, June 6, 1990.

43. Edmund M. Silvestre, "Fil-Am Widow Fearful No More," *Filipino Reporter*, Feb. 21, 2002.

44. Jonathan Yardley, "Risking Society for Literature?," *Washington Post*, Jan. 25, 1982.

45. Jay Maeder, "The Worth of Culture," *Daily News* (New York), Nov. 12, 1998.

46. Farber, "Killing Clouds Ex-convict Writer's New Life."

47. Mailer, preface to Abbott, *In the Belly of the Beast*, xvi.

48. Clive Davis, "The Killer Instinct," *Times* (London), Mar. 1, 2002. Retrieved from Lexis/Nexis database, Nov. 15, 2003.

49. Norman Mailer, "The White Negro: Superficial Reflections on the Hipster," in *Advertisements for Myself* (New York: Putnam's, 1959), 337–58; Mailer, *The Executioner's Song* (Boston: Little, Brown, 1979).

50. Kakutani, "The Strange Case," 36.

51. Ibid., 37.

52. Bernard Weinraub, "Mailer Tells a Lot. Not All, But a Lot," *New York Times*, Oct. 4, 2000.

53. Jerzy Kosinki, quoted in Joyce Wadler, "Violence's Intellectual," *Washington Post*, Aug. 11, 1981.

54. Ibid.

55. "Radical Rage and Chic," *New York Times*, Aug. 18, 1981.

56. Abbott, *In the Belly of the Beast*, 18.

57. Des Pres, "A Child of the State," 14.

58. Huey P. Newton, "Eulogy for Jonathan Jackson and William Christmas," delivered at St. Augustine's Church, Twenty-Seventh and West Streets, Oakland, Calif., in *Off the Pigs! The History and Literature of the Black Panther Party*, edited by G. Louis Heath (Metuchen, N.J.: Scarecrow, 1976), 322–23.

59. Leonard Munker, quoted in Wadler, "Violence's Intellectual."

60. Yardley, "Risking Society."

61. Farber, "Freedom for Convict-Author."

62. Roderick Nordell, "Prisons: View from behind the Bars," *Christian Science Monitor*, Aug. 10, 1981.

63. "Prose and Cons," *Saturday Night Live*, season 7, episode 1, transcript at snltranscripts.jt.org/81/81aprose.phtml.

Conclusion

1. He took the alias because he was on the run from a Texas chain gang. Charles K. Wolfe and Kip Lornell, *The Life and Legend of Leadbelly* (New York: HarperCollins, 1999), 85.

2. Ibid., 87.

3. Ibid., 100.

4. "Leadbelly: Bad Nigger Makes Good Minstrel," *Life*, Apr. 19, 1940, 38–40. The title of the *Life* story offensively captured some of the dominant views that helped explain the appeal of Ledbetter's legend.

5. Ibid., 39. The performance at the Modern Language Association is described in John A. Lomax, *Adventures of a Ballad Hunter* (New York: Macmillan Company, 1947), ix.

6. Kevin Fagan, "Death Row Poet's Final Pleas: Murderer Who Won Writing Awards Is Scheduled to Die Tuesday," *San Francisco Chronicle*, Jan. 27, 2002. See also "Governor Davis Denies Clemency Request of Stephen Wayne Anderson," press release, Jan. 26, 2002, Governor Gray Davis Digital Library, ⟨http://www.gray-davis.com/ViewLibraryItem.aspx?ID=6269⟩.

7. I take this idea of a "quest for a revolutionary culture" from Julie Marie Bunck,

Fidel Castro and the Quest for a Revolutionary Culture in Cuba (University Park: Pennsylvania State University Press, 1994).

8. U.S. Department of Justice, Bureau of Justice Statistics, *Report to the Nation on Crime and Justice* (Washington, D.C.: U.S. Government Printing Office, 1988), 120.

9. James Austin et al., *Unlocking America: Why and How to Reduce America's Prison Population* (Washington, D.C.: JFA Associates, 2007), 1; Farnsworth Fowle, "Study Shows Prison Population Rose 13% to Set a Record," *New York Times*, Feb. 18, 1977.

10. Charles B. A. Ubah, "Abolition of Pell Grants for Higher Education of Prisoners: Examining Antecedents and Consequences," *Journal of Offender Rehabilitation* 39, no. 2 (2004): 76.

11. Michele F. Welsh, "The Effects of Elimination of Pell Grant Eligibility for State Prison Inmates," *Journal of Correctional Education* 53, no. 4 (2002): 154.

12. Goldie Blumenstyk, "Use of Pell Grants to Educate Inmates Provokes Criticism," *Chronicle of Higher Education*, June 5, 1991, 37–38.

13. U.S. Department of Education, Office of Correctional Education, "Pell Grants for Prisoners: Facts/Commentary," 1995; Daniel Karpowitz and Max Kenner, *Education as Crime Prevention: The Case for Reinstating Pell Grant Eligibility for the Incarcerated* (Annandale-on-Hudson, N.Y.: Bard Prison Initiative, n.d.).

14. Robert Bruce Slater, "Locked in but Locked Out: Death Sentence for the Higher Education of Black Prison Inmates?" *Journal of Blacks in Higher Education*, no. 6 (1994–95): 103.

15. Jesse Helms, "Amendment 938," *Congressional Record*, July 20, 1991; S|1330. Helms, quoted in Jon Marc Taylor, "It's Criminal to Deny Pell Grants to Prisoners," *World & I*, Mar. 1995, 88.

16. U.S. Department of Justice, "Violent Crime Control and Law Enforcement Act of 1994: Fact Sheet," NCJ FS000067, Oct. 24, 1994.

17. Abby Ellin, "Cons in Class," *New York Times*, Aug. 3, 2003.

18. Ubah, "Abolition of Pell Grants," 79.

19. Jonathan E. Messemer, "College Programs for Inmates: The Post–Pell Grant Era," *Journal of Correctional Education* 54, no. 1 (2003): 34.

20. Quoted in Ellin, "Cons in Class."

21. Karl O. Haigler, Caroline Harlow, Patricia O'Connor, and Ann Campbell, *Literacy behind Prison Walls* (Washington, D.C.: U.S. Department of Education, 1994). The verbal arts, however, are alive and well despite the high rate of illiteracy. See Douglas Taylor, "Prison Slang and the Poetics of Imprisonment," in *Prose and Cons: Essays on Prison Literature in the United States*, edited by D. Quentin Miller (Jefferson, N.C.: McFarland, 2005), 233–45.

22. Results of a Louis Harris poll reported in Sol Stern, "The Campaign to Free Angela Davis . . . and Ruchell Magee," *New York Times Magazine*, June 27, 1971, 8.

23. James Baldwin, quoted in Jackson, *Soledad Brother: The Prison Letters of George Jackson* (Chicago: Lawrence Hill, 1994), x.

24. Sandow Birk, "Incarcerated: Visions of California in the Twenty-First Century" (Santa Barbara, Calif.: Santa Barbara Contemporary Arts Forum and LAST GASP, 2001).

25. For a broad overview of the postrelease struggles and successes of people exonerated by DNA evidence, see Janet Roberts and Elizabeth Stanton, "A Long Road Back after Exoneration, and Justice Is Slow to Make Amends," *New York Times*, Nov. 25, 2007. In June 2009 the Supreme Court ruled 5–4 that inmates have no constitutional right to DNA testing to prove their innocence. *District Attorney's Office for the Third District, et al. v. Osborne* (08–6).

26. Medill Innocence Project, "Who We Are and What We Do," ⟨www.medill innocenceproject.org⟩; accessed May 27, 2009.

27. Jennifer Eckroth, "Tainted DNA Evidence and Post-Conviction Reversals in Houston, Texas: Suggested Solutions to Curb DNA Evidence Abuse," *American Journal of Criminal Law* 31, no. 3 (2004): 433–56; "Errors at FBI May Be at Issue in Three Thousand Cases," *New York Times*, Mar. 17, 2003.

28. Adam Liptak, "The Death Penalty: A Witness for the Prosecution," *New York Times*, Feb. 15, 2003.

29. Michael Sneed et al., "Ryan to Commute All Death Row Sentences," *Chicago Sun-Times*, Jan. 11, 2003.

30. *What I Want My Words to Do to You*, documentary film produced by Eve Ensler, Carol Jenkins, and Judith Katz (Washington, D.C.: Public Broadcasting System and Borrowed Light Productions, 2003).

31. Bruce J. Schulman, *The Seventies: The Great Shift in American Culture, Society, and Politics* (New York: Free Press, 2001), 25.

32. Abbott, *In the Belly of the Beast*, xii.

33. Angela Davis, foreword to Rena Fraden, *Imagining Medea: Rhodessa Jones and Theater for Incarcerated Women* (Chapel Hill: University of North Carolina Press, 2001), xii.

34. Easy Waters (William Eric Waters), "Chronicling Sing Sing Prison," in *Doing Time: Twenty-Five Years of Prison Writing*, edited by Bell Gale Chevigny (New York: Arcade, 1999), 73–76. Waters was released from prison in 2000.

INDEX

www.ingramcontent.com/pod-product-compliance
Lightning Source LLC
LaVergne TN
LVHW091048080826
845145LV00002B/670

9780807871171